Nursery Smart Pages

Sheryl Haystead, Editor

Gospel Light

HOW TO MAKE CLEAN COPIES FROM THIS BOOK

You may make copies of portions of this book with a clean conscience if:
• you (or someone in your organization) are the original purchaser;
• you are using the copies you make for a noncommercial purpose (such as teaching or promoting your ministry) within your church or organization;
• you follow the instructions provided in this book.

However, it is ILLEGAL for you to make copies if:
• you are using the material to promote, advertise or sell a product or service other than for ministry fund-raising;
• you are using the material in or on a product for sale;
• you or your organization are **not** the original purchaser of this book.

By following these guidelines you help us keep our products affordable.

Thank you, Gospel Light

All Scripture quotations, unless otherwise indicated, are taken from the *Holy Bible, New International Version* ®. *NIV* ®. Copyright © 1973, 1978, 1984 by International Bible Society. Used by permission of Zondervan Publishing House. All rights reserved.
Other versions used are:
KJV—King James Version. Authorized King James Version.
NKJV—From the *New King James Version.* Copyright ©1979, 1980, 1982 by Thomas Nelson, Inc. Publishers. Used by permission. All rights reserved.

NOTE

Because church liability laws are inherently complex and may not be completely free of doubtful interpretations, you are advised to verify that the legal rules you are following actually apply to your situation. In no event will Gospel Light be liable for direct, indirect, special, incidental or consequential damages arising out of the use, inability to use or inappropriate use of the text materials, forms or documentation, even if Gospel Light is advised of or aware of the possibility of such damages. In no case will Gospel Light's liability exceed the amount of the purchase price paid.

Gospel Light in no way guarantees or warrants any particular legal or other result from the use of the *Little Blessings* program.

While Gospel Light attempts to provide accurate and authoritative information regarding the subject matter covered, it is sold with the understanding that Gospel Light is not engaged in rendering legal or other professional services, and is sold subject to the foregoing Limited Warranty. If legal or other expert assistance is required, the services of a competent professional person should be sought.

Forms are shown for illustrative purposes only. They should not be relied on for any legal purpose or effect until they have been reviewed by a competent attorney in your state who is experienced in laws relating to churches.

EDITORIAL STAFF: **Publisher,** William T. Greig • **Senior Consulting Publisher,** Dr. Elmer L. Towns • **Publisher, Research, Planning and Development,** Billie Baptiste • **Senior Editor,** Lynnette Pennings, M.A. • **Senior Consulting Editors,** Dr. Gary S. Greig, Wesley Haystead, M.S.Ed. • **Editor, Theological and Biblical Issues,** Bayard Taylor, M.Div. • **Editor,** Sheryl Haystead • **Writers,** Mary Gross, Kathleen McIntosh • **Associate Technical Editor,** Linda Mattia • **Contributing Editors,** Valjean Aycock, Cheryl Balinski, Elsa Barber, Emmy Bonja, Sherry Budke, David Epstein, Rhonni Greig, Jan Harvey, Linda Hoover, Willamae Myers, Everett Scott, Jackie Scott, Linda Young • **Designer,** Carolyn Thomas • **Illustrator,** Chizuko Yasuda

Gospel Light

Contents

A Step-by-Step Plan for Your Nursery

Gospel Light's *Little Blessings* nursery kit is the most complete resource available for churches who either want to begin or maintain a quality ministry to children in the first two years of life. Whether your church is large or small, you can use these resources. Here is a step-by-step plan for what to do.

1. Start with the basics: health and safety.

❖ Evaluate the nursery room, procedures and staff according to the Organizing Your Nursery section of this book.

❖ Set several short- and long-term goals for improving the operation of your nursery based on your evaluation.

2. Help your staff introduce a Bible-based theme for each month.

❖ At the beginning of every month, display in the nursery the two appropriate posters from the *Nursery Posters*. Caregivers, whether serving for several months, a few weeks or even as substitutes, will be able to see at a glance on the informational poster the monthly theme, a simple song, finger fun and Bible story to use with children in the nursery. The photo poster will not only help make your nursery attractive, but will provide caregivers with a theme-related picture to talk about with children.

❖ Use Tips: Display informational posters at an adult's eye level. Display photo posters where children can see them.

Purchase enough *Nursery Posters* so that each nursery room has its own supply of posters.

❖ Bonus Idea: Ask every caregiver to watch the *How to Grow and Nurture a Quality Nursery* video for ideas on how to make your nursery a healthy, happy place where babies and toddlers are introduced to God's love.

3. Add a musical touch!

❖ Provide the *I Love to Sing!* cassette or CD for caregivers to play and sing along with in the nursery. The upbeat, simple Active Time songs will give teachers ways to play with children as they talk about the monthly theme.

The gentle, soothing Quiet Time songs are perfect for calming babies and toddlers.

❖ Use Tip: Reproduce cassettes/CDs for parents in your nursery program to use at home or in the car.

4. Keep going with Bible story pictures!

❖ Place a copy of the *I Love to Look!* picture cards in each nursery room. Instruct each caregiver to use the card for the month to tell and talk about a short Bible story with children, one-on-one.

❖ Use Tips: Where many staff are in the same room, provide two or three copies of *I Love to Look!* for designated caregivers to use.

Purchase an *I Love to Look!* for each child. At the beginning of the month, make the cards available for parents (mail cards, set them out on a counter or in a pocket on your nursery bulletin board for parents to take copies, caregivers place cards in diaper bags). Or in September, give the entire *I Love to Look!* to each family, giving new families a copy during the year.

Don't stop now!

5. Use the Teacher's and Parent's Home Pages to communicate with and train caregivers and parents.

❖ Photocopy the monthly Teacher's Home Page (on pages 189-238), mailing it to each caregiver during the week before he or she will serve in the nursery. (It's a quick and easy way to remind rotating staff of their nursery commitment!)

❖ Photocopy the monthly Parent's Home Page (on pages 139-188) and distribute to parents (mail them, set them out on a counter or in a pocket on your nursery bulletin board for parents to take copies, caregivers place pages in diaper bags). Combine the Parent's Home Page with the *I Love to Look!* by stapling or clipping each month's page and picture together.

❖ For two full years of parent tips and activities, alternate Years A and B Parent's Home Pages.

❖ Bonus Idea: Supplement the learning ideas on the Home Pages with the instant activities in the *I Love to Wiggle and Giggle!* easel book. Each nursery room needs at least one easel book. Additional books should be purchased if the room is large and has more than two caregivers. Encourage parents to purchase an easel book to have at home, using the activities with their child to reinforce the learning that has taken place at church.

How do we teach babies and toddlers?

The best session for babies and toddlers is one in which children freely play in a safe and interesting environment. Caregivers interact with children, participating with children in a variety of activities (singing, playing with toys, reading books, telling a simple story) and caring for physical needs. Young children are not developmentally ready for structured group activities, so while two or more children may occasionally gather to listen to a story, or do the motions to a song, don't expect toddlers to participate in a group learning time. Babies and toddlers learn best when the activity is one they have initiated, or when they express obvious enjoyment and interest in a teacher-initiated activity.

Where can our nursery staff find all the good stuff they need?

Designate a specific shelf or cupboard where all curriculum-related materials will be stored. At this same location, post one or more sheets which clearly tell the procedures each caregiver needs to follow (for example, how to set up the room—show a photo of how the room should look; how to check in children—include a copy of the check-in form; how to connect children's activities with the monthly Bible theme—provide the curriculum materials needed; how to clean up the room—give a brief checklist of what needs to be done).

How can we make sure the posters and pictures last?

Posters and pictures can be laminated or covered on both sides with clear Con-Tact paper for greater durability. Lamination will also allow for occasional cleaning with a bleach and water solution.

How can I make sure our nursery makes the best use of these nursery materials?

Ask parents of children in the nursery to take the responsibility for one or more of these tasks: display the appropriate posters each month and store posters for reuse, distribute the Teacher's and Parent's Home Pages, reproduce and distribute cassettes/CDs and *I Love to Look!* picture cards to parents. In larger churches, the nursery coordinator or members of the nursery committee can do these jobs. Members of an adult Sunday School class, a Grandparent's Club or the church youth groups can help with collating tasks.

Organizing Your Nursery

This section contains concise and practical information that can help you build a quality nursery ministry from the ground floor up. There are two ways to find specific information you need:

  (1) Use the index at the back of this book;

  (2) Read the section containing information
      on the subject you need help with.

Procedures are suggested for the following categories:

Caregivers: Describes everything you need to know about staffing a nursery. Includes recruiting tips, job descriptions, screening and application forms, scheduling and training ideas.

Health/Safety: Provides vital information about making your nursery safe for the children God has entrusted to your care. You'll find suggestions and tips for keeping the nursery clean, checking in children and their belongings, handling diapering and feeding of children, safety checklists, ways to respond to illnesses and emergencies and more.

Partnering with Parents: Gives guidelines for communicating with parents and making it easy for parents to communicate with you. Describes and provides samples for nursery handbooks and brochures, check-in forms and record keeping, plus a bonus Problem Solving with Parents section.

Room/Supplies: Provides complete descriptions of everything in the well-equipped nursery environment. Includes equipment and furniture lists, room diagrams, guidelines for toy selection (as well as a section describing safe nursery toys you can make) and tips for handling specific room problems.

Caregivers

VIPs in the Nursery

The adults in the nursery come in all shapes and sizes—some with lots of experience and some with very little. They're called by many names: workers, caregivers, aides, baby-sitters, attendants, helpers. But no matter what you call the adults who staff your nursery, realize that these people are very important people: they're teachers. They may not consider themselves teachers, but at no other time in little ones' lives are children learning so much, and learning so quickly. Almost everything caregivers do teaches and influences the babies and toddlers in their care.

As a teacher, the nursery caregiver creates a safe and interesting environment with age-appropriate activities, provides physical and emotional care and encourages interaction among children and adults (among other caregivers and parents, too!). The caregiver's influence is so significant, yet it cannot be measured, and here's one reason: First impressions are often lasting impressions. A church nursery is often the first place the child is cared for away from home. The response of a child to the church nursery likely will affect his or her response to other new places. A church nursery is also often the first time a child is cared for in a group setting. Again, a child's nursery experience will help shape future interaction with other children.

Not only are the children affected by what goes on in the nursery, but parents are deeply influenced by their child's reactions. Nursery caregivers have the opportunity to make a significant impression on people who are just beginning their lives as parents. When a child is born, many parents find themselves overwhelmed by the responsibility, and for the first time may see a need for some kind of church experience. New parents may feel uncertain about what to do and how to properly meet the varying needs of their children—both physical and spiritual. A loving caregiver can be just the resource—and friend—a new parent needs.

Caregiver Ratio

Many variables affect the number of caregivers needed in the nursery. Generally, one teacher can adequately care for three or four babies and toddlers (use the lower number for infants, the higher number for the oldest toddlers). Always plan for at least two caregivers to work together in the nursery, no matter how few children are present. Requiring two staff members to be present with each group of children allows emergency situations to be dealt with and protects the caregivers and the church from unsupported parent complaints.

Recent research has shown that maintaining the proper ratios of caregivers to children helped children experience fewer tantrums, develop more advanced language skills, play in more complex ways with each other and their toys, and develop increased attachment to their caregivers. Caregivers also demonstrated gentler means of guiding children when they were responsible for smaller numbers of children.

Options for Staffing

Churches use a variety of staffing options: paid workers (church members, members of other churches who meet at different times, licensed caregivers obtained through a referral agency, students at a nearby Christian college), volunteers (parents or other adults in the church) or a combination of options.

Sample application forms for both paid and volunteer staff are provided on the next pages. Adapt these forms according to specific guidelines your church has adopted and any applicable laws in your state. Some churches require fingerprinting and police background checks for all staff who work with children. All churches should have a well thought-out screening process for all caregivers. If your church has not yet developed guidelines for screening children's workers, consult a legal expert in church liability issues.

Set up an interviewing team of at least two people for all paid positions (member of church staff who has oversight for the nursery program, nursery committee member, parent). Pay rates should be comparable to pay scales in your community. Follow any applicable state or federal laws for reporting income and withholding taxes.

Using paid caregivers has some advantages:
❖ higher expectations of workers to fulfill the job description;
❖ continuity of caregivers in the nursery;
❖ increased value to the position.
Using volunteer caregivers has advantages, too:
❖ staff has a higher degree of commitment to the nursery—workers are present because they've chosen the job;
❖ volunteers are more likely to view their job as a ministry.

Volunteer Application

Name _____   Telephone _____

Address _____

Date _____   Age _____   Birthday _____   Marital Status _____

Are you CPR certified or do you have any medical training? _____

Does your health limit your ability to lift children? _____

Describe your experience with children (paid or volunteer): _____

_____

How long have you attended our church?
(If less than one year, list previous church name, address and phone number.) _____

_____

In what programs in our church do you participate on a regular basis? _____

_____

Why do you want to work in the nursery? _____

_____

When are you available to work in the nursery? (Days of week; day or evening.) _____

_____

What do you enjoy about being with babies and toddlers? _____

_____

Statement of Faith _____

_____

References (two people who know you well)

1. Name _____   Telephone _____

   Address _____

2. Name _____   Telephone _____

   Address _____

Have you ever been convicted of a crime? If yes, when and for what? _____

Applicant's Signature _____

Paid Application

Name _____ Telephone _____

Address _____

How long have you lived at this address? _____

Date _____ Social Security _____ Are you over 18? _____

Are you CPR certified or do you have any medical training? _____

Does your health limit your ability to lift children? _____

Describe your experience with children (paid or volunteer): _____

_____

Why do you want to work in the nursery? _____

_____

When are you available to work in the nursery? (Days of week; day or evening.) _____

What do you enjoy about being with babies and toddlers? _____

_____

Statement of Faith

_____

Personal References (two people who know you well)

1. Name _____ Telephone _____

   Address _____

2. Name _____ Telephone _____

   Address _____

Employment References

1. Name _____ Telephone _____

   Address _____

2. Name _____ Telephone _____

   Address _____

Have you ever been convicted of a crime? If yes, when and for what? _____

Applicant's Signature _____

No matter what combination of paid and volunteer nursery staffing you use, always make feedback possible. Leave copies of this form in nursery rooms for caregivers to complete at any time. In addition, several times a year give forms to all caregivers to complete. Caregivers who feel their concerns are listened to and acted upon will be more likely to continue in their nursery ministry.

Tell Us What You Think!

Date _____

Name (Optional) _____

Describe any concerns you have about health and safety, staffing and equipment needs.

_____

_____

_____

What do you think needs to be improved in the nursery? Why?

_____

_____

_____

What ideas do you have for improving the nursery?

_____

_____

_____

Thanks for your help in making our nursery a friendly, safe place to be!

Scheduling Do's and Don'ts

The number of options for scheduling caregivers is probably equal to the number of nursery programs in existence! However, one overriding principle to keep in mind is that continuity of familiar caregivers is a high priority in nursery programs. Babies and toddlers (and nervous parents!) need the security of familiar faces and voices. Continuity of care is the ideal to strive for constantly.

Children and their parents aren't the only ones who benefit from familiar caregivers. Adults who spend their time in the nursery will also find their experience much more enjoyable (and hopefully serve more often) if they are given the opportunity to get to know the children in their care, learning about and appreciating their growth and development. Building relationships with children and their parents leads a caregiver to truly experience the benefits of a nursery ministry!

The ideal plan is to schedule caregivers in the nursery for six to twelve months at a time. Shorter time commitments of two to five months can also be effective. If caregivers serve for one month at a time, schedule their terms of service so that they overlap, resulting in some new and some familiar faces each week. Sample reminder notices that can be mailed to caregivers are provided on the following pages. Also include information about nursery procedures and learning activities, such as those suggested on the monthly Teacher's Home Pages (pages 189-238).

When possible, build teams of caregivers who can encourage each other in this important ministry to young children, and who will enjoy serving together. Caregivers are more likely to continue in service when their experiences have been positive. It's also helpful to pair an inexperienced caregiver with someone who is familiar with your nursery procedures and who is experienced in childcare techniques.

If you find it necessary to recruit caregivers for a week at a time, try one of these alternatives to lessen the negative impact of such a "revolving door" policy: (1) caregivers serve one session each month (over a period of several months, children will come to recognize these caregivers); (2) hire or recruit at least one caregiver who is present regularly (at least a month at a time) and is the familiar face that welcomes families to the nursery.

Post a schedule of caregivers in the nursery (particularly if you use a rotating staff), give caregivers child-safe name tags to wear (adhesive tags work well) and post their names near the nursery entrance so parents know who is caring for their children.

IT'S YOUR TURN!

DURING THE MONTH OF OCTOBER

YOU ARE SCHEDULED FOR:

☐ Crib Nursery, 8:30 Service

☐ Toddler Nursery, 8:30 Service

☐ Crib Nursery, 9:45 Sunday School

☐ Toddler Nursery, 9:45 Sunday School

☐ Crib Nursery, 11:00 Service

☐ Toddler Nursery, 11:00 Service

If you are unable to serve at your scheduled time, please call Jonelle Smith at 555-5555.

Dear Lisa,

I'm so glad you will be teaching in our toddler room during the month of May at the 10:30 Worship Service. Even though we don't have a formal lesson time with children this age, each child you talk with and play with will be learning from you. I've enclosed the Teacher's Home Page which suggests activities for this month's theme: People at Church Help Me.

Here are some tips that will make your time in the toddler room enjoyable:

☐ Dress comfortably. Wear low-heeled shoes.

☐ Arrive at 10:15. Everything goes smoother when the adults are in the room ready for the children's arrival.

☐ Read the nursery instructions on the bulletin board for information about checking in children, changing diapers and feeding.

☐ Use the children's names frequently throughout the session.

Please call if you have any questions. Thanks!

Mark Thomas, Nursery Coordinator, 222-2222

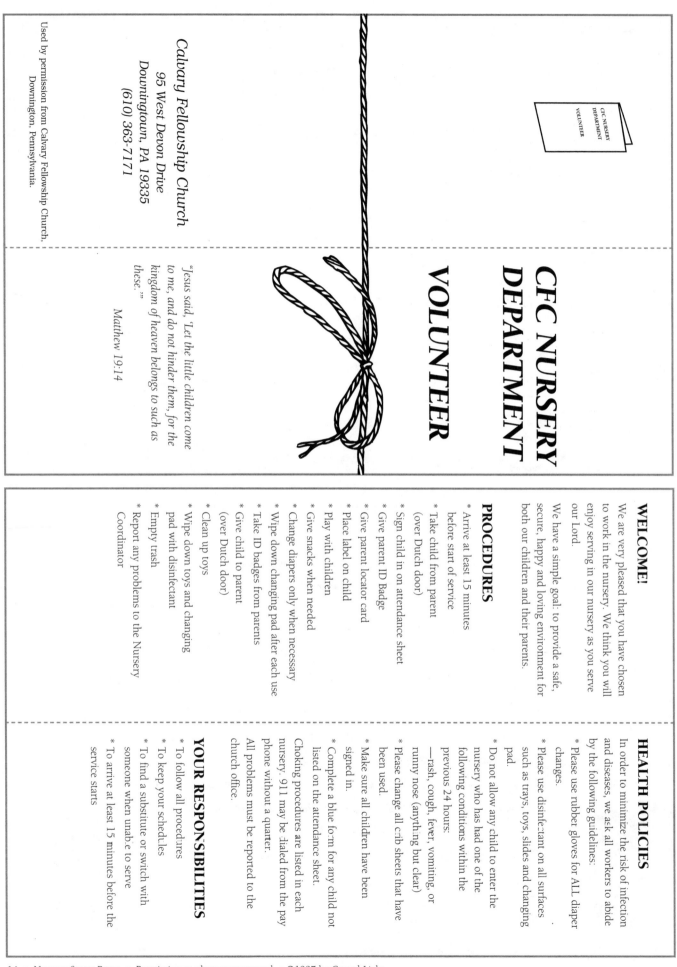

CFC NURSERY DEPARTMENT VOLUNTEER

WELCOME!

We are very pleased that you have chosen to work in the nursery. We think you will enjoy serving in our nursery as you serve our Lord.

We have a simple goal: to provide a safe, secure, happy and loving environment for both our children and their parents.

PROCEDURES

* Arrive at least 15 minutes before start of service
* Take child from parent (over Dutch door)
* Sign child in on attendance sheet
* Give parent ID Badge
* Give parent locator card
* Place label on child
* Play with children
* Give snacks when needed
* Change diapers only when necessary
* Wipe down changing pad after each use
* Take ID badges from parents
* Give child to parent (over Dutch door)
* Clean up toys
* Wipe down toys and changing pad with disinfectant
* Empty trash
* Report any problems to the Nursery Coordinator

HEALTH POLICIES

In order to minimize the risk of infection and diseases, we ask all workers to abide by the following guidelines:

* Please use rubber gloves for ALL diaper changes.
* Please use disinfectant on all surfaces such as trays, toys, slides and changing pad.
* Do not allow any child to enter the nursery who has had one of the following conditions within the previous 24 hours:
  —rash, cough, fever, vomiting, or runny nose (anything but clear)
* Please change all crib sheets that have been used.
* Make sure all children have been signed in.
* Complete a blue form for any child not listed on the attendance sheet.

Choking procedures are listed in each nursery. 911 may be dialed from the pay phone without a quarter.

All problems must be reported to the church office.

YOUR RESPONSIBILITIES

* To follow all procedures
* To keep your schedules
* To find a substitute or switch with someone when unable to serve
* To arrive at least 15 minutes before the service starts

"Jesus said, 'Let the little children come to me, and do not hinder them, for the kingdom of heaven belongs to such as these.'"

Matthew 19:14

Calvary Fellowship Church
95 West Devon Drive
Downingtown, PA 19335
(610) 363-7171

Used by permission from Calvary Fellowship Church, Downington, Pennsylvania.

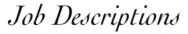

Job Descriptions

Nursery caregivers will find their jobs easier if their assigned tasks are clear and specific. Develop a job description for each position in your nursery. Distribute the job descriptions to the appropriate staff, and use the descriptions as an aid for recruiting. If you have a rotating staff, post the job descriptions in the nursery rooms at the appropriate locations.

Depending on the size of your church, your nursery staff may include a variety of jobs: coordinator, caregiver, greeter, substitute, laundry, supplies, record keeping. Combine jobs in small churches. All job descriptions should include starting and ending dates (preferably six months to a year), the purpose of the job, specific tasks and what support will be provided. Job descriptions for caregivers may also include expected times of arrival and departure, how to maintain cleanliness in the room during and after the session, suggested activities and experiences to provide for children and what to do in case of emergencies or problems.

Adapt the following job descriptions, adding information specific to your church.

COORDINATOR
Job Description

TASK: To recruit and schedule caregivers, overseeing their training and the nursery environment.

TERM: One year, beginning September 1

RESPONSIBILITIES:

☐ Recruit the following positions:
Caregivers (Use the screening procedures established by our church)
Supply Coordinator
Snack Coordinator
Greeters

☐ Post and distribute caregiving schedules

☐ Distribute parent and teacher newsletters each month

☐ Plan at least one training event for caregivers

☐ Develop a budget for the year

☐ Update and distribute Nursery Handbook

☐ Communicate regularly with church staff liaison

Caregiver
Job Description

TASK: To lovingly care for babies and toddlers.

TERM: Three months, September through November

RESPONSIBILITIES:

❑ Be present in the nursery from 11:00 A.M. until 12:15 P.M. each Sunday morning

❑ Upon arriving, quickly scan the room for safety hazards and remove any potential problem items (broken toys, coffee cups, etc.)

❑ Provide physical and emotional care for children

❑ Engage children in the learning activities suggested in the newsletter you received

❑ Follow guidelines for diapering, feeding and caring for children as described in the Nursery Handbook

❑ Attend at least one training event previous to term of service

Supply Coordinator
Job Description

TASK: To purchase and distribute nursery supplies.

TERM: One year, beginning September 1

RESPONSIBILITIES:

❑ Inventory and purchase needed supplies (obtain approval from Nursery Coordinator for purchases over $25.00)

❑ Turn in receipts to church office for reimbursement

❑ Keep records of all purchases

❑ Help determine nursery budget

Supply List:

❑ Snack (crackers and juice). Label with date of purchase and store on nursery shelves

❑ Diapering (baby wipes, disposable gloves, hand soap, diapers, changing table covers)

❑ Cleaning (trash can liners, bleach, sponges, paper towels)

❑ Care items (crib sheets, blankets, cloth diapers, toys)

Greeter
Job Description

TASK: To greet families and check in children as they arrive in the nursery.

TERM: Six months, September through February

RESPONSIBILITIES:

❑ Be present in the nursery from 9:30 A.M. until 10:00 A.M. each Sunday morning

❑ Put out a new check-in form each Sunday. Place previous check-in form into the Attendance Form box in the reception office.

❑ Offer a friendly greeting to each family.

❑ Assist parent(s) as needed to check in (following the procedures described in our Nursery Handbook)

❑ Be alert for symptoms of illness. Do not admit baby with signs of illness, such as a cold or fever

❑ Encourage parents and older children to stay outside of nursery area

❑ Assist parents in updating information cards every 2–3 months

❑ Pay special attention to visitors (give Nursery Handbook, provide directions to adult programs)

Getting and Keeping Caregivers

Keeping a positive attitude about recruiting nursery volunteers can be a challenge. A lack of congregational awareness of the nursery program, adults who feel they've done their time in the nursery or the attitude that the nursery is just a place where baby-sitting takes place are barriers many churches face.

1. Publicize the positive benefits of the nursery ministry. Before beginning any recruiting effort, plan several ways to increase awareness of the nursery program. People do not want to make a commitment to a program about which they are unfamiliar or have only heard negative comments.

❖ Let others know the positive aspects of your nursery through newsletter or bulletin inserts. Periodically publish a brief humorous or heartwarming story about a child's interaction with a caregiver, or an eye-catching photo of your nursery's ministry.

HERE'S ONE OF THE MANY LITTLE REASONS WE HAVE A CHURCH NURSERY:

(photo of baby)

Did you know that over 45 children are lovingly cared for each Sunday in our nursery?

Did you know that a minimum of 15 adults work together each Sunday to provide loving care in our nursery?

Did you know that you can support our nursery by helping out when asked, by donating a new toy and by saying thank-you to one of our many nursery caregivers?

Overheard in the Nursery

"I MEET MORE VISITORS TO OUR CHURCH WHEN I WORK IN THE NURSERY THAN IN ANY OTHER PROGRAM I'VE EVER HELPED IN."
NURSERY CAREGIVER

"I HOPE THAT FRIENDLY LADY WITH THE BIG SMILE IS HERE TODAY."
ONE-YEAR-OLD

"THERE'S NO BETTER WAY TO GET A FRESH LOOK AT LIFE THAN TO WATCH A TODDLER EXPLORE."
NURSERY CAREGIVER

"I'VE BECOME A BETTER PARENT FROM WORKING IN THE NURSERY."
PARENT VOLUNTEER

"YOU FOUND MY FAVORITE BLANKET. YOU MUST LOVE ME!"
TWO-YEAR-OLD

❖ Put up bulletin board displays identifying and picturing babies and toddlers at play with caregivers in the nursery. Or feature nursery caregivers, displaying their names and pictures and perhaps a quote about why they enjoy working in the nursery.

❖ Briefly interview nursery caregivers, during worship services or in adult classes, about the reasons they enjoy being in the nursery. Ask questions such as, "What do you remember about your first day in the nursery?" "What's your favorite thing to do in the nursery?" "How have you benefited by being in the nursery?" Take advantage of baby dedications or baptisms and new baby announcements to invite the congregation to visit the nursery. Periodically update the church staff or leadership about the number of visitors who have attended the nursery as a way of increasing their awareness of the nursery's importance.

❖ Organize parents of nursery children to help you form a baby/toddler parade during a worship service. While playing fun music from a baby/toddler cassette or CD, children and parents gather at the front of the church (carry babies or put them in strollers, toddlers walk or travel in wagons). Children may carry favorite toys or stuffed animals; tie helium-filled balloons to strollers, wagons or children's wrists. While children and parents are gathered at the front of the church, the pastor prays briefly for these families and the nursery caregivers who serve them.

❖ Another popular way to publicize your nursery is to show a video or slides of the babies and toddlers in your nursery. Show the pictures in adult education classes or as part of a worship service. Preface the pictures with a statement such as "Here are some of the many little reasons our church has a nursery" or "These are the little ones we welcome in Jesus' name each week in our nursery." As the pictures are shown, play a song from a children's music cassette/CD.

2. Let others know when you are in need of nursery staff. Talk to leaders of all children's ministries, church staff, coordinators of new members' classes, etc. Communicate the goals and needs of your nursery, asking for names of possible volunteers and inviting prayer support. If recruiting is made the responsibility of just a few people, they tend to become overworked and discouraged; also, recruiting efforts tend to be made again and again to the same limited pool of people.

3. Continually maintain a prospect list. Avoid the trap of only looking for prospects when you face a vacancy. An ongoing prospect list helps change the focus from finding any available person as quickly as possible to finding the person who fits the position.

❖ Obtain names from the church membership list, new members' classes, adult class lists and survey forms.

❖ Consider parents, singles, seniors and collegians.

❖ Since young teens often want to help in the nursery, invite these youth helpers and their families to participate together in the nursery for a month at a time.

❖ Don't forget to recruit men! Using men in the nursery ministry benefits both the babies and the men involved. While some men may resist the idea of teaching babies or toddlers, little ones can greatly benefit from warm associations with male teachers. In fact, some babies respond better to men than to women! For a child without a strong or consistent male presence in the home, godly men in the nursery become important role models.

Men are an essential part of a quality nursery staff. Some churches are reluctant to involve men because they believe parents are comfortable only with women caregivers. But by using well-thought-out caregiving policies (such as having two adults present in each room at all times), there should be no problem with parent discomfort or possible abuse allegations. Adhering to clearly outlined policies eliminates confusion and frees adults to minister in the nursery by focusing their time and energy on the children.

Legal advisers suggest that no persons be allowed to supervise children of any age until they have been members or regular attenders of your church for at least six months, preferably a year. See "Options for Staffing," page 8, for other safety and liability issues regarding paid or volunteer nursery staff.

Parents as Caregivers

While some parents (especially single parents) may need time away from their children in order to refresh and renew themselves, most parents benefit from participating in the nursery ministry. Some churches request that all parents assist in the nursery for one month during the year. Helping four or five weeks in a row is a better learning experience for parents and children alike than a rotating system of assisting one session each month. Arrange parent participation far in advance of the dates you expect parents to assist.

Let parents know the benefits they will receive as nursery caregivers. Parents will have an opportunity to see their child among other children of a similar age. Many parents find this experience increases their understanding of normal behavior at particular age levels.

Parents can work with an experienced caregiver who is able to share valuable insights gained from teaching many children. Effective learning comes when parents observe this teacher dealing with a variety of situations. As parents participate in specific learning activities with children, they have an opportunity to practice skills they can use at home. Also, parents develop a better understanding of the procedures in the nursery. Participating in one session will convey more than a caregiver can ever explain about how the department operates. In addition, caregivers, while observing the interaction between parent and child, can learn which caring techniques work best for the child. Parents and nursery staff working together can often do more to build and strengthen relationships between church and home than any other approach.

Sample parent recruiting letters are provided on the next page.

Dear Mommy and Daddy:

Please don't be shocked that I am writing to you. While crying, smiling, fussing and pointing have usually sufficed to get what I needed, my present need requires a more sophisticated form of communication.

To come right to the point, I need you to volunteer to help in my room at church during one session each Sunday morning (Sunday School or Worship) for one month during the coming year. I need you to do this to help ensure that there are always enough caring, capable adults to take care of me and my friends when we're at church. Besides, I think it's fun to show off my parents to my friends. (I won't always feel that way.)

One of the grown-ups at church (someone who talks better than I do) will be calling you in a few days to see if you'll do this for me. The grown-up who calls will help you settle on which month will be best for you. Also, you'll get a chance to find out about the great materials and activities our church provides to help me start learning about God and Jesus and other stuff I'm going to need to know.

So, I'm counting on you. I've already told the other kids at church that I've got the greatest parents in the whole wide room. Please don't let me down.

Sincerely,

Jasmine

TIP: Enclose a picture of their child with each parent's letter.

A GREAT PLACE FOR BABIES & TODDLERS...AND MOMS AND DADS

One of the BIG reasons our baby and toddler rooms are such terrific places for little ones is because so many parents volunteer to help out. Little ones feel safe and comfortable with a mom or dad who enjoys giving hugs, smiles, and a little comfort when needed. Having enough parent volunteers ensures that each child gets plenty of friendly, personal attention, so our baby and toddler rooms are usually very happy, enjoyable places for everyone.

Our plan for scheduling parents is to invite you to be part of our Baby/Toddler Teaching Team during one session each Sunday morning (Sunday School or Worship) for one month during the coming year. Being in the same room for a full month lets children get to know the parent volunteers, and lets the parents feel comfortable and successful.

Each month we have a different theme, guiding children in positive experiences related to simple but important truths about God and Jesus. Your one month of ministry will be a time of enjoyable growth as a parent, because everything we do with babies and toddlers at church is also beneficial for parents to do with little ones at home during the week.

One of our committee members will be calling you in a few days to see if you'll be able to take advantage of this opportunity and to schedule the month when you'll be sharing your love, and God's love, with little ones.

If there's a month when you really would prefer to serve, call (insert name and phone number) right away. The schedule does get built on a first-come, first-served basis.

Teen Helpers

Junior high and high school boys and girls often express an interest in helping care for little children. And many times, these young people are truly liked by energetic toddlers. Be aware that some churches choose not to use any nursery staff under the age of 18 for liability reasons, or to limit their participation to toddler rooms. However, many churches have planned effective ways of training and using youth in the nursery—always as helpers, and never as the primary caregivers. A youth helper's length of service should be limited to one to three months so that the helper does not miss out on youth church programs. Here are some guidelines for setting up a youth helper program:

First, determine with your church staff the minimum age and grade level for youth helpers and any other needed requirements, such as get parent's permission to participate, regularly attend church youth classes and worship services, attend a specified number of training classes, and be recommended by a youth supervisor/leader in the church. Ask youth to complete the volunteer or paid nursery application forms (see pages 9 and 10).

Second, plan one or more training classes for potential youth helpers and their parents. Including parents in the classes is helpful not only because it acquaints the parents with what their children are doing, but it also encourages parents to follow up at home on the training.

At the training classes, provide job descriptions, explain nursery procedures and safety guidelines, tour the nursery and include a time of child-care training. (Several sample worksheets are provided on page 23.) Emphasize that the job of a youth helper is an important task because of the way in which early experiences influence young children and because of the service youth helpers provide to the church family. Clearly state to helpers how important it is that they focus on children, and not on other helpers in the room.

Teen Helper
Job Description

TASK: To assist adult leaders in providing loving care for toddlers.

TERM: Three months, September through November

RESPONSIBILITIES:

☐ Be present in the nursery from 11:00 A.M. until 12:15 P.M. each Sunday morning.

☐ Follow the directions of the adult leader to provide physical and emotional care for children.

☐ Read the Nursery Handbook to become familiar with our nursery guidelines.

☐ With a parent, attend one training event.

Recommendation

_____ has applied to

☐ Work as a teen helper in the church nursery.

☐ Be placed on a recommended baby-sitter list.

*Ability to follow adult leadership?

*Ability to make friends with young children?

1. How would you describe this young person's

*Relationship with God?

2. Do you have any reservations about this person's ability to work with babies and toddlers?

Thank you for your help. Please return this form to the Director of Christian Education. Your comments will be kept confidential.

Worksheet #1

Answer these questions:

Why is it a good idea to...

make sure children don't share bottles, crackers or other snacks?

_____

_____

let the adult leader know if you bring a child in or out from the outdoor play area?

_____

_____

ask the adult leader before offering crackers to a child?

_____

_____

close all gates to the outdoor play area when you first go out?

_____

_____

Worksheet #2

Fill in the blanks with words from the box.

shoes	imitate
eat	sand
fussy	make fun
toddlers	alone

1. Try to distract a _____ toddler before picking him or her up.

2. Be sure never to leave a child _____ in the outdoor play area.

3. Please _____ before you come to the nursery. Crackers are for the children.

4. Empty _____ from a child's _____ before coming inside.

5. Please remember not to _____ of a child's speech or _____ what they say.

Worksheet #3

Draw lines to match each question with the appropriate answer.

What should you do if:

1. Michael and Noah both want the same truck?

2. your friends come to visit you in the nursery?

3. Kimberly throws sand?

4. Adam cries when he first comes into the room?

5. Jonathan needs his diaper changed?

6. Michael quits playing with the blocks and goes to ride on the horse?

7. Natalie, who has been asleep in a crib, wakes up and starts to cry?

a. Pick up the blocks unless someone else begins playing with them right away.

b. Tell your friends you'll talk to them after church.

c. Reassure him that his parents will come back. Then invite him to play with you.

d. Distract one child with a different toy.

e. Say, "You need to play with the sand, not throw it."

f. Quietly ask the leader what to do.

g. Talk to her; check the sign-in sheet to see if she needs a comfort toy or bottle. If she continues to cry, ask the adult leader what to do.

(Answers: 1-d; 2-b; 3-e; 4-c; 5-f; 6-a; 7-g.)

Guidelines for Recruiting

Prayerfully prioritize your prospect list. Then personally contact each prospect with a letter or phone call. Personalize the letter or call by telling the recipient the purpose of your contact—"I'm calling because I'd like you to think about becoming a part of our nursery team." Then describe why you think the person would be able to contribute to the nursery ministry—"I've noticed that you are really patient with young children and you seem to really know what they are like" or "You're such a friendly person and easy to get to know, and I thought you would be especially good at building relationships with the parents of the nursery children."

❖ Briefly explain what commitment you are asking for—"I'd like you to think and pray about being a caregiver in the toddler room during the worship service. There are two other adults you'll be working with and 10 to 12 children. Our caregiver teams serve for six months at a time." Add any other pertinent details.

❖ Always end your contact with an invitation for the prospect to observe the nursery ministry in action before making a final decision (be sure the staff being observed are doing a capable job) and encourage the prospect to take time to prayerfully consider your offer. Follow up the contact about a week later. If the answer is yes, be ready to offer orientation and training to help the new staff member make a good beginning. (If the answer is no, thank the prospect for taking the time to consider the ministry.)

❖ Sample recruiting flyers and inspirational clip art to put on your own letters are provided on the following pages. If you choose to send a form letter to your prospects, add a personal note to the letter. Avoid placing recruiting announcements in church bulletins or newsletters; it's best to recruit from a pool of people who have been recommended to you or who have demonstrated the characteristics of the kind of caregivers you're looking for. General announcements of "We need help in the nursery" give the impression that your ministry is desperate for volunteers because no one is really very interested in it.

❖ If someone unknown to you or other members of your church requests to help in the nursery, sincerely thank the person for his or her offer. Explain that all nursery staff are required to have regularly attended the church for a minimum of six months to a year (or whatever your church's policy specifies). Be ready to suggest a way the person might help in the nursery until the time requirement has been met (send birthday cards to children, decorate bulletin boards, etc.) or another area of service in the church.

I've noticed that you are really patient with young children.

Here's What We Need to Build Our Nursery Staff!

CAREGIVERS
Sit on the floor
Sing songs and tell stories
Give TLC to show
God's love

DECORATIONS
Good with masking tape
Can design
bulletin boards
Looks at life from
a child's view

SUPPLY COORDINATOR
Make lots of lists
Drive to the store
Purchase diapers
and graham crackers

GREETER
Have big smile
Give encouraging
words
Talented with
name tags

Plant a seed of faith!

Lots of little plants are waiting to be cared for in our nursery.
You have been recommended as someone who is capable of helping
a little child grow by joining our team of faithful "gardeners."

❏ I'd love to be a gardener in the nursery!

❏ I can't be a gardener in the nursery right now (but call me in a few months).

❏ I'm gardening in a different plot right now!

I prefer to work in the garden of the

❏ Sprouts (Babies) ❏ (Toddlers) ❏ Any garden is fine!

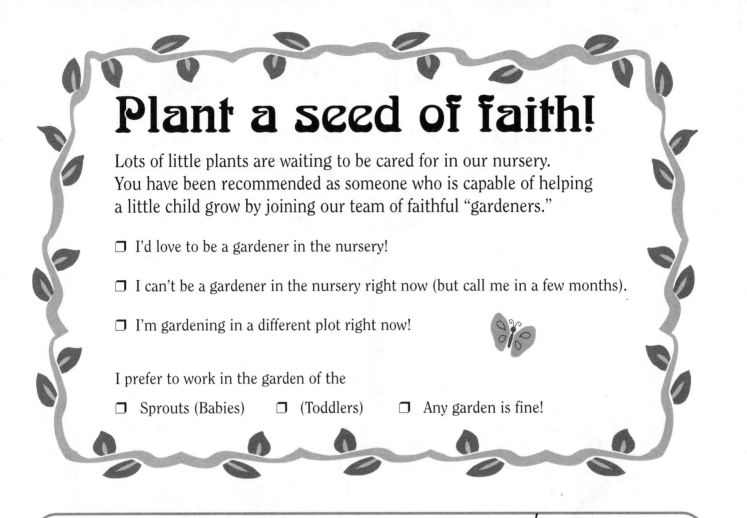

Touch the hand of a little one!

We've heard that you'd be a good person to help us provide safe and loving care for the children in our nursery. Hands-on opportunities for ministry in the nursery include giving hugs, playing with toys, clapping hands, turning the pages of a book, and giving gentle back pats!

If you can give us a hand, please call

_____

_____

_____

Top 5 Reasons to Join Our Nursery Staff

5. SMILES ARE GIVEN AWAY FOR FREE.

4. YOU'LL SEE KIDS GROWING RIGHT BEFORE YOUR VERY EYES.

3. BABIES AND TODDLERS WILL THINK ANYTHING YOU DO, SAY OR SING IS PERFECT.

2. YOU'LL MAKE LOTS OF FRIENDS.

1. AND THE NUMBER ONE REASON TO JOIN OUR NURSERY STAFF:

You'll be following Jesus' example of welcoming children to the family of God!

Open Up Your Heart to a Child's Love!

Show You Care!

More than diapers and toys! The ministry of the nursery touches lives for eternity.

An A for Appreciation

One of the best ways to recruit nursery staff is to keep the staff you already have! Here are some tips for ways to offer support and appreciation to your caregivers.

Plan ahead for substitutes. Agreeing to help in the nursery should not mean that a person can never take a needed break. Maintain a list of names and phone numbers of people who have already agreed to serve as nursery substitutes. In a larger church, the nursery coordinator may need to be the keeper of the list, ensuring that a variety of people are called. In a smaller church, you may distribute the list to the caregivers themselves, requesting them to notify you or another supervisor whenever a change is made.

Write personal notes. Periodically write a personal note of thanks to a nursery staff member. Depending on the size of your staff, make a plan to regularly write at least one note each week or month. Thank the person for a specific action he or she has demonstrated. For example, "I've noticed that you are especially good at calming fussy babies. They love to hear you sing" or "I appreciate your buying and sorting the snacks without any reminders." Or mention the number of families that were able to experience a worship service because of the volunteer's presence in the nursery.

Plan church-wide features. Several times a year, list the names of the nursery staff in a church bulletin or newsletter. Or take their pictures and display them on a bulletin board. Some churches include nursery staff in their regular teacher dedication or recognition events (dinners, lunches, pizza nights to which all family members are invited, etc.).

Give award certificates or gifts. Thank-you gifts can be purchased or homemade. Refrigerator magnets, mugs or plants will express appreciation to a volunteer. Give small gifts at the end of a volunteer's term of service, on his or her birthday or at holiday times. Or ask a nursery parent to make a half-dozen muffins or bag of cookies to give a nursery worker who has cared for his or her child recently.

Purchase or make your own certificates to give at the end of each volunteer's length of service. Sample certificates are provided on the following pages.

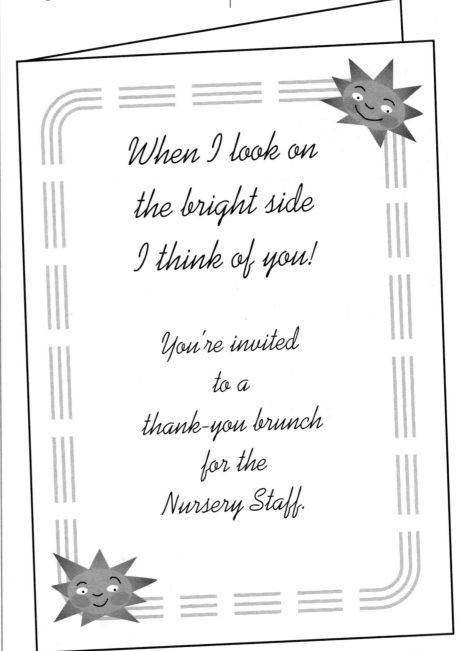

When I look on the bright side I think of you!

You're invited to a thank-you brunch for the Nursery Staff.

Thanks for your help!

Wee Care Certificate
Awarded to

_____

For

_____

• Nursery Smart Pages • 29

If smiles and hugs
were worth money,
you'd have
spent a million!

Thanks for investing
in the lives of our little ones!

Dear _____

My mommy told you thank-you today for taking care of me. I wish I could talk, too! Here's what I would say.

I'm glad you noticed how much fun I was having playing with the blocks! First, I built towers. But then I banged the block on lots of things—the ball, the car, the wall, and even your leg! (I'm sorry that hurt you. Thanks for giving me a train to bang on instead!) You let me figure out how a block works! I learned a lot!

Whenever I come into the room, you smile at me. It makes me feel so good to see you! Sometimes I'm a little sad that my mom is leaving, so I can't smile back. But deep inside, I know you care for me. Thank you.

I heard you talk about Jesus today. I don't exactly know who He is, but if He loves me as much as you do, He must be pretty special!

I love you!

ONE, TWO, WE THANK YOU.

THREE, FOUR,
WE LOVE YOU MORE.

FIVE, SIX AND SEVEN,
THE REWARD'S IN HEAVEN.

EIGHT, NINE AND TEN,
COME BACK AGAIN!

FAVORITE FRIEND AWARD

TO _____

FOR _____

Training Your Nursery Staff

Every nursery caregiver can benefit from one or more training events. New caregivers need basic instruction in what their jobs are (give them a copy of the job description on page 16), and how the nursery program functions (give them a copy of your nursery brochure or handbook).

Even experienced workers need to be made aware of procedure updates, program improvements and changing health and safety guidelines. Most caregivers also feel a renewed sense of dedication and excitement about their nursery ministry after meeting for even a brief time of training and inspiration.

Each training event (at least once a year) should include a brief focus on the importance of the nursery ministry, reminders and updates about nursery procedures and tips for interacting with babies and toddlers. Show a video (such as *How to Grow and Nurture a Quality Nursery*) designed to help nursery caregivers understand how best to provide a safe and enjoyable program for babies and toddlers. You may wish to provide training in a particular skill, based on one of the training articles found in this book:

❒ "Communication with Nontalkers," page 104

❒ "Crying: Understanding a Baby's Cry," pages 105, 106

❒ "Welcoming a Baby to the Nursery," page 131

❒ "Take a Look at Babies" and "Take a Look at Toddlers," pages 101, 102

❒ "Teaching Babies About God," page 117

❒ "Extending Your Nursery Ministry," pages 113, 114

❒ "Why Use Curriculum?" page 107

The nursery coordinator can provide the training, or ask a knowledgeable person in your church or community.

Help build relationships among the nursery staff by providing name tags, offering refreshments and asking participants to answer a few ice-breaker questions such as, "What's your favorite thing to do with a baby or toddler?" or "What's the first word that comes to your mind when you hear the word 'baby'?" Ask each worker to answer this question from the perspective of a particular child in your nursery: "What is the purpose of our church's nursery?"

Personally meet with any new staff who are not able to attend a training event, giving them a copy of your nursery brochure or handbook and the video to watch at home.

Health/Safety

Health and Safety Guidelines

Nothing speaks louder to parents of your loving care for their children than clean and safe rooms. While following health and safety guidelines does not guarantee a quality nursery, an effective nursery ministry cannot function without them.

Well-thought-out health and safety procedures benefit everyone connected to the nursery. Babies and toddlers and their parents are, of course, the prime beneficiaries: In a safe environment that is planned just for them, young children are encouraged to learn and grow. Secure in the knowledge that everything possible is being done to keep their child safe and happy, parents can take advantage of time away from their children to build their own relationships with God and others in the church family.

Nursery caregivers also find that making health and safety issues a priority makes their service a positive experience. For example, a nursery without a firm well-baby policy may find their caregivers (not to mention other children) frequently exposed to illnesses. Establishing guidelines for specific nursery procedures (checking in, feeding, diapering, emergencies, etc.) also helps the staff to know and fulfill what is expected of them. Other safety guidelines (child/adult ratios,

etc.) protect caregivers in the event of a complaint.

In discussing health and safety procedures with caregivers and parents, communicate instructions with a positive approach. For example, "In order to help our nursery be the best it can be, these are the health and safety guidelines we follow" or "So that you can concentrate on caring for and enjoying the babies in our nursery, here are the health and safety procedures we've established." Frequently thank parents and caregivers for their attention to these issues.

Occasionally a parent or caregiver may question the need for a certain health procedure. Acknowledge the person's feelings ("It does seem like it takes a lot of time to put on the gloves just to change a diaper") but reaffirm the need for such a procedure ("Using the gloves means that no one has to worry about a child or caregiver being exposed to an illness while changing diapers").

Health and safety guidelines are best developed by a committee of people. Many churches have found

it helpful to create a nursery committee which meets several times a year, or more frequently if needed, to establish the policies and procedures of the nursery. This committee may be made up of several parent representatives, several people who serve in the nursery, a member of the church staff or governing body who is charged with the responsibility of the nursery program and a health professional (doctor, nurse, etc.). Some churches request that a lawyer familiar with church liability issues review their health and safety procedures. (If your church has a licensed infant/toddler facility, state health regulations must be adhered to any time the nursery is in use.) You may also request that a consultant from your state's Occupational Safety and Health Agency (OSHA) visit your nursery to evaluate the facility for safety and health hazards.

It is most helpful if the people on this committee are familiar with all of the information provided in the Organizing Your Nursery section of this book.

After establishing policies and procedures such as deciding on the number of staff members and their duties, how the nursery will be staffed, necessary equipment and supplies, and how children will be greeted and dismissed, this committee meets to evaluate and modify procedures and guidelines as necessary.

The Big Picture of Cleaning

Keeping things clean is always an issue of concern in any program involving children—especially one in which children spend so much of their time on the floor or putting things in their mouths (often both at the same time!). You may want to provide charts (see next page) on which to record cleaning assignments.

❏ Laundry (crib sheets, towels, blankets, caregiver smocks) and toys that have been in a child's mouth or drooled upon need to be cleaned after each use by a baby or toddler. Provide a laundry basket or plastic dishpan into which items needing to be washed can be placed. At the end of a nursery session, used fabric items should be washed with a hypoallergenic detergent. Hard-surfaced toys should be washed or wiped thoroughly, first with soapy water, then with a disinfecting solution, and finally rinsed with hot water. The hot water temperature of any sink accessible to children should be 110°F or less. (Some toys can also be washed in a washing machine or dishwasher.) Make sure toys are completely dry before returning them to the nursery.

❏ Wipe the surface of any furniture (crib rails, infant seats or swings, etc.) with disinfecting solution after use by a child. Also disinfect frequently touched surfaces such as doorknobs.

❏ Vacuum carpets or mop tile floors after each session, cleaning up any spills immediately.

❏ Disinfecting solutions, such as Lysol, can be purchased or made fresh for each session (mix 1 tablespoon household bleach in a quart of water, or for a larger amount, mix ¼ cup bleach in a gallon of water). All solutions must be clearly labeled, identifying the contents as well as the action to be taken if solution is ingested, splashed in eyes or on skin. It is preferable for solutions to be kept in original containers. Post poison control phone number near the closest telephone. Store all cleaning supplies out of reach of children, preferably in cabinets that either lock or have safety latches.

Less Frequent Cleaning

Once or twice a month wash windows, blinds, shelves, throw rugs, chairs and large toy items. Wash window curtains every six months. Once or twice a year wash the walls (paint as needed with lead-free paint) and shampoo the carpets. More frequent carpet shampooing may be required if the nursery receives heavy use.

Cleaning Staff

Some churches ask volunteers (parents or other adults in the church) to do the cleaning. For example, each week after the last nursery session, a volunteer may come to gather laundry items, take them home, wash and return items before the next nursery session.

Other churches request that the nursery staff be responsible for cleaning all items used at a particular session (wash surfaces and toys before leaving the room, take home laundry items to wash and return).

Less frequent types of cleaning can be done by a cleaning committee or other church group that "adopts" the nursery. Church custodians may be asked to do heavy-duty cleaning (shampoo carpets, mop floors, etc.).

Cleaning assignment charts, such as those on the next page, can be posted in each nursery room.

Daily Room Care

_____

Today's Date:

☐ Wash Laundry

☐ Wash and
Disinfect Toys

☐ Disinfect
Furniture
Tables
Door Knobs
Light Switches

☐ Vacuum
Mop Floor

☐ Spot Clean
Spills or
"Spit-Ups"

Long-Term Room Care

Room: _____

MONTHLY: _____

Date: _____

☐ Wash Windows

☐ Wash Rugs

☐ Wipe Off and Disinfect
Large Toy Items

SIX MONTHS: _____

Date: _____

☐ Wash Window Treatments

☐ Shampoo Carpet

YEARLY: _____

Date: _____

☐ Wash/Paint walls

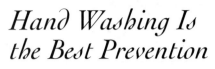

Hand Washing Is the Best Prevention

Frequent hand washing will do much to prevent the spread of infections. Encourage workers to wash their hands when they arrive in the nursery room, before handling food or bottles, after going to the bathroom, after changing a child's diapers or helping a child with toileting, after any contact with body fluids, and after cleaning nursery equipment or supplies.

Wash hands with running water and antibacterial soap, rubbing front and back of hands together for 15 to 30 seconds. Dry hands with disposable towels. Use a disposable towel to turn off the faucet so that hands are not contaminated again. Display hand washing instructions near each sink.

If your nursery does not have nearby sink facilities, provide a commercial no-rinse hand solution for caregivers to use.

Hand Washing Is the Best Prevention

Wash and wipe your hands together, live in health forever!

TAKE TIME TO WASH:

✓ when you first arrive

✓ before handling food or bottles

✓ after using the restroom

✓ after changing each child's diaper

✓ after any contact with body fluids

✓ after cleaning up

EVERYTHING YOU EVER WANTED TO KNOW ABOUT WASHING HANDS:

✓ wash with running water and antibacterial soap

✓ wash front and back of hands

✓ wash for 15–30 seconds

✓ dry hands with disposable towel

✓ turn off faucet with disposable towel

Guidelines for Safe Child Care

Establish and communicate clear guidelines about safe and healthy child care practices. Each nursery caregiver should be aware of how to interact with babies and toddlers in routine nursery activities such as feeding, sleeping, playing, diapering and toileting.

During these routine activities, emphasize the importance of focused attention on children's needs rather than conversation with other adults. Encourage caregivers to view routines such as diapering and feeding as opportunities to interact with the child, building a loving and caring relationship with him or her.

Changing Diapers

Direct caregivers to check each child's diaper at least once each hour, changing diapers when wet or soiled. If children are likely to be present in the nursery for more than one hour or with rotating staff, caregivers may find it helpful to keep a record of each diaper change.

Time for a Change!

Date: _____

Child's Name: Time Diaper Was Changed:

_____   _____

_____   _____

_____   _____

Note if diaper was wet or soiled.

The first step in changing diapers is to be prepared. Make sure that all the materials needed are at hand before picking up the child (clean diaper, disposable sheeting placed on changing table, disposable gloves, premoistened towelettes, clean clothes if needed, plastic bag for trash disposal).

Wash your hands, put on a pair of disposable gloves, talk with the child about what you are going to do, and then place the child on the changing table. Remove the wet or soiled diaper and place it in a plastic bag. Gently cleanse the diapered area with premoistened towelette, cleansing from front to back. Place towelette into plastic bag containing diaper, tie shut and place bag into wastebasket. (For cloth diapers: place towelette in wastebasket; place diaper in plastic bag; tie shut the plastic bag and place in diaper bag). Put clean diaper on the child and remove child from changing table. After settling the child elsewhere in the room, remove the disposable sheeting from the changing table and clean the table with disinfecting solution. Remove disposable gloves and place in wastebasket. Wash your hands.

Post a step-by-step description of how diapers are to be changed near the changing table. It is now accepted practice to have two adults present when diapers are changed. For the protection of male caregivers, some churches do not allow men to change diapers in the nursery. At no time in the diapering process should a caregiver turn his or her back to child on changing table or leave child alone on the changing table. If you have any concerns or questions about the safest procedures for diaper changing, contact your local health department for more information.

Ten Steps to Changing Diapers

1. Collect all necessary supplies (gloves, clean diapers, plastic bags, premoistened towelettes, etc.).

2. Wash hands and put on gloves.

3. Talk with child about what you are going to do.

4. Place the child on a clean, disposable surface (wax paper or paper towels). Never turn away from a child on a changing table, even if child is strapped onto the table.

5. Remove the wet or soiled diaper. Place in a plastic bag.

6. Use a premoistened towelette to clean the diaper area, wiping from front to back. Place towelette in plastic bag containing soiled diaper. Close and knot bag and throw it away. (For cloth diapers: dispose of wipes in wastebasket, place diaper in plastic bag, tie shut and place in diaper bag.)

7. Put clean diaper on child and remove child from changing table.

8. Remove disposable paper cover from changing table. Spray area thoroughly with bleach solution, wiping with paper towel.

9. Remove gloves and place in wastebasket.

10. Wash hands thoroughly.

Toilet Training

Request that toddlers who are being toilet trained always be brought to the nursery in diapers or in disposable training pants. Provide a potty chair or a low toilet in an adjacent bathroom to assist toddlers who are in the process of potty training. Leave the bathroom door open while a child is using the toilet. If the toilet is located away from the nursery, two adults should accompany the child. Some churches stipulate that same-sex caregivers should assist the child.

Feeding Babies

Always be sure that each child's bottle is labeled. If possible, store bottles in a small refrigerator or an insulated bag. Never feed a child a bottle that has warmed to room temperature—any bacteria in the milk or formula will rapidly multiply at room temperature. Bottles may be warmed, if needed, in a bottle warmer. (If bottle has been warmed, before feeding the baby, test the temperature of the milk or formula by placing a few drops on the back of your forearm.) Feeding babies is most satisfying in a peaceful place with no bright lights or loud noises.

Wash hands before feeding a baby. Hold the child in a slightly upright position (the upright position is thought to prevent ear infections) while holding him or her securely in your arm. A rocking chair with arms is comfortable for caregivers and babies. Tilt the bottle so the nipple is always full. Some parents may provide a cloth to use in burping the baby after the feeding, or caregiver may use a paper towel.

Feeding Toddlers

Many churches keep a supply of snacks and juices to serve toddlers. Supplies should be purchased by a trusted, long-term caregiver who is careful about where the food is purchased. Store foods in a locked cabinet where they cannot be tampered with. Before serving foods, be sure they are still fresh and free from obvious signs of deterioration.

Always check each child's information card (see pages 62, 63) or check-in sheet (see pages 64-67) for food allergies. Severe or life-threatening food allergies should be written on a masking tape strip and placed on the child's back or attached to name tag. Common nursery snacks are graham crackers, fish-shaped crackers, mini rice cakes, dry unsweetened cereals, diluted apple juice and water. Never serve items which could cause a child to choke: popcorn, nuts, raisins, raw carrots, grapes, etc. Always supervise toddlers while they are eating.

Use premoistened towelettes to clean a child's hands before eating, or children may wash their own hands if a child-size sink is in the room. Toddlers may sit around a table, or sit on the floor for eating. (Some churches place a large sheet on the floor, encouraging children to sit on the sheet while eating. After snack time, the sheet is gathered up to be laundered.) Say or sing a short prayer with children before and during their snacks.

Treat spills in a matter-of-fact way, providing a damp sponge for children to use in helping to clean up spills.

In order to prevent toddlers from sharing bottles, restrict the child's movements while he or she is drinking from a bottle (caregiver holds the child on his or her lap, places the child in a crib or playpen). In a small nursery, it may be possible to closely supervise the toddler so the bottle is not left where other children can get it.

Sleeping

During each session, be sensitive to babies and toddlers who appear to need a rest. Occasionally a parent may indicate to you on the check-in sheet that a child is accustomed to napping during the session. Realize, however, that the extra stimulus of a nursery may make it difficult or impossible for a child to fall asleep.

A tired child may benefit from a brief time of rocking by a caregiver, or listening to a soothing song. Or the child may feel rested after lying in a quiet area of the nursery with a favorite toy or blanket. A comfort item brought from home may help the child relax and eventually fall asleep. When a child awakens, don't necessarily rush to pick up the child, but look for clues to indicate the child's preference.

Sometimes a parent will indicate to you the child's preference for sleeping (side, back or stomach). Health specialists now recommend placing babies on their backs to sleep and not wrapping babies too tightly. Use firm bedding materials

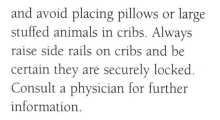

and avoid placing pillows or large stuffed animals in cribs. Always raise side rails on cribs and be certain they are securely locked. Consult a physician for further information.

Safety Checks

Because the church nursery may be used by a variety of groups, some of whom may not be familiar with safety and health guidelines, a care-

giver or other nursery staff member should inspect the room at the beginning of each session.

✓ Look for potentially dangerous objects (small objects, pins, buttons, coins, broken toys, hot beverages or purses brought in by staff, etc.) on floor or shelves.

✓ Be sure all electrical outlets are covered with safety plugs and that all cords (including cords for blinds) are out of reach of children.

✓ Check that furniture or climbing toys are placed away from windows and that window screens are firmly fastened.

✓ Confirm that all cleaning supplies are put away out of the reach of children (on high shelves or in locked cabinets).

✓ Look for chipped paint or splinters on furniture and walls and loose wallpaper on walls. Until repairs can be made, masking tape can be used to cover small areas of peeling paint or wallpaper.

✓ Remove any broken toys, or toys which are inappropriate for babies and toddlers. All toys need to be large enough so they can't be swallowed. (Choke testers are available from educational supply stores.)

Adapt this sample checklist for use in your church. You may need to include information about disinfecting furniture, checking to be sure doors or gates are open or closed, etc. Give the checklist to the nursery coordinator or to a designated caregiver for use at the beginning of each session, or post the checklist on a bulletin board in the nursery for all caregivers to refer to.

On page 41 is a flyer which can be given to groups using the nursery on a one-time or occasional basis.

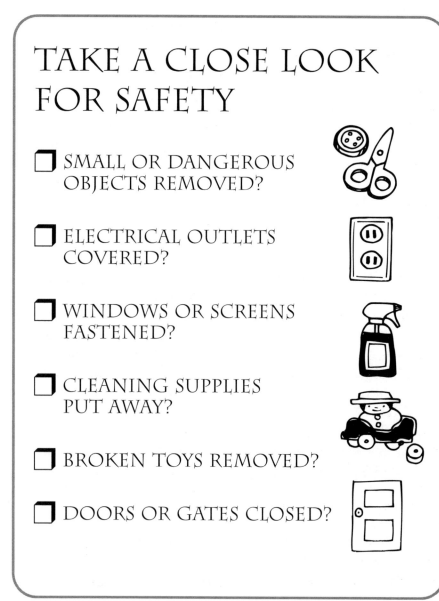

TAKE A CLOSE LOOK FOR SAFETY

☐ SMALL OR DANGEROUS OBJECTS REMOVED?

☐ ELECTRICAL OUTLETS COVERED?

☐ WINDOWS OR SCREENS FASTENED?

☐ CLEANING SUPPLIES PUT AWAY?

☐ BROKEN TOYS REMOVED?

☐ DOORS OR GATES CLOSED?

WELCOME TO OUR NURSERY!

PLEASE HELP US KEEP OUR NURSERY SAFE, CLEAN AND READY-TO-USE!

WHILE IN THE NURSERY:

- [ ] USE THE NAME TAGS, CHECK-IN SHEETS AND SECURITY TAGS PROVIDED IN THE ROOM.

- [ ] MAINTAIN A SAFE CHILDCARE RATIO (ONE ADULT FOR EVERY 3-4 CHILDREN) WITH TWO ADULTS BEING PRESENT IN THE ROOM AT ALL TIMES.

- [ ] WASH AND DISINFECT CHANGING TABLE AFTER EACH DIAPER CHANGE. (FOLLOW THE DIAPER-CHANGING INSTRUCTIONS POSTED ABOVE THE CHANGING TABLE.)

- [ ] WASH YOUR HANDS AFTER DIAPERING EACH CHILD OR ASSISTING A CHILD IN BATHROOM.

BEFORE LEAVING THE NURSERY:

- [ ] WASH AND DISINFECT ANY TOYS USED BY CHILDREN. (CLEANING INSTRUCTIONS ARE POSTED BY THE SINK.)

- [ ] PUT CLEAN SHEETS ON ANY CRIBS USED BY CHILDREN. PLACE ANY USED LAUNDRY (CRIB SHEETS, BLANKETS, ETC.) IN THE LAUNDRY BASKET.

- [ ] WASH AND DISINFECT ALL EQUIPMENT THAT WAS USED (CRIB RAILS, BABY SWINGS, ETC.).

- [ ] VACUUM THE CARPET AND/OR SWEEP THE FLOOR.

- [ ] EMPTY THE WASTEBASKET.

- [ ] CLOSE AND LOCK WINDOWS AND DOORS.

Thanks for your help!

Illnesses

One of the most frequent concerns of parents who are choosing whether or not to place their child in a group child-care setting is whether or not the other children are healthy. Your nursery committee needs to carefully plan how the health of children and caregivers is monitored.

Healthy from the Start

1. Well-baby policy. The basic foundation for a healthy nursery is a well-baby policy. Establishing, communicating and firmly adhering to a well-baby policy will reassure parents and caregivers alike and make your nursery a welcoming place. A well-written policy will answer questions of parents who are concerned about the health of their children in the nursery. Several sample guidelines are on the next page.

Communicate your well-baby policy by including it in a nursery handbook or brochure, in parent newsletters, and in letters to families who visit your nursery. Display well-baby guidelines on nursery bulletin boards or entry areas. At the beginning of the winter cold-and-flu season, many churches send home a letter reminding parents of health guidelines.

It is also important to acquaint your church staff with the nursery's well-baby policy. Enlist the help of staff members in making it possible for parents to stay home with an ill child. Explain that following the well-baby policy will increase attendance and parent participation in the programs of the church because the nursery will become known as a safe, healthy place for babies and toddlers.

Some churches designate a caregiver or the nursery coordinator to do a quick visual health inspection as babies and toddlers are checked in at the nursery. While some symptoms are not visible at a quick glance, a runny nose or frequent cough should prompt a conversation with the child's parents. Simply state what you have observed in a friendly manner and invite the parent's response. "I hear Joshua coughing a lot. How does he feel today? Does he have a fever?" or "Allie's nose seems to be running. How is she feeling? Does she have a cold?"

It's difficult to exclude a child from the nursery, but most parents will respond to a conversation that makes it clear the parents and caregivers are a team working together for the child's health. For example, you might say, "I'll ask Mrs. Smith to keep an eye on Nathan. If his runny nose continues, he'd probably feel more comfortable if you took him home." Then the nursery caregiver monitors Nathan's health while keeping him in an isolated area of the nursery. Another way to converse with the parent is to say, "The nursery committee has asked us to pay special attention to our well-baby policy during this time of colds and flus. We're sorry, but it looks (or sounds) as if Megan would be better off at home today."

Occasionally a child has been determined to have allergies that cause a continual runny nose (clear discharge), rash or cough. Ask parents to note allergies of this nature on the child's information card.

Always introduce the well-baby policy with a positive approach: "We want to keep our babies healthy!" or "Your child's good health is our goal!"

2. Caregiver substitutes. Encourage nursery caregivers to limit their participation in the nursery when they are sick by having a ready list of substitutes. Nursery coordinators or designated caregivers should not hesitate to ask a caregiver with symptoms of ill health to go home.

Good Health Guidelines

We want to provide a healthy environment in our nursery, so we ask you to keep your baby at home when you observe any of the following:

Fever/Vomiting

Discharge in or around the eyes

Green or yellow runny nose

Excessive coughing

Diarrhea

Questionable rash

Any communicable disease

If your baby becomes ill while in the nursery, you will be notified promptly.

If your child is being treated with an antibiotic, he or she should have received treatment for at least 24 hours before coming to the nursery.

For your child's protection, we ask our caregivers to follow these same guidelines.

Dear Parents of Nursery Children,

Young children are very susceptible to colds, flus and other diseases. We realize a child's illness can be a difficult time for a parent, and that it's often frustrating to rearrange your schedules to provide care for a sick child at home.

We want to help eliminate these concerns as much as possible. This requires that our nursery has the healthiest environment possible. The best way to prevent illness is to prevent exposure. The purpose of this letter is to help our nursery caregivers and parents work together to provide a healthy environment.

1. Please keep your child at home if any one of the following is true: your child has a fever or has had a fever in the past 24 hours; your child has vomited or had diarrhea in the past 24 hours.

2. A quick health check will be conducted when you bring your child to the nursery. A child will not be admitted with any of these symptoms: matter in the eyes, frequent coughing, runny nose (anything but clear discharge).

Thanks for letting us care for and love your child. Please do not hesitate to call if you have any questions or comments about the nursery.

Nursery Coordinator
555-5555

Adapted by permission from First Presbyterian Church, Santa Barbara, California.

When a Child Becomes Ill

Occasionally a baby or toddler develops symptoms of illness during a nursery session. The child may be particularly fussy, cry continually in pain, appear lethargic, have a flushed face or sudden rash, cough frequently and sound very congested, discharge from nose or eyes may be apparent, or the child may feel overly warm. Babies may indicate pain by drawing their legs up to their abdomens while crying. If any of these symptoms appear, contact the parent and request that the child be taken home for his or her own comfort and health. Until a parent arrives in the nursery, a caregiver should remain with the child in an isolated area of the nursery.

If a child has recently been ill and is no longer contagious but still receives medication, parents should administer the medication. (Medications brought by parents should be stored properly away from the reach of children, in a refrigerator if needed.) Health professionals recommend that a child be on antibiotics for at least 24 hours before he or she is no longer considered contagious.

Infectious Diseases

Children with infectious diseases such as mumps, measles, chicken pox, conjunctivitis and impetigo should be kept at home. Occasionally a child may develop symptoms of a disease later in the day after spending a session in the nursery.

In these cases, it's helpful to send or post a notice to alert parents to the possibility that their children were exposed to the disease. Include possible symptoms and the time period in which children may show symptoms of the disease.

The health and safety guidelines developed by your nursery committee should include guidelines for responding to children who have hepatitis (HBV) or AIDS, or who may be HIV positive. Write guidelines for handling these diseases in conjunction with church-wide guidelines. Include facts about the disease, information about the infection control procedures followed in your church (e.g., cleaning and disinfecting procedures, use of disposable gloves, etc.), and confidentiality policies. A sample infectious disease policy and a related form are on the next three pages. Because laws about the treatment of people with infectious diseases are subject to change, it is best to consult a state health agency and a competent local attorney for further information about state and federal laws at the time you are developing your church's procedures and policies.

Parent Note:

We thought you'd want to know!

While in the nursery at First Church on May 29, your child was exposed to chicken pox.

Symptoms of chicken pox usually include small raised pimples that may have tiny yellow water blisters on top, fever and headache. Symptoms are likely to appear between 11 and 19 days after exposure.

For further information, consult your child's doctor.

INFECTIOUS DISEASE/AIDS & HBV POLICY

STATEMENT OF PURPOSE

We commit ourselves to being knowledgeable and informed about Infectious Diseases/AIDS & HBV (Hepatitis B Virus), and to be a support network that is nonjudgmental, compassionate and Christ-centered, capable of providing spiritual and emotional support to those infected as well as affected family members and friends. While we do not condone the behaviors that sometimes result in AIDS, we know Jesus loves every individual and desires for all to come to Him in repentance. We believe we are assisting God's work in the person's life when we extend compassionate care to infected people. It could well be that our loving ministry to an HIV-infected person is what will successfully communicate God's love to him or her.

MEDICAL FACTS ABOUT AIDS

Acquired Immune Deficiency Syndrome (AIDS) is a serious life-threatening condition. The best scientific evidence indicates that AIDS is caused by a virus known as HIV (Human Immunodeficiency Virus), which is transmitted through exposure to infected blood or semen through sexual contact, injury, sharing of contaminated needles, or from an infected mother to child before or around the time of birth. Not every infant who tests positive is actually HIV infected. One-half to two-thirds will be completely free from evidence of infection by eighteen months, after antibodies from the mother have dissipated from the infant's blood.

OUR RESPONSE

Any individual who has been diagnosed with any infectious disease and/or is HIV Positive or has AIDS should be treated similarly to any other individual attending our church. In general, we will not reject or ostracize anyone who has an infectious disease, is HIV Positive or who has AIDS as long as that individual presents no real threat to the safety of others in the congregation (example: open sores or inability to control bodily functions). Confidentiality regarding individuals who have infectious diseases or are HIV Positive or have AIDS will be respected.

United States Public Health Service guidelines for infectious diseases will be followed for all individuals including infants and children in the Nursery, Sunday School and Day/After School Care. Nursery and Children's Workers and other appropriate groups will be trained accordingly, using universal precautions.

"Universal precautions" refers to the handling of body fluids from all students and not just those known to be infected with a blood-borne pathogen.

Universal precautions require the use of protective barriers such as gloves, protective eye wear, gowns and masks. Precautions beyond the use of gloves would only be required in unusual circumstances in the school setting. Gloves do not, however, prevent possible exposure due to penetrating injuries from needles or sharp instruments.

Adapted by permission from Calvary Assembly of God, Winter Park, Florida and Westlake Bible Church, Austin, Texas.

The AIDS Committee

A standing AIDS Committee will be established to help anyone in our congregation who is HIV positive. The Committee will assess how the church can be most supportive of the person/family and will administer the guidelines of this policy to ensure that the patient's church experience is as good as the experience of any other church attender.

The specific duties of the committee include the following:

1) When a person identifies him-/herself or his/her child as HIV positive to anyone in the congregation, the person should be told about the AIDS Committee and encouraged to contact the chairman. The chairman will arrange for one or more committee members to visit with the person or family and assess the needs and desires of the patient.

2) One member, preferably a health-care professional, will volunteer to receive calls from anyone in the congregation who has a question or concern about AIDS. The person's phone number will be published in appropriate church publications.

3) The committee will meet on a case-by-case basis to talk to and help any family bringing an infected child to church. The committee or its representative will convey the goals of the church and initiate the procedures adopted for infected children.

Each case will be examined individually and flexibility maintained. The child's physician, parents or guardian, and the AIDS Committee will decide how to bring such a child to church.

While these decisions are being made, an adult will be assigned to personally minister to and monitor the HIV-infected child.

Toddlers and infants with HIV infection will be integrated slowly into the classroom. The child will begin in a playpen and an assigned monitor will stay with the child at all times. This monitor might initially be a doctor or nurse who would care for the child, keep his/her toys away from others, and change diapers. Later the monitor could be any responsible adult. (The close observation is not necessary to prevent transfer of HIV disease but to alleviate the anxieties of other parents.) Play outside the playpen and full integration into the class will depend on the child's behavior and the sentiment of the parents of the other children.

Infants through 6th grade children who are infected will be identified to the parents of the other children in the Sunday School class and to the Sunday School teachers. The AIDS committee will be in charge of a concentrated communication and education effort with the desired effect of reducing anxieties and providing a quality church environment for the HIV-infected child. If the anxiety of the parents and other children is so high that the infected child is in danger of being ostracized, then the committee will find at least two people who can play with the infected child, teach the Sunday School lesson, and serve him/her in every need.

EDUCATION FOR THE CONGREGATION

According to the most recent research data from the Center for Disease Control, "No documented cases of HIV infection have been traced to casual contact." Since knowledge can dispel fear and set the groundwork for compassionate understanding, we shall commit to educating the church regarding infectious diseases and HIV-related issues.

Protective Measures

The best way to prevent the spread of blood-transmitted infections such as HIV is to utilize "universal precautions," which means the blood of everyone is considered potentially infectious. Since the vast majority of people who have HIV are unaware of their infection, the greatest danger is exposure to the blood of an infected child or adult who is assumed to be uninfected. Therefore all blood spills will be handled with caution.

Latex examination gloves will be worn when contact is anticipated with blood, open sores, cuts, or the inside of a person's mouth. Gloves will also be used when handling objects that are contaminated with blood. Children's workers with open sores on the hand will wear gloves. Open sores elsewhere on the body will be covered with an adequate-sized bandage.

Gloves will be readily available throughout the church. They will be stored in the nursery, in children's Sunday School rooms, in the kitchen and on the playground.

Since HIV is destroyed by household bleach, a solution of one part bleach to ten parts water will be kept in the first-aid cabinet. The bleach solution will be stored at room temperature in closed, opaque plastic containers and made fresh at the beginning of each session. Small blood spills will be cleaned while wearing gloves, using disposable towels moistened with the bleach solution. If a large spill of blood occurs, the area will be cleaned with disposable paper towels or linens while wearing gloves. The bleach solution will then be poured over the area, and the area cleaned again.

PARENTAL RELEASE FORM FOR HIV POSITIVE CHILD

As a parent of _____,

I do give my consent for a bona fide need-to-know person to be informed that

my child is HIV positive so that she or he can be attended to in case of emergency.

_____

Signed

Accidents

Nursery caregivers need to be familiar with efficient procedures for handling accidents, even though they may never need to put the procedures into practice. Often, a quick hug and sympathetic ear are enough to calm a child's outward distress. However, alert caregivers to be watchful no matter how slight the injury appears. Questions to ask are:

❏ Is the child unresponsive?

❏ Is the child having difficulty breathing?

❏ Is the child's cry unusual?

❏ Is the child's pulse weak or rapid?

❏ Is the child vomiting?

If any of these questions are answered in the affirmative, call for medical help immediately.

Each nursery room should have an up-to-date first aid manual (available from your local American Red Cross agency) clearly in view and a first aid kit stored out of children's reach. Once a month the nursery coordinator should check the kit contents and replace items as needed. Consider posting basic first aid information (what to do for insect bites and stings, head or nose injuries, falls and cuts, seizures, choking, poisoning) on nursery bulletin boards.

Caregivers should also have quick access to a telephone if emergency medical services are required. Post emergency phone numbers (9-1-1 or local hospital, police and fire departments and poison control centers) near each telephone, along with directions to your facility and how to get to the building in which you are located.

Consider these additional tips for handling accidents:

❖ During each nursery session, designate a person in the building or on the premises who is trained in CPR for infants and toddlers. (Provide CPR and first aid classes for caregivers on a regular basis.)

❖ During each nursery session, schedule a doctor or nurse to be on the church premises. Post his or her name and location, or use a pager system.

❖ Never hesitate to offer first aid to an injured baby or toddler, but when possible wear disposable gloves in cleaning up blood or other bodily fluids.

Any time a child sustains an injury, verbal and written reports need to be completed. (See forms on pages 49, 50.) Parents and a designated person on the church staff should be informed of the injury and the circumstances in which it occurred and how the injury was treated. (Follow any guidelines that have already been established by your church.)

If a caregiver, whether paid or volunteer, is injured in the nursery, follow the insurance and liability procedures your church has already established for employees and volunteer workers.

Emergencies

All churches should have planned procedures in case of fire and emergency evacuation plans. Depending on your church's location, you may also need to provide information for emergencies such as earthquakes, tornadoes and floods. Ask your local American Red Cross agency to provide you with the appropriate posters and/or handouts to display or have on hand in your nursery. Summarize pertinent emergency information at caregiver training sessions.

Plan and post two emergency exits from each nursery room. (Ask your local fire department to help you determine the safest routes and where fire extinguishers should be mounted.) Designate a meeting place for all children and caregivers.

Additional tips for emergencies:

❖ Keep a bag of emergency supplies (snacks, diapers, disposable gloves, first aid kit, flashlight, portable radio, water, etc.) elsewhere on the church premises or quickly accessible to caregivers in case of evacuation.

❖ Always have at least one working flashlight available in each nursery room, in case of a power outage or if an evacuation takes place at night.

❖ Keep several baby slings or backpacks in the nursery for carrying babies in an emergency. Several children may also be placed in a crib with wheels. Roll cribs out the doors to a predetermined safe area.

Parent Notification
I Was Hurt Today (But I'm OK Now!)

Where I Was:

_____

What Happened:

_____

_____ helped me by

_____

Parent Notification
I Was Hurt Today (But I'm OK Now!)

Where I Was:

_____

What Happened:

_____

_____ helped me by

_____

Church Office Notification Injury Report

Name, Age and Gender of Child Who Was Injured:

_____

Address: _____ City/Zip: _____

Name of Parent: _____ Phone: _____

Date and Time of Accident: _____

Describe in detail how the child was injured, including location, names and actions of all children and adults involved.

_____

_____

_____

Describe the child's injuries and what action was taken to treat the injuries.

_____

How and when was the parent notified?

_____

Please list names and phone numbers of witnesses to the accident.

1. _____

2. _____

3. _____

Additional Comments: _____

Your name, address and phone number: _____

_____

Child Abuse Prevention and Reporting

Developing safety procedures for preventing and reporting child abuse is somewhat like taking a CPR class. While never expecting to have a problem, it is wise to take necessary precautions. People who minister to children need to be trained to know how to respond if there is a situation calling for action, praying that it will not be needed.

Adapt the sample policy on this page to help your church create a safe place for both children and adults in your nursery, including guidelines for caregiver selection, caregiver practices, reporting obligation and response to an allegation. All caregivers (and other children's workers) should be familiarized with these guidelines on an annual basis. (It is recommended that a lawyer evaluate your policies to be sure they conform to your state's laws regarding child abuse.) Some churches use security video cameras in their nurseries (similar to those in convenience stores), both as a safety precaution and as a means of having positive proof of innocence in case of allegations.

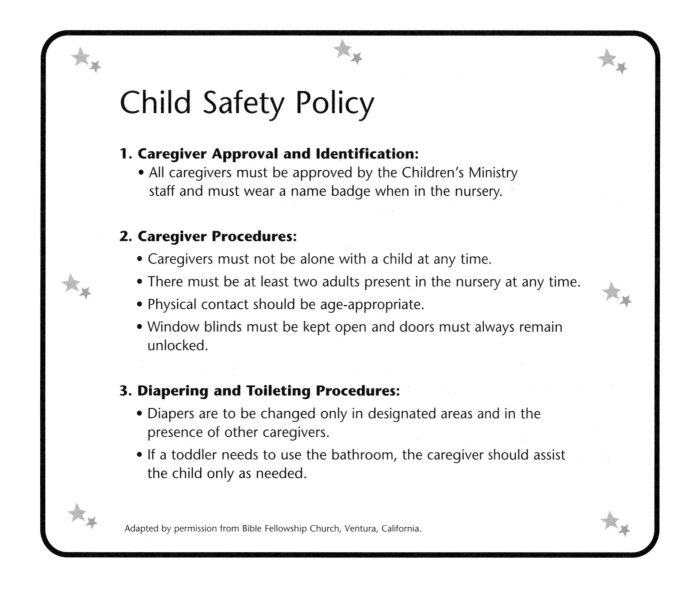

Child Safety Policy

1. Caregiver Approval and Identification:
- All caregivers must be approved by the Children's Ministry staff and must wear a name badge when in the nursery.

2. Caregiver Procedures:
- Caregivers must not be alone with a child at any time.
- There must be at least two adults present in the nursery at any time.
- Physical contact should be age-appropriate.
- Window blinds must be kept open and doors must always remain unlocked.

3. Diapering and Toileting Procedures:
- Diapers are to be changed only in designated areas and in the presence of other caregivers.
- If a toddler needs to use the bathroom, the caregiver should assist the child only as needed.

Adapted by permission from Bible Fellowship Church, Ventura, California.

How to Report Suspected Child Abuse

1. All caregivers are to be familiar with the definitions of child abuse (see below).

2. If a caregiver suspects that a child in the nursery has been abused, the following steps are to be followed.
   • Report the suspected abuse to your supervisor.
   • Do not interview the child regarding the suspected abuse. The interview process will be handled by trained personnel.
   • Do not discuss the suspected abuse. It is important that all information about the suspected child abuse (victim and abuser) be kept confidential.

3. Caregivers reporting suspected child abuse will be asked to complete the Suspected Child Abuse Report (available from your state's Department of Social Services). Confidentiality will be maintained where possible. This report must be completed within 24 hours.

4. Once a suspected child abuse case has been reported by a caregiver to a supervisor, it will be reported to the designated reporting agency.

Adapted by permission from Bible Fellowship Church, Ventura, California.

Definitions of Child Abuse

Defined by The National Committee for Prevention of Child Abuse

Physical Abuse: Nonaccidental injury, which may include beatings, violent shaking, human bites, strangulation, suffocation, poisoning, or burns. The results may be bruises and welts, broken bones, scars, permanent disfigurement, long-lasting psychological damage, serious internal injuries, brain damage, or death.

Neglect: The failure to provide a child with basic needs, including food, clothing, education, shelter, and medical care; also abandonment and inadequate supervision.

Sexual Abuse: The sexual exploitation of a child by an older person, as in rape, incest, fondling of the genitals, exhibitionism, or pornography. It may be done for the sexual gratification of the older person, out of a need for power, or for economic reasons.

Adapted by permission from Bible Fellowship Church, Ventura, California.

Partnering with Parents

Involving Parents at the Start

Any ministry to young children involves ministering to parents as well. Long-term, positive results in child guidance and nurture are increased when parents and nursery caregivers become partners working together. Conversely, whenever parents are ignored, the impact of any program involving their child is greatly reduced. Whether you are just beginning a nursery program, or your nursery program has been functioning for many years, it will benefit you to involve parents in the oversight of the nursery program, policies and procedures. If you have a nursery committee overseeing the nursery, include one or more parents on the committee. (See page 33 for additional information on nursery committees.)

Communicate with Parents

When parents and nursery caregivers share similar goals and use similar approaches, effectiveness is greatly increased. Parents and the nursery staff need to work together to develop common understandings of ways babies and toddlers learn and how they are cared for. The child will sense the continuity between church and home. A clearly defined and consistent plan for communication is vital to developing this link between church and home.

1. Parent Handbook.

Develop a handbook or brochure that describes the procedures of your nursery. Parents are usually very willing to comply with these procedures when they clearly understand what is expected of them and the reasons for the procedures. Periodically evaluate your brochure or handbook and update the policies as needed.

Distribute the handbook to parents the first time they bring their child to the nursery. Each person working in the nursery should have a copy. Make copies available in the narthex or entryway to your church and make sure church ushers or greeters know not only the location of the nursery, but where the handbooks are kept so they can give them to interested visitors. (Note: Whenever making handbooks, brochures or flyers to distribute to parents, make ample extra copies. Store the copies in a "new family" folder. When a new family becomes a part of your nursery, it's easy to compile a packet of the information they need.)

The handbook should include information on the following topics:

❖ A brief statement about the goals of your nursery.

❖ Well-baby guidelines for children in the nursery.

❖ Which personal items should be brought to the nursery and how they should be labeled.

❖ Greeting and dismissal procedures, including your church's plan for child and parent identification.

❖ How you would like parents to provide information about the child (name of child and parents, phone numbers, feeding instructions, food allergies, etc.).

❖ Name and phone number of nursery coordinator or a church staff member who may be called for further information.

❖ Depending on the size of your church, you may also provide information about room locations for different ages, facility map, age at which children are promoted into a two-year-old class and programs in which parents of young children may be interested. Keep in mind that the brochure or handbook must provide the essential information parents need to know, but not so much information that only the most dedicated parent will read it!

Several sample brochures are provided on the following pages.

PARENTS— WELCOME TO THE NURSERY!

We believe your child is a special gift from God—so we want to provide the best love and care possible. Please label your child's diaper bag and bottle, and complete the sign-in sheet.

We provide loving care and teaching during both morning worship services as well as during the Sunday School hour. It helps avoid upsetting confusion if you indicate which sessions your child will attend. It is easier on your child if you do not check on him or her between sessions. (No child should have to endure two separations in one morning.)

All children cry sometimes when being left by parents. We understand and expect it. In most cases, crying stops a few moments after you leave. (Yes, it's a plot to make you feel guilty.) If your child continues to cry after five or ten minutes, we will send someone to notify you.

WELL CHILDREN ONLY! For the health of all (and the peace of mind of every parent), children with symptoms of illness should not be brought here. Thank you!

We are delighted that you brought your baby to our Baby/Toddler Department. We will do our best to provide good care while your baby is with us.

Here are several important things to remember that will make your baby's time at church enjoyable and worthwhile:

1. To protect the health of all our babies, we cannot accept a baby who is ill with a cold or fever.

2. Please put your child's name on your diaper bag and its contents: plastic bottle (with enough food to see him or her through the session), diapers, pacifier, etc. We are happy to warm a bottle, but we cannot feed your baby food other than what you bring in a bottle.* Our toddlers (ages 12-24 months) receive a small snack, usually crackers and juice. Please notify us of any food allergies your toddler has.

3. Please check your child's Information Card at least once a month to mark any changes in schedule, preferences or other information that will help us care for your child. Information Cards are kept near the entrance in a file box.

4. Your child may cry when left with us. This reaction is a normal healthy show of preference for parents. The child's fussing usually stops within a few minutes, and becomes less common with regular attendance.

We hope you feel confident that your little one will receive loving care and understanding. Ask us about any of our policies and procedures. We are happy to answer your questions.

Signed, _____

* (NOTE: A department with only a few children may not need this restriction.)

Nursery

Birth through 27 months

The nursery is open every Saturday and Sunday during the Celebrations and for special church events as announced. Located in the main hallway of the Celebration Center, the nursery is divided into separate rooms for different age groups. The nursery rooms are open 15 minutes before a Celebration or event and remain open for the duration of the activity. Please remember to be prompt in picking up your children after the Celebration or event is over.

You are encouraged to help your child feel comfortable with the nursery experience by staying in the room as long as necessary.

Our Nursery is a Volunteer Co-op.

If your child attends regularly, you are expected to serve in our nursery for at least one Celebration a month, unless you are actively involved in children's ministries.

Dads and Moms are encouraged to team up together for nursery duty. We need to have a specific ratio of adults to children so that no adult is supervising more than 3 infants, 4 crawlers, or 5 toddlers. Because of this requirement, when you check your child in, you may be asked to stay and work during that Celebration.

We have a Visual Paging System!

The number you receive when you check your child in (birth through 3 years) serves as a security check as well as a pager number. Should your child need you during Celebration, the number will appear on either side of the Celebration Room near the ceiling on the black wall area. Please, go immediately to your child's room!

We welcome you and your child to

Children's Ministries

at

Calvary Community Church.

We want your child to feel welcome and a part of our program through the people and activities that God has placed in this ministry area.

Children's Ministries

Birth Through Grade 6

From infancy you have known the holy Scriptures...

which are able to make you wise for salvation through faith in Christ Jesus. All Scripture is God-breathed and is useful for teaching, rebuking, correcting and training in righteousness, so that the man of God may be thoroughly equipped for every good work.

(2 Timothy 3:15,16)

If everyone follows these guidelines, the Nursery will flow along very smoothly.

CFC NURSERY DEPARTMENT

What's expected of you?

We simply ask that you follow the following checklist every time you come to the Nursery.

1. Diaper bag labeled with child's name?
2. Bottles and pacifiers labeled?
3. Hand child over the door to awaiting nursery worker?
4. Pick up ID badge?
5. Fill out locator card?

Calvary Fellowship Church
95 West Devon Drive
Downingtown, PA 19335
(610) 363-7171

Jesus said, "Let the little children come to me, and do not hinder them, for the kingdom of heaven belongs to such as these."

Matthew 19:14

Used by permission from Calvary Fellowship Church, Downington, Pennsylvania.

WHAT IS THE PURPOSE OF THE NURSERY?

The purpose of the nursery department is to provide a safe, loving, fun, and comfortable environment for both you and your child. To accomplish this our workers will walk, rock, read, feed and play with the children to insure that they are content.

The nursery department is made up of three rooms: Infants (Birth–6 months), Crawlers (6–12 months) and Walkers (12–24 months). Each room is staffed by a team of 2–4 workers. Each team is scheduled 1 week per month.

The nursery has implemented an ID badge system that prevents anyone other than the parent from picking up a child. As you sign in your child, you will receive an ID badge with your child's name on it. Simply return the ID badge to a nursery worker when picking up your child.

Parent locator cards are given to each parent while leaving the child in the nursery. A diagram of the Worship Center is on it. Simply place an *X* where you will be sitting, write your name on it and give it to an usher. If your child needs you during the service, we will be able to find you quickly.

INFANTS

This room is for children Birth–6 months. All babies in this room are cared for by adults only. Men are not scheduled in this room in order to provide privacy for nursing Moms.

Swings and cribs are used in this room and no snacks are given.

When your child is crawling you may move him/her up to the next room.

CRAWLERS

This room is for children 6–12 months.

All babies in this room are cared for by adults only. Snacks (Cheerios) are provided in this room unless otherwise specified.

When your child is walking you may move him/her up to the next room.

WALKERS

This room is for children 12–24 months.

The children in this room are cared for by adults and teenage apprentices. We feel that this is a great training tool for the youth of our church.

Snacks are provided.

Your child will stay in this room till after his/her 2nd birthday.

You will be notified when it is your child's turn to graduate to the Wonderworks Department.

HEALTH POLICIES

IN ORDER TO INSURE THE SAFETY AND HEALTH OF OTHER BABIES AND WORKERS, PLEASE REFRAIN FROM BRINGING YOUR CHILD IF HE/SHE HAS HAD ANY OF THE FOLLOWING SYMPTOMS WITHIN THE PAST 24 HOURS.

DIARRHEA

VOMITING

FEVER

RASH

OPEN SORES

RUNNY NOSE (ANYTHING BUT CLEAR)

We are striving to make the nursery as healthy and safe as possible. Some ways we are doing this are by using rubber gloves for diaper changes, parent locator cards, personal ID badges, and periodic CPR classes.

If you have any questions, problems or suggestions, please feel free to call the church office.

Our goal is to provide a secure and happy environment for you and your child.

Children will be promoted within the Nursery the first Sunday of each month.

Children will be promoted from Nursery into Preschool twice a year.

Parents will be advised of the promotion day for their child.

For a successful family ministry, parents of nursery-age children will serve one service in the nursery per month.

The purpose of the enclosed policies is to promote unity and understanding between the parents and Nursery Staff at the Valley Cathedral.

THE VALLEY CATHEDRAL

Sharing, Caring and Loving God

Phoenix, Arizona

Used by permission from
The Valley Cathedral,
6225 North Central Avenue
Phoenix, Arizona 85012.
(602) 265-6225
Dan Scott, Senior Pastor
Keith deLaet, Children's Pastor

The Valley Cathedral

Welcome to the Valley Cathedral Nursery

Sunday A.M. & Wednesday P.M.—
Birth Through 3 Years

Sunday P.M.—Birth Through Kindergarten

General

1. Nursery facilities will be open 30 minutes prior to regular church services and approximately 15 minutes after church services.

2. A parent should call for the child IMMEDIATELY following the service or function.

3. It is suggested that only one parent call for their child. This will save confusion at the classroom door.

4. No children above nursery age will be permitted in any Nursery room.

5. Children may be brought to the Nursery only if the parent(s) or adult guardian(s) (at least 18 years of age) wish to attend a church service or function.

6. Nursery bedding is changed after each use. Beds and toys are wiped down with a sterilized solution after each session.

7. Please do not "look in" on your child. This may cause your child to be unnecessarily upset, as well as cause disruption to the other children.

8. All nursery-age children must be signed into their rooms and labeled by their parent or adult guardian. A number tag will be pinned on your child and the parent will keep the corresponding Nursery Number Card. If your child needs your attention, this number will be flashed on the Number Boards in the Worship Center (ask an usher to point them out to you if you are not familiar with their location). Children will only be released to the parent or guardian possessing a Nursery Number Card. This is for security and the protection of

your child. Please do not enter the room.

9. Parents should indicate on the sign-in sheet where they will be during all classes and services. This will expedite finding you in case of an emergency.

10. It is strongly recommended that babies and toddlers not be left for a period longer than 3–4 hours. Children become very tired and frustrated when left for long periods of time. We want them to have a positive attitude about church and God.

Clothing, Etc.

1. Diaper bags, clothing and other personal items MUST BE LABELED with the child's full name. Please include a change of clothing and an empty plastic bag in the diaper bag for wet or soiled clothing.

2. It is suggested that your child be dressed in comfortable loose-fitting, machine-washable clothing that will not restrict free movement.

3. Disposable diapers are preferred in all rooms.

4. Nursery-age children undergoing toilet training should have with them a change of clothing in a labeled bag.

5. Do not allow your child to bring personal toys or other possessions unless it is a "security" item (pacifier, blanket, etc.).

Illness

1. Children who are sick (fever, colored mucus from the nose, coughing, vomiting within the last 24 hours, skin rash, etc.) will not be allowed in the Nursery.

2. If your child develops a fever or other illness symptoms, you will be asked to take your child home.

3. No medication will be given to any child in the Nursery Department.

4. Parents should report any allergies to their child's teacher.

Food

1. Under normal circumstances, nursery-age children are not to be fed any meals during Bible Study, Worship Services, or Training Sessions. For safety reasons, the Nursery Staff cannot mix formula for babies.

2. If your child has a food allergy or a special need related to food, please notify the teacher.

3. A nursing area is provided for nursing mothers.

4. Please refrain from giving your child gum or candy before coming to class. It can be dangerous, and is very messy.

For the safety of your child, the Nursery Staff cannot be responsible for special instructions unless they are in writing and attached to your child or diaper bag.

2. Parent Bulletin Board.

Near the entrance to each nursery room, mount a bulletin board on which you can display items of interest to parents. For example, post a copy of your church's well-baby policy or suggestions about what to include in each child's diaper bag.

Displaying the names (and photos) of the caregivers in the nursery can be especially helpful for visitors or even for regular attendees if the staff in the nursery rotates frequently. Also post invitations to church programs planned for parents of young children, such as play groups or parent education classes. Keep in mind that the nursery is one of the best places to build bridges with visitors to your church. Change the bulletin board display about once a month, updating it with new information, pictures of new babies and new families and a seasonal picture or two. (Purchase seasonal borders at educational supply stores. Double-knit polyester fabric makes a colorful backing for bulletin boards.)

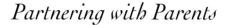 

3. Parent's Home Pages (pages 139-188 of this book).

Most parents of young children are looking for ways to effectively guide not only their child's physical growth, but also all aspects of the child's development. Parent's Home Page is a reproducible monthly newsletter for parents that provides tips about child care, updates parents on child care procedures and guidelines, and describes at-home activities parents can enjoy with their children. These newsletters also encourage parents to become partners with the nursery caregivers in reinforcing the Bible teaching presented at church. (Note: If you wish to create your own monthly newsletters including specific information related to your church, the information on the Parent's Home Pages can be used to supplement your own material.) For two full years of parent tips and activities, alternate Years A and B Parent's Home Pages.

Reproduce the Parent's Home Pages (including the introductory page) and, at the beginning of each month, place them in children's diaper bags or mail them. You may also wish to post a copy of the page on a bulletin board near the nursery entrance with copies available for parents to take.

When a new family begins attending, it's helpful to personally deliver the introductory page and the appropriate monthly Parent's Home Page. Call ahead of time to arrange for a convenient time to deliver the newsletter. While you are visiting, point out the features of the Parent's Home Page. Explain the method by which parents will receive each newsletter. Keep your stay brief. Answer any questions the parents may have about the nursery's policies and procedures.

4. Parent Location Plan.

Occasionally, because of a child's illness or prolonged crying, it is necessary to ask a parent to return to the nursery. When parents check in their children, they should be asked to designate the location(s) or program(s) where they will be (see check-in and parent location forms on pages 65-69). A caregiver or aide contacts parents if they are needed.

Some churches use a coupon system. At the nursery, the parent is given a coupon to fill out and give to a church usher. The coupon tells the names of the parents and child as well as the parent's seating location.

Another option is to ask parents to sit in a certain section of the sanctuary, such as the back row on a particular side of the room. (Rope off or label a certain number of seats for this purpose.) It is helpful to acquaint the ushers ahead of time with whatever plan you use to find parents.

Some churches give parents low-range beepers or vibrating pagers to use while on the church property. Or mount a message board in the sanctuary that displays the assigned numbers of children whose parents are needed in the nursery.

If the parents cannot be easily located and there is an emergency, ask an usher to communicate with the worship leader, requesting that the leader announce the names of the needed parents.

5. Parent Notes.

Some churches give brief written comments to the parents about their children's experiences in the nursery. This type of written note is most helpful in larger churches where the number of children and parents limits the time available for personal feedback. Each note includes a place for the child's name, the date, information about sleeping, feeding and diaper changing, as well as a brief comment about the child's overall behavior in the nursery.

Another option is to have a space on the check-in sheet for a caregiver to jot a brief comment about the child's morning in the nursery. When signing out the child, the parent notes the caregiver's observation. Or you may provide small pads of paper and pens for a caregiver to write a brief note to the parent, placing it in the child's diaper bag.

Of course, none of these written notes will ever take the place of a caregiver's friendly greeting to a parent with a personal comment about an experience the child enjoyed in the nursery, or a new development the caregiver has noticed! Parents appreciate teachers who are aware of their child as an individual.

Name:

_____

Date:

_____

Favorite Activity Today:

_____

_____

TODDLER TALK

NAME: _____

DATE: _____

I WAS:
- ❏ HAPPY
- ❏ FRIENDLY
- ❏ BUSY
- ❏ QUIET
- ❏ CURIOUS
- ❏ SLEEPY
- ❏ TEARY
- ❏ CHATTY

I HAD FUN:

_____

DIAPERING INFORMATION:

_____

_____

Peek into Our Nursery

In our nursery today, _____,

I saw _____

_____ had a good time playing with toys

_____ took a nap for_____

_____ cried a little when you left

_____ ate a snack _____

_____ drank from the bottle _____ oz.

_____ cried off and on

Diaper Information: _____

From: _____

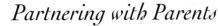
Record Keeping

Since much of what the nursery caregiver needs to know about a child in his or her care cannot be communicated by the child, it's especially important for a church to set up effective means for parents to communicate needed information. Often the most chaotic time in a church nursery is the arrival and dismissal time. If the majority of parents and the nursery staff are well acquainted with the procedures established by your church, the chaos will be reduced. Everyone— from the babies and toddlers to the caregivers and parents—will find their nursery experience more enjoyable.

Each church needs to evaluate the number of children in the nursery and the size of the room and decide if parents will be asked to check in their children at a counter or reception area, or if they may enter the nursery itself to leave their children. In order to reduce confusion during arrival and dismissal— not only for the caregivers, but also for the children—many churches limit traffic in and out of the nursery. Visitors can be invited to briefly observe in the nursery room if they are interested.

Note: The extensiveness of the check-in procedures you set up will often be determined by the size of your church, the community in which you live and the number of children cared for in your nursery. However, some form of these procedures needs to be established in ANY nursery so that each child is safe and protected. Safety guidelines also provide needed legal protection for nursery caregivers.

1. Labeling Children's Belongings.
Every item a parent brings for the child should be labeled: bottles, pacifiers, diapers, diaper bag, clothing, etc. Suggest that parents print the child's name on a masking tape strip attached to each item. Labeling can be done at home, or at church with tape and pens provided.

Some churches make or purchase identification tags for each child's diaper bag, keeping the tags at church and making them available for use each time the nursery is open. These tags can be made from colored vinyl fabric (circles, teddy bear or lamb shapes are popular), punched with a hole at the top and fastened with a large safety pin to the diaper bag. (Matching tags for children can also be made to be fastened to a child's clothing on his or her back.) Keep a supply of blank tags or make masking tape labels for visitors. Make permanent tags when the visitor becomes a regular attender.

Draw details on name tags with fine line permanent marking pens.

2. Information Cards.

In order for nursery caregivers to be aware of each child's specific needs, parents need to complete an information or registration card and then update the information on the card periodically. Keep cards in a file box near the room entrance. Occasionally post an "Update Reminder" notice on a bulletin board near the entrance to your nursery or on the nursery door. In addition to name, address and birth date, you may request information about food or medical allergies or preferences, napping suggestions, names of the child's siblings and activities the child enjoys.

Caregivers refer to information cards as needed during the session (before serving a snack, when a child seems sleepy, etc.). If you have a large number of children in the nursery with one or more staff changes during the session, you may want to write a child's food allergies on child's name tag or on a masking tape strip to be placed on the child's back. Use names and addresses for maintaining home contacts (mailing birthday cards to children, sending invitations to parenting programs, mailing the Parent's Home Pages, etc.).

A church may choose to ask a parent to complete a more extensive registration form which includes name of family doctor, name of person who will care for child if parent cannot be reached, medical insurance information, social security number of child, and liability release statements to be signed by the parent. If your church desires to use such a registration form, consult a book about church liability issues (available from your local Christian bookstore) and contact a lawyer who is familiar with the laws in your state for help in designing a legal and appropriate form.

Some churches display a dry erase board titled "Handle with Care" on which critical information about children is written (serious allergies, asthma, etc.).

Baby/Toddler Information Card

Date _____

Child's Name _____
           First   Last

Nickname _____

Address _____
        Street number   City   State   Zip

Phone (_____)_____ Birth Date _____

Comments (Serious allergies, minor allergies, medical conditions)

_____

_____

Sleeping Time _____ Position _____

Comments (Child's preferences, ideas for comfort)

_____

Parents' Names _____

Siblings _____

Emergency Contact _____

NURSERY REGISTRATION SHEET

Child's Name: _____   Nickname: _____

Birth Date: _____   Today's Date: _____

SIGNIFICANT OTHERS

Mother: _____   Father: _____

Services usually attended: _____

Where will parents be: _____

Siblings Names & Ages: _____

_____

_____

Address: _____

Home Phone: _____   Work Phone(s): _____

OTHER SAFE ADULTS Who I Can Go Home With:

_____

_____

_____

MY FAVORITE THINGS

_____ Blanket: _____

_____ Pacifier: _____

_____ Toy: _____

_____ Game/Song: _____

_____ Other: _____

SNACKS

_____ Are OK: _____

_____ Do not give: _____

_____ Allergies: _____

_____ In diaper bag: _____

_____ Concerns: _____

Diaper Size: _____

Outside Play OK? _____

When I'm sleepy: _____

When I'm crying: _____

Used by permission from Eastminster Presbyterian Church, Ventura, California.

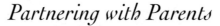

3. Caregiving Tips.

Parents have labeled their child's belongings and completed an information card. Now it's time to consider what happens at the beginning and end of the nursery session. How can a parent provide the essential information needed by the caregiver to properly care for the child and to return the child to the parent in a safe and orderly manner?

❑ **Check-in Forms.** The first step in this process is for the parent to fill out a nursery check-in form. These forms typically ask for the child's name and age, parents' names and where they will be located and comments from the parent or instructions for child care. A space for caregivers to record notes about feeding, sleeping or diaper changing can also be included.

Place check-in forms on a clipboard to be kept in each nursery room. Designate a caregiver in each room be make sure parents complete the check-in form. Collect check-in forms at the end of each session or day in which the nursery is used in order to compile attendance figures. Several sample check-in forms are included on the following pages.

Encourage EVERYONE, even your most regular attenders, to completely fill out these forms. One reason is that if a visiting parent sees that others have left several spaces blank, he or she may follow that example. Important information may then not be available for the caregiver. Also, in a busy or large nursery, staff may not always remember a verbal instruction or something which was written several weeks or months ago. Make the form easier for parents to complete by reducing the amount of time it takes to fill in the desired information. For example, provide forms with children's names already preprinted. Visitors add their names at the bottom of the list. Or preprint the variety of locations where parents might be, asking parents to simply check off the appropriate locations.

❑ **Child Name Tags.** The second step in this check-in process is for each child to receive a name tag. Print the child's name on a masking tape strip and place it on the child's back, or purchase adhesive name tags. Vinyl name tags in a variety of shapes can also be made (see page 61).

❑ **Child and Parent Identification.** The third step involves giving the parent a tag, coupon or number which must be presented at the end of the nursery session by a parent or another adult designated by the parent. While a small church may feel that this is a burdensome detail, developing a child identification system will ensure that children are only released to approved adults, and protect caregivers from parent complaints.

Consider these ideas for child identification systems, choosing one that best fits your church. A sample tag and coupon are provided on page 69. (It is also possible to purchase commercially-made child/parent identification systems. Contact your local Christian bookstore for possible sources.)

❑ **Coupon with date and child's name.** Coupon is given to parent when the child is checked in. Only the person with the coupon is allowed to pick up the child at the end of the session.

❑ **Number ID.** Card or paper with date and number assigned to the child. A tag with the corresponding number may also be attached to the child's diaper bag. (Some large churches also purchase an electronic system in which a message board is mounted in the sanctuary. If a parent is needed to return to the nursery, the number assigned to the parent's child flashes on the message board.)

Wallet-sized, permanent identification cards with parents' and children's names and personal family identification number can be given to parents. A child is only released to an adult who shows the identification card.

❑ **Photo ID.** Take photos of each child with his or her parents. Mount photos on a bulletin board near the entrance to each room. Have an instant camera available to photograph visitors.

❑ **Parent Designation.** Provide a section on the check-in form in which the parent writes the name of the person who will be picking up the child. Person picking up the child would be requested to show identification if not known to the nursery staff.

Nursery Check-In

Date: _____

Child's Name and Number	Age of Child	Parent's Name	Parent's Location in Church Buildings				Special Instructions
			Sat. P.M.	Sunday 8:00	Sunday 9:15	Sunday 11:00	

Nursery Check-In Form
Parents Check Appropriate Information

Child's Name	Age (mos.)	Feeding Time	Breast-Fed	Bottle-Fed	Juice OK	Water OK	Crackers OK	Pacifier	Parent's Name and Location	Comments

Special Instructions Below

Today's Date _____

Child's Name _____
         First   Last

Birth Date: _____   Phone: _____

Parent's Name _____

Parent's Location (circle one or more of the following):

Church Service	1	2	3	Evening
Sunday School Class	1	2	3	Rm# _____
Other: _____				Rm# _____

BABY'S ROUTINE:

FEEDING:

❑ Breast-fed   ❑ Bottle-fed (warm/cold)
❑ Bottle Water/Juice   ❑ Rock While Feeding
❑ Needs Burping   ❑ Holds Own Bottle
❑ Snack   Ritz   Graham   Cheerios

SLEEPING:

❑ Sleeps at: _____ O'clock
❑ Sleeps on: Back   Tummy
❑ Sleeps with: Blanket   Pacifier
❑ Needs to be: Patted   Rocked

TODDLER'S ROUTINE:

❑ Snack OK   Ritz   Graham
❑ Bottle   ❑ Water from a Cup
❑ Pacifier   ❑ Blanket
❑ Diaper   ❑ Potty Training

Other: _____

	Care Given	Time	Initials
Feeding:			
Sleeping:			
Diapering:			
Taken to Potty:			
Other:			

Parent's copy must be returned when child is picked up!

Grace Community Church, Tempe, AZ,

Used by permission from Grace Community Church, Tempe, Arizona.

Form in duplicate.

Welcome to Our Nursery!

In order for us to provide safe and loving care for your child, please:

1. Attach a name tag to your child (on his or her back).

2. Label everything (bottle, diaper bag, pacifier, etc.) with masking tape.

3. Sign in your child on the check-in form, adding any special instructions.

4. When you hand your baby and diaper bag to a caregiver, he or she will give you a numbered coupon. To pick up your baby, please return the coupon.

Thank you!

PARENT LOCATOR CARD

CHILD'S NAME _____

PARENTS _____

8:30 _____ 10:30

PARENTS: Complete the above information. On the other side of this card, indicate your location with an X. Please give this card to an usher. If you are needed in the nursery, we'll use this card to help us find you.

Nursing mothers are asked to sit in the back of the Worship Center near the open door.

PLATFORM

Nursing Moms

Please find my parents: _____
(Child's Name)

Parent's Name _____

Please check child's age and classroom:

Nursery —10 ☐	3 years—13 ☐
Walkers —11 ☐	4 years—14 ☐
2 years —12 ☐	5 years—15 ☐

Location in worship building:

Section: 1 2 3 4 Row _____

Balcony: 1 2 3 4 Usher _____

Parents:

Please give this card to the usher where you sit.

STAGE

Jubilee

CHILDREN'S MINISTRIES

NAME _____

NUMBER _____

DATE _____

TO PROTECT YOUR CHILD, PLEASE RETURN
THIS COUPON TO THE NURSERY
WHEN PICKING HIM OR HER UP.

Presbyterian Church

Baby & Toddler Security Tag

Date _____

This tag must be returned in order for your child to be released from the nursery.

If it is necessary for you to return to the nursery,
your child's number will flash on the box
at the front of the sanctuary.

We appreciate your cooperation!

Your child's number is: _____

4. Parent Feedback Forms.

At least once a year, distribute a questionnaire to the parents of the children in the nursery. Invite their comments about what they like and what they would improve. Use their comments as your nursery committee evaluates policies and procedures.

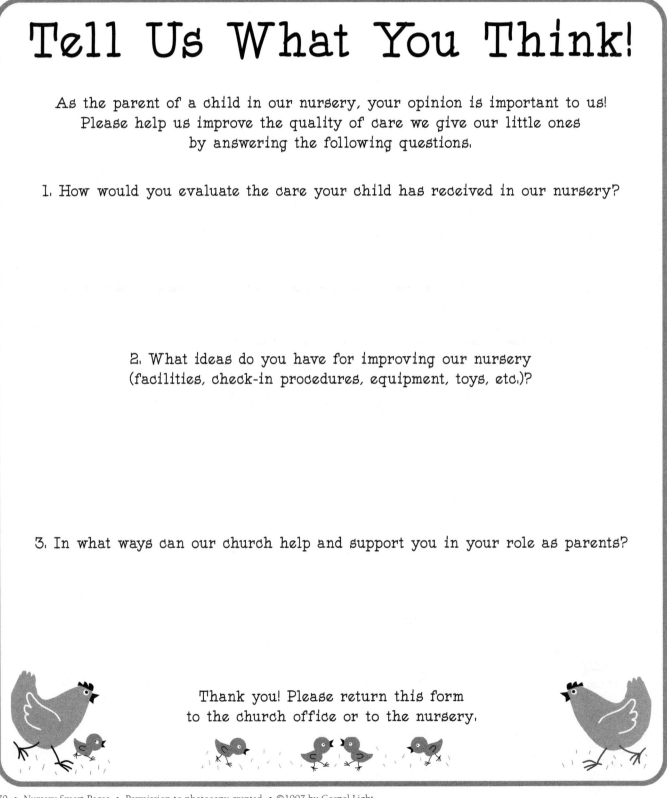

Tell Us What You Think!

As the parent of a child in our nursery, your opinion is important to us!
Please help us improve the quality of care we give our little ones
by answering the following questions.

1. How would you evaluate the care your child has received in our nursery?

2. What ideas do you have for improving our nursery
(facilities, check-in procedures, equipment, toys, etc.)?

3. In what ways can our church help and support you in your role as parents?

Thank you! Please return this form
to the church office or to the nursery.

Problem Solving with Parents

In any nursery program, despite the best-laid plans and policies, situations may occur in which parents and nursery staff need to work together to solve a problem. All nursery staff need to respect parents as the people who know the child best and can give good ideas for helping him or her to grow. Building effective communication with parents is a significant part of the nursery ministry.

What should we do when a parent has forgotten to label the child's belongings or to send a diaper?

The parent may never have received a nursery brochure or handbook describing this important procedure. Check to be sure! If time permits, when the parent arrives to pick up the child, offer a brief, friendly reminder. Another idea is to provide caregivers with a form that is quickly completed and placed in the child's diaper bag as a reminder. See these sample forms.

Sometimes a child will cry when being left, settle down and then when the parent comes back to check on the child, begin crying again.

Often parents simply don't realize the disruption they cause by frequent appearances in the nursery. Help parents understand that more than one tearful good-bye is all any child should be expected to handle in one day. When a parent returns unexpectedly and is seen by the child who immediately begins to cry again, ask the parent to stay. "Since your child has seen you, it would be best if this time you stayed for the rest of the session. Next time we'll be glad to notify you if your child doesn't stop crying after a short time."

Some churches install one-way windows in nursery doors so that parents can check on their children without being seen.

Sometimes we get very

busy

in this Nursery—too busy even to mark your child's belongings at the time you bring him/her to us.

HELP!

Please mark your child's

❏ Diaper bag

❏ Bottle(s)

❏ Single diaper(s)

❏ Blanket

before you bring him/her next time.
Thank you!

Today we needed a

Diaper

for _____

*Next time, please send an extra diaper marked with your child's name.
(If your child does not need it, you'll get it back.)*

Thank you!

Our church has a well-baby policy that most parents follow. However, one family regularly brings their sick child to the nursery.

Many churches, at the onset of the winter cold-and-flu season, post a reminder of their policies regarding sick children at the entrance to the nursery. This reminder is usually enough of a gentle prompt.

In any discussion with a parent about a sick baby, try to emphasize that a consistent policy of allowing only well babies and toddlers in the nursery is for everyone's protection.

Occasionally a child's symptoms may not have been apparent to the parent or may worsen during the time the child is in the nursery. In that case, nursery caregivers should contact the parents and ask them to take the baby out of the nursery.

If a child's symptoms are not severe and you are able to isolate the child from others, you may decide to keep the baby in the nursery. When the parents return to the nursery, mention the child's symptoms. Some churches provide notes for caregivers to complete, as friendly reminders of the well-baby policy. See this sample note.

One of the toddlers we care for bursts into tears whenever he is startled or in any way bothered by another child. Should we talk to the parents?

The first thing to do is to help the child avoid any further upsets by perhaps holding the child, positioning yourself next to the child, or placing him or her in a more secluded area of the room. Ask other caregivers who regularly care for the child if they are aware of any factors in the room that might be causing the child's unhappiness. If no solution seems to help, contact the parents during the week and ask for any ideas they may have for calming the child. For example, the parent may be aware that the child is teething and suggest a particular method of soothing the teething soreness.

We love your child, but...

we noticed today that

_____

has a:

☐ *Runny nose*

☐ *Cough*

☐ _____

Please bring your child back only after this is cleared up. Thank you for your cooperation.

The Workers in Room _____

Used by permission from Grace Community Church, Tempe, Arizona.

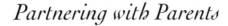

Some parents regularly let their children bring favorite blankets or toys from home. Other children, especially at the toddler age, want to play with the toy and it's difficult for the young owner to share.

Sometimes carrying that favorite toy or blanket helps a young child feel secure in an unfamiliar environment. In that case, don't immediately try to separate the object from the child. Later in the session, when the child is feeling more secure, ask the child if he or she is ready for you to put the toy in his or her diaper bag.

If bringing toys continues to create problems among the children, talk with the parent by phone. "Your daughter's doll is so pretty that all the little girls want to play with it. I'm concerned the doll may get spoiled or dirty, and it's probably not fair to ask your daughter to always share her doll with others. Maybe you can put the doll to 'bed' at home before you come to the nursery next week." Try to help parents understand the difference between a security item (sometimes needed) and play toys (not needed).

A new family in our church often asks if their older daughter (a six-year-old) can stay in the nursery with their toddler. They always comment how much the daughter enjoys playing with the babies. We don't want to hurt their feelings, but we don't have space in the nursery for extra people.

"Can I help in the nursery?" is a request often heard at churches. Older girls and boys often express an interest in helping care for little children. Some churches have a guideline stating that all nursery staff must be at least 18 years old. In that case, you may explain to the parents, "Thanks for offering your daughter's help, but the church's rule is that workers need to be 18."

If your church has decided to allow youth helpers, a well thought-out program of training and supervision needs to be established. (See "Teen Helpers" on page 21.) Then, in responding to the one-time or occasional request, simply state, "I'm glad you want to help in the nursery. I can't let you come in today, but in a few months there's a training class you can attend if you really want to help in here."

We've asked that parents return to pick up their children as soon as possible after the worship service ends. One mom always stops to talk with friends on the way and comes late every week.

It's good that parents have friends at church, but often parents don't realize the effect their late arrivals have upon their children. Once the first parent arrives, babies and toddlers often seem to have a heightened anxiety level: "When's my daddy going to come?" Sometimes that anxiety increases to the point of tears. A comment to the parent may help: "Nathan seems to worry when he's the last child to be picked up." Or the caregiver may make a more direct request: "The nursery closes for cleanup at 12:15. Can you come back by that time so I can clean up?"

• Nursery Smart Pages • 73

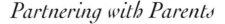

In our Toddler Room, one child seems to regularly disturb the other children, pushing them and grabbing away toys. Several parents have noticed the child's behavior, expressing concern about what can be done to safeguard the other children.

First, consider what needs to happen in the nursery for the safety of all the children. For awhile, it may be necessary for a nursery caregiver to constantly monitor the child's behavior, sitting close enough to the child to prevent any hurtful actions toward others and redirect the child's behavior. When the child starts to grab a toy held by another child, for example, gently pull back the child's hand and comment, "Ethan is playing with that toy now. You can have a turn later. Here's a ball we can play with." If the child resists your attempt at distraction, you may need to gently restrain the child, perhaps picking up the child and moving to another area of the room. Often, the child's misbehavior may lessen with the patient, helpful guidance of a loving adult.

Secondly, in response to the comments of other parents, let them know the specific steps you are taking for the protection of all the children. Keep in mind that some problems of this nature may occur repeatedly because the nursery room is too crowded for the number of children, the available toys are not age-appropriate, there are no duplicates of popular toys, or the child is in the nursery for too long a time period.

On a particularly busy day in the nursery, we neglected to change a baby's soiled diaper before the parents returned to get the child. The parents were upset.

The best approach is to apologize to the parents. In your apology, let them know what you will do to make sure each child's diapers are checked on a regular basis. Many nurseries have a policy assuring that each child's diaper is checked at least once every hour, and the time is recorded on a record sheet or the nursery check-in sheet. (See page 37 for a sample form.) Your openness and willingness to improve the nursery care may help to disarm any negative feelings.

Parent Outreach Ideas

What are the benefits of a nursery program that seeks to involve and build relationships with parents of babies and toddlers? Immeasurable! Many new parents are in awe of their responsibilities in caring for and nurturing a little one. At this time of transition in their lives, parents are often quite open to the friendship and help offered by the church family.

Some of these outreach ideas can be established on a permanent basis, while others will be effective for a few months at a time. Periodically throughout the year, evaluate what your nursery is doing to build relationships with parents and consider one or more of these ideas. Because young families may have significant financial needs, plan low-cost programs and events.

Father's Day/ Mother's Day

Take an instant close-up picture of each baby or toddler in the nursery on one of these special days. Trim the picture and mount it on a poster board circle approximately 2 inches (5 cm) in diameter. Punch a hole through the picture and attach a large safety pin. (If you have access to a button-making machine, buttons can also be made.) Give picture tags or buttons to mom or dad when they return to the nursery.

Parent Library

Establish a shelf, table or corner near the nursery where books and magazines of interest to parents of young children can be displayed. Stock this useful library with books about child rearing, activities to enjoy with young children, age-level characteristics, etc. Encourage parents to sign out these books, returning them in a week or two. Invite parents whose children have grown beyond the infant/toddler stage to donate books or videos they found helpful as parents of young children.

New Baby News

When a baby is born or a new family begins attending your church, introduce them to the church family by taking their pictures (including any brothers and sisters) and placing the labeled pictures on one or more bulletin boards—one by the nursery, and perhaps another one in a well-traveled location.

Birth announcements can also be a feature of all-church newsletters. Many churches celebrate the good news of a baby's birth with a rose or other flower placed in the sanctuary along with a public announcement of the baby's birth.

Some churches keep track of birth announcements published in community newspapers. (Addresses may be published in the newspaper, or find them in your telephone directory.) Shortly after the baby's birth, send a card of congratulations to the new parents, acquainting them with your nursery program and inviting them to attend your church. You may also include brochures or pamphlets about other church programs, or self-addressed and stamped cards which can be returned to request further information.

Hospitals provide packets of helpful items to parents of new babies. Ask a hospital administrator if you can provide an invitation to visit your church, along with a brief description of your nursery program.

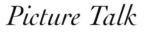
Picture Talk

Take pictures of children with nursery caregivers, or take pictures of children enjoying an activity together at church. After developing the pictures, cover them with clear adhesive-backed paper. Send the pictures home with children, encouraging parents to talk with children about their enjoyable times at church.

If you have an instant camera, take pictures of children (looking at a book, playing with blocks, sleeping, etc.) and send them home as instant feedback about the children's experiences at church.

Video cameras can also be used to record a segment of the nursery session. Parents and even toddlers will enjoy observing these video-tapes of the child's morning at church.

Special Occasions

Celebrate with families the special events in their lives and the lives of their children.

When a baby is born, send or deliver flowers to the family. If there is an older child, bring him or her a small gift, too.

Consider giving the parents a gift subscription to a parenting maga-zine, or give the parents a book that presents helpful parenting informa-tion.

Send birthday cards for the child's first and second birthdays.

When a baby is dedicated or baptized, give the child a certificate. Ask your pastor to write a personal letter to the child, to be saved by the parents and presented to him or her at 12 years of age.

On the day of a baby dedication or baptism, offer a tour of the nurs-ery after the dedication service, tak-ing advantage of the interest aroused in the nursery ministry.

Nursery Get-Acquainted Tours

Once or twice a year offer a tour for prospective and new parents. Dis-tribute copies of your nursery brochure and handbook. Answer questions about the policies of the nursery. Provide a brief time with refreshments for nursery staff and parents to talk together. Parents will always feel more comfortable leav-ing children in the nursery if they are familiar with the room, staff and procedures.

You may wish to invite a parent whose child has been in the nursery for six to twelve months to attend the open house or tour. He or she may be able to reassure new parents about leaving babies in the nursery, pass on some helpful hints about getting babies and toddlers to and from the nursery (not always an easy experience!), and describe how their family has benefited from the caregivers in the nursery.

Church Update

When parents have missed church because of a sick baby or toddler, deliver a cassette tape of the worship service and a church bulletin to them. Offer to help if needed: provide a meal, pick up a prescription, baby-sit a child while the sick child is taken to the doctor, etc. Consider maintaining a list of people in the church who wish to help young families in these ways.

"Welcome Wagon" Visits

Visit a new family or prospective parents at home, offering a small, homemade fabric diaper bag to the family. Fill the diaper bag with helpful items such as a diaper, personalized bib, a copy of the nursery brochure or handbook, information card to be completed by parents, small toy, etc. (Offer the task of making and assembling items for the diaper bags to a group of retired people, or to those who enjoy sewing.)

Birthing/Lamaze Classes

Offer classes in the nursery for parents-to-be. Relationships formed in classes such as these can help provide the support and friendship new parents often need. Holding the classes in the nursery give the extra advantage of acquainting parents with the nursery facilities.

Baby-Sitting Support

Maintain a list of reliable adult and youth baby-sitters. Many parents of young children, especially those who do not have an extended family in the area, find it difficult to find reliable baby-sitters. Follow your church's procedure for screening volunteers, setting several requirements to be met by baby-sitters whose names are included on the list (be a member or regular attendee of your church for at least one year, be recommended by a member of the church staff, complete a first aid/CPR class, etc.).

Friday Nights Out

Once a month offer free baby-sitting to parents of young children during the dinner hour. Parents can eat at home or at a restaurant, enjoying a special time of "adults only" conversation. Follow your usual policies for safety and health in the nursery including these additional guidelines: (1) Parents reserve space a week ahead of time; (2) When checking in their children, parents leave a phone number where they can be reached and sign a permission slip.

First Aid/CPR Class

Offer a first aid and/or CPR training class for parents of young children. Contact your city's Red Cross chapter to arrange for class leaders. Encourage your nursery staff and youth in the church who are potential baby-sitters for church families to participate as well.

Parent Support Groups

Mothers, dads, grandparents—anyone involved in the regular task of caring for young children—will enjoy a once-a-week or once-a-month time of fellowship for support, study and just plain fun! Offer child care in your nursery, or ask participants to take turns serving in the nursery.

Invite a speaker (a knowledgeable person in your church or community) to address an issue of interest to parents—discipline, activities to do at home, holiday celebration ideas, safety in the home, etc. Include a time for parents to talk together, trading ideas and thoughts about the challenges of child rearing.

Support groups can also be organized around a specific interest of the participants: aerobics, quilting, golf, tennis, book/video reviews, cooking, computers or crafts. Offering six to eight sessions at a time will encourage participation by parents whose time is limited.

Dads Only groups are a popular way to encourage fathers to feel significant in the lives of their children. Older, experienced fathers serve as group leaders, offering tips and ideas for how to care for babies and toddlers.

Grandmothers' Club

Many older women in the church either do not live near their own grandchildren or have no grandchildren to love and care for. Similarly, many young families either do not live near their parents or their parents are no longer living. Plan some occasional informal meetings between the two groups, such as refreshments in the backyard of a church member's home, holiday craft class (grandmas and mothers take turns caring for the little ones), or recipe exchanges (grandmas bring the food to taste, everyone brings a recipe or two).

Participants of a grandmothers' (or grandfathers') club may also enjoy helping with nursery tasks—laundering sheets, washing toys, making blankets, or building shelves.

Parenting on the Go

Periodically send copies of articles in this book to provide information and training for busy parents. Choose articles such as "Exploring Books Together," page 100; "Communication with Nontalkers," page 104; "Discipline in the Nursery," page 111; "Teaching Babies About God," page 117; "Babies at Work," pages 127, 128; "Helping Little Ones Feel Secure," page 130. If your church has access to a cassette duplicating machine, record a clear reading of an article, make copies of the cassette and send them home for parents to listen to. Make a recording of a new article each month.

Room/Supplies

The Nursery Environment

Children under the age of two have very special needs that require very special care. The key words for baby/toddler rooms are space, cleanliness, safety and comfort. The environment in which these little ones are cared for helps set a new life (and often, the lives of the parents) on the path of either enjoying or resisting church experiences. Ask yourself, "If I were a baby or toddler, would I want to be in this room? Why or why not?"

When the nursery rooms are inviting in their appearance, recruiting nursery caregivers is also made easier. Although an attractive, spacious room does not automatically insure quality care, facilities can either assist the nursery staff in providing a good program, or they can hinder the process. Staff who feel frustrated by poorly organized supplies or crowded conditions are not likely to return.

The goal of a well-designed nursery, however, is not only to enable the staff to safely and comfortably care for babies and toddlers, but to help parents feel that their children will enjoy and benefit from their time at church. Visitors to your church nursery will naturally evaluate the room and equipment, and are more likely to feel comfortable leaving children in a room that is attractive, safe and orderly rather than one that is poorly lighted, crowded and chaotic.

Size and Number of Rooms

One of the first issues to consider is the number and size of the rooms needed to provide safe care for babies and toddlers. Each person in attendance (caregivers and children) needs 25 to 35 square feet (7.5 to 10.5 sq. m) of space. Rectangular rooms, rather than square or long, narrow rooms allow for maximum flexibility in room arrangement.

What are the benefits of all this space? Young children need the freedom to discover and enjoy many activities. Open space, age-appropriate equipment and safe, interesting play materials help children feel that their room at church is a good place to be.

Depending on the size of your church, you may wish to group children of similar ages or physical development together: infants, crawlers, toddlers, walkers. Other ways of grouping children are:

❖ Birth to 3 months; 4 to 8 months; 9 to 12 months; 13 to 18 months; 19 to 24 months.

❖ Birth to 12 months; 1-year-olds.

❖ Babies; younger toddlers; older toddlers.

❖ Babies to 6 months; 7 to 12 months; 13 to 18 months; 19 to 24 months.

(If children of widely differing ages are in the same room together, perhaps even including preschoolers, read "Older Children in the Nursery" on page 121 for helpful guidelines.)

Once each year, reevaluate room designations, considering the number of children and their ages. Many churches move children from room to room as they mature in physical and language skills, designating the two-year-old class as a "holding department." (A holding department receives children from a younger group more than once a year, but promotes the children to the next older group all at one time—"Promotion Sunday.") The two-year-old class often works best as a holding department, since the nature of twos already requires very flexible procedures and schedule.

Keep in mind that a small group size is especially important for babies and toddlers. Young children are likely to be stressed by large groups (even with an adequate number of caregivers) and lots of activity and noise. If your nursery rooms are so large that more than 12 children are cared for in each room, consider ways of using sturdy dividers or other furniture to create smaller areas of space within the room.

Room Location

The ideal location for all nursery rooms is at ground level, with quick and easy access to a safe outside area (avoid locating the nursery near the parking lot or busy streets). Rooms on the first floor allow efficient safety precautions and are convenient for parents. An adequate number of exits are essential in case of emergency. Locating a nursery near the church sanctuary can help first-time visitors find their way.

Regardless of where the nursery is located, make sure it's clearly marked and that ushers, greeters and the welcome/information center staff know its location. Provide a labeled facilities map to direct parents to the appropriate rooms in which their children are cared for.

Room Appearance

While every church is unique in its facility design, there are basic guidelines that can be followed to make your nursery look and feel safe as well as comfortable. As you review these checklists and sketches, ask yourself, "How can we arrange our present facilities to include the features described in these rooms? What can we do to make our room more efficient and attractive?" Visit nurseries at other churches or day care centers (or interview their staff) to gain tips on what works and what doesn't (particularly if you're fortunate enough to be remodeling or building new facilities).

❏ **Room Surfaces.** Floor coverings should be nonporous cushioned vinyl tile or a high density synthetic carpet with substantial rubber backing, and need to be thoroughly cleaned after each session. Invest in good quality floor surfaces which will last with frequent use. Consider using carpet tiles that can be replaced one at a time. (If throw rugs must be used in the nursery, securely fasten edges to avoid tripping.) Some churches run vinyl tile or carpet up the walls to the height of children.

Ceilings should be covered with acoustical tile or plaster to reduce sound; walls should be soundproofed, well-insulated and painted with cheerful pastel or light colors. Bright colors can be added as highlights. Use wall paint that can be easily washed (usually semi-gloss). Place electrical outlets out of children's reach or cover them with safety plugs. Make sure all cords are out of reach.

❏ **Lighting.** Lighting should be even and without glare. Subdued light is desirable in a room where babies sleep and are fed. Consider using a dimmer switch. Windows should be of shatterproof clear glass, with the bottom sill about 2 feet (60 cm) from the floor so that children will be able to see out. Window screens need to be securely fastened. Provide window coverings only if needed to reduce glare and provide insulation.

❏ **Temperature.** Adequate ventilation is a must! Maintain room temperature between 68 and 72° F. (20 and 22° C.). Check for drafts from windows and doors. Radiators or floor heaters must be covered for safety.

Equipment and Furniture Needs

Consider these lists of equipment and furniture as ideals for which to strive. If you are in a new or small church, it may be overwhelming to think about providing all this equipment at once. After you've obtained the basics, continue to evaluate the priorities of your nursery, upgrading or adding equipment as your church budget allows. The number of each item listed will vary depending on the size of your church.

All rooms, whether for babies or toddlers, need to have access to sinks and toilets. When a nursery is not equipped with a sink and running water, provide commercially made rinseless hand washing solution for caregivers use. Ideally, a toddler room should have child-size sinks, and toilets (11 inches [27.5 cm] in height) or potty chairs to assist in toilet training.

Furniture

❒ **Cribs (hospital type).** Height of mattress should be about waist level for most teachers, reducing the strain of lifting and bending. Avoid stacking cribs, which can easily result in trying to group too many infants in too small a space. In addition, the close proximity of stackable cribs can contribute to the spread of illness among babies. For safety, slats of cribs must be no more than 2⅜ inches (5.9 cm) apart, and the space from the top of the mattress to top of rail should be 36 inches (90 cm). Placing cribs at least 3 feet (.9 m) apart from each other ensures that babies do not breathe directly on each other and allows enough space for workers to care for children.

   Toddler Notes: Few toddlers will nap during a session, but one or two cribs should be available for those who do.

❒ **Playpens.** Lightweight, easy-to-clean nylon mesh playpens are helpful when a child needs a protected area in which to briefly play.

❒ **Bouncy seats.** Babies not old enough to sit up or crawl may safely sit in these seats and observe the nursery surroundings.

❒ **Adult rocking chairs.** Keep rockers separated, reducing the temptation for teachers to visit with each other.

   Toddler Notes: Be alert to children crawling or walking nearby. Gliders prevent hurt fingers or toes.

❒ **Changing tables.** Place changing tables near a sink in a well-ventilated area, away from food areas. If a changing table is temporarily unavailable, diapers may be changed in a crib or on a pad on the floor. (If you have the opportunity to design a nursery, arrange changing tables or stations so that the caregiver faces out toward the room, allowing the caregiver's actions to be observed at all times. This arrangement protects caregivers from complaints.)

❒ **Infant swings.** Use only for brief intervals. Do not place swings in rooms where children who are crawling or walking are cared for. (Walkers are not recommended for use in nurseries because of potential accidents.)

❒ **Toy shelves.** Low, open shelves allow toddlers to see what materials are available, help themselves and then return materials to the shelves. Avoid storing toys in large bins or boxes—children see chaos rather than an orderly display of materials.

❒ **Storage shelves or cabinets.** Use for storing diaper bags, nursery supplies and the nursery staff's belongings. Wall-mounted cabinets above the children's reach are preferred. (If cabinets are at children's level, they must be securely fastened with child-proof locks.) Wall hooks above the child's reach may be used for hanging diaper bags and adult sweaters and coats. Diaper bags may also be placed on counters. Cubbyholes work well, but in toddler rooms need to be placed above children's reach. Bolt shelves to walls, especially in areas susceptible to earthquakes.

   Toddler Notes: Store toys that need teacher supervision and extra toys (rotate toys periodically to maintain children's interest). Clearly label shelves. Coat racks may be placed outside the nursery room so that parents can handle outdoor clothing.

❒ **Low table** about 14 inches (35 cm) high, 18 inches (45 cm) wide and 30 inches (75 cm) long on which toddlers may enjoy art experiences. Chairs, about 8 inches (20 cm) in height are optional.

❒ **Cassette or CD player.** Place out of children's reach.

❒ **Small refrigerator (optional).** Use for storing bottles and juice.

Supplies

❑ **Crib blankets and sheets.** Wash sheets and blankets after each use.

❑ **Changing supplies: disposable diapers in a variety of sizes, disposable gloves, premoistened towelettes, disposable covers for changing tables** (wax paper, large paper towels, computer paper or commercial covers), **plastic bags for diaper disposal and soiled clothing.** Keep changing supplies out of reach of children.

　Toddler Notes: Store several hand toys near the changing area to occupy the child during diaper changes. Rotate and wash these hand toys with the rest of the toys in the nursery.

❑ **Safety items.** Purchase safety items as needed: plug guards and/or covers for all electrical outlets, safety locks for window-blind cords, safety door latches, one-piece door stoppers, window guards, security gates, safety latches for all cabinets and drawers and toilet seat locks.

　Provide fire extinguishers and flashlights for each nursery room.

❑ **Anti-bacterial soap** for washing hands; tissues and disposable towels. Soap dispensers should be attached directly over sinks so that soap drips into the sink and not onto counters or floors. (Purchase rinseless hand washing soap if nursery does not have access to running water and sink.)

❑ **Disinfecting solution.** Wash and disinfect toys, crib and playpen rails, infant seats, etc., after each use. Check with a druggist about safe, effective disinfecting solutions such as Lysol, Triquat, Mytar, Sage, Wescodyne, ethyl or isopropyl alcohol (70%). For a homemade disinfectant, mix 1 tablespoon household bleach in a quart of water. For a larger amount, mix ¼ cup bleach in a gallon of water. Make the solution fresh each day and keep in a labeled spray bottle out of reach of children.

❑ **Covered wastebasket with liners.** Wastebaskets near the changing table should be foot operated. Empty after each session.

❑ **Laundry basket.** Place all used sheets and blankets in basket. Toys on which babies have chewed are also placed in this basket to be sterilized before use.

❑ **Soft, washable or disposable slippers** for caregivers to wear in the infant room. Shoes are dangerous with crawling babies.

❑ **Snack items, paper cups, napkins and pitchers for toddler snack times.** Provide finger foods and small amounts of liquid in cups so children can feed themselves while seated on floor. Optional: Place a sheet or flannel-backed vinyl tablecloth on the floor on which toddlers sit while eating.

❑ **First Aid manual and kit.** Store supplies out of reach of children.

❑ **Record keeping supplies.** Keep an adequate supply of check-in forms, pencils, name tags, masking tape, etc., near the nursery entrance. Store supplies out of reach of children.

❑ **Bottle warmer (optional).** Keep out of children's reach. One possible solution to warming bottles is to fill a Crock-Pot three-quarters full with water and turn it on approximately one hour before the nursery session begins. (Place Crock-Pot and cord out of reach of children.) Warming a baby's bottle in the heated water usually takes less than a minute.

❑ **Smocks (optional).** When caregivers wear smocks, children have a clean surface on which to rest their heads, the caregiver's clothing is protected and a professional appearance is presented. Wash smocks after use.

❑ **Camera (optional).** Frequently take pictures of children, displaying pictures on bulletin boards or giving to parents.

❑ **Room deodorizers (optional).** If your nursery rooms are not well-ventilated, place deodorizers in each room in a place where children cannot reach them.

Room Layout

Arrange nursery rooms to provide open space in which caregivers and children may move freely. In determining your room layout, keep in mind these safety guidelines:

✓ Arrange furniture so that there are no hard-to-supervise blind spots.

✓ Bolt shelves and cabinets to the wall.

✓ Attach safety hinges to doors so they open and close slowly, preventing caught fingers or toes.

✓ Place furniture away from windows, protecting children who may climb on it.

✓ Evaluate the ways in which children will move from one area of the room to another, making sure that movement is not impeded.

✓ Include space for nursery staff to store their own belongings (Bibles, purses, etc.).

✓ Do not block any entrance, exit, or adjacent hallways with unused furniture. Every exit should be clearly marked. Contact your local fire department or state licensing agency to help you determine proper placement of fire extinguishers, fire alarms, emergency exits and other safety considerations. (For example, all doors, even when locked, should be openable from the inside.) Post fire and other emergency (tornado, storm, earthquake, etc.) plans next to every doorway.

✓ Corners of furniture, shelves and counters should be rounded or padded when possible.

✓ If possible, arrange changing tables or stations so that caregiver is facing out to room while changing diapers. Caregivers' actions are then in full view of other adults in the room, providing protection for the caregiver in case of unwarranted complaints.

Adapt the room arrangements on the next three pages to your facilities. Avoid creating rooms too small to be flexibly used as the needs of your nursery change over the years.

Since welcoming and checking in children is one of the most important aspects of a nursery room, carefully plan how your nursery will handle this procedure (check-in options described on pages 64 and 87).

Floor Plan Options

MORE THAN TWO ROOMS

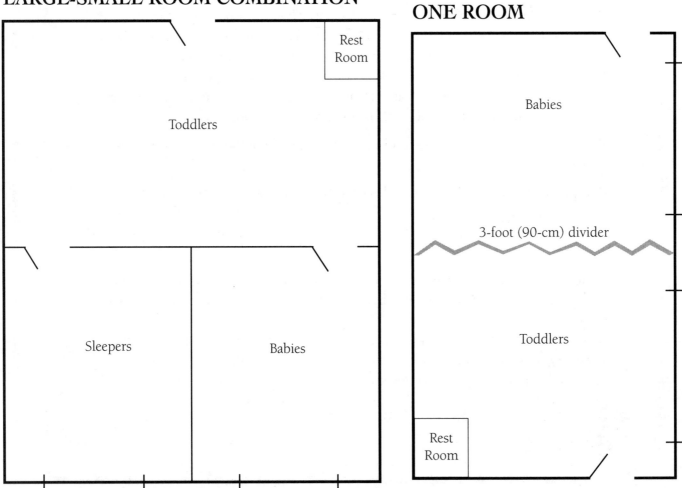

Babies (0–8 months)

Crawlers (8–14 months)

Toddlers (15–24 months)

Rest Room

Rest Room

LARGE-SMALL ROOM COMBINATION

Rest Room

Toddlers

Sleepers

Babies

ONE ROOM

Babies

3-foot (90-cm) divider

Toddlers

Rest Room

Floor Plan Options

MULTIROOM

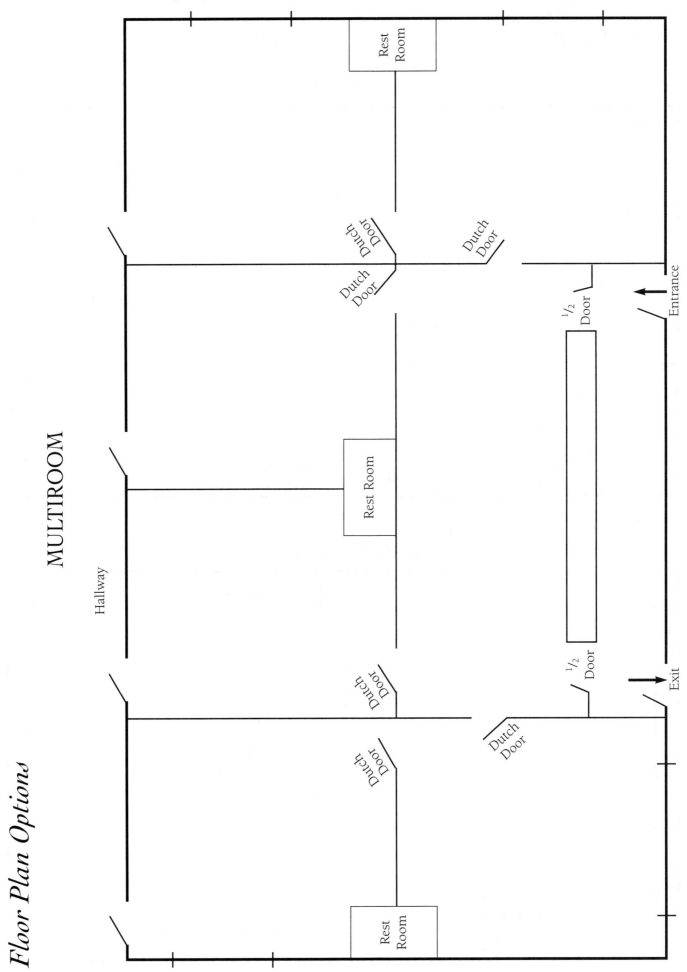

Room Diagrams

See pages 81-82 for complete lists of furnishings.

BABIES

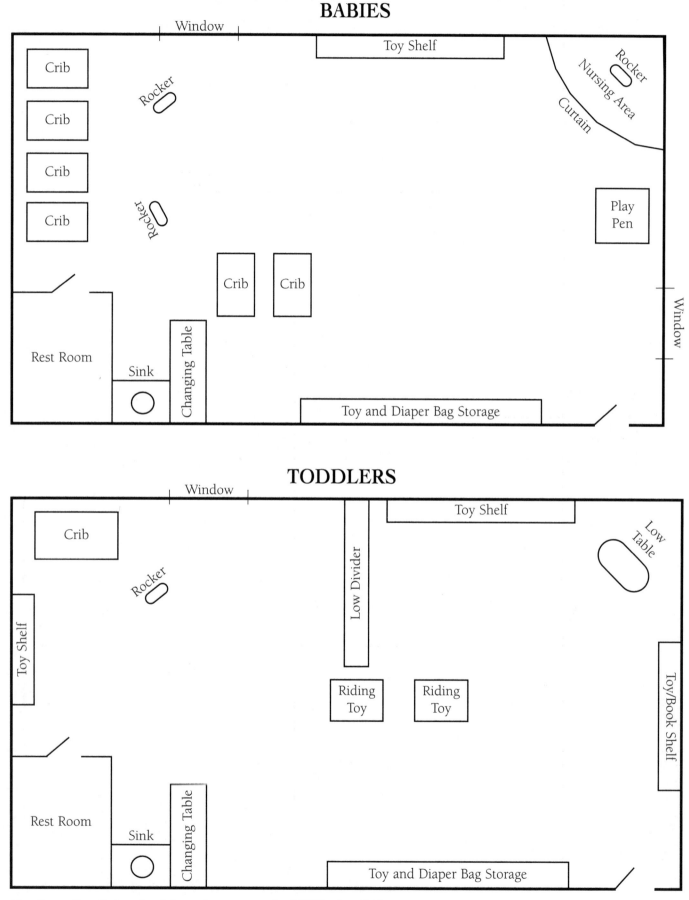

TODDLERS

Ways to Greet and Welcome Children

Scene 1

Parent checks in child at the classroom.

Scene 2

Parent checks in child at desk, attaches child's name tag and labels belongings before taking child to his or her classroom.

Scene 3

Parent checks in child at counter inside the classroom.

Nursery Room Questions and Answers

What's the best setup for a nursery check-in area?

Plan a counter or clearly defined area where parents hand their child to a caregiver. Except in the smallest of churches, if every parent and sibling of a child accompanies the child into the nursery room itself, the traffic conditions become very crowded and cause considerable confusion and chaos. Limiting access to the nursery ensures a much calmer atmosphere for babies and toddlers. In planning the layout of the nursery room, try to signal the drop-off area with visual clues (a low counter over which the baby or toddler is handed, a portable gate which prevents access to the room). Of course, any visiting parent who requests entrance to the nursery should be accommodated.

Each church is likely to find a different solution to the check-in procedure, usually depending on the available facilities and the number of children using the nursery. Here are some options: (1) All babies and toddlers come to a large, central reception area with caregivers ready behind a long counter to greet families, check in babies and bring them to their appropriate rooms. (2) Parents bring their children to the appropriate room which has a counter, table or Dutch door at the entrance where check-in takes place.

How can we help nursing mothers feel comfortable feeding their babies?

Some churches like to provide a special area of privacy for nursing mothers. A small room adjacent to the nursery works well. In many churches, however, nursing rooms are not available. A curtain or folding screen can be used to section off a portion of the room. If two rooms adjoin, a sliding door can be pulled shut to provide privacy when needed. Sometimes a room designed for sleeping babies can be used. One or two rocking chairs with arms are a nice addition to a nursing area. Many mothers are very comfortable nursing among the activity of other children, but often a quieter area is less distracting to the infant.

Our church has one large room for both babies and toddlers. What's the best way to divide the room?

Folding partitions can be added to the room to divide it in two, or sturdy low shelves or bookcases can create a visual barrier between two sections of one room. (See the room diagrams on page 84 for additional ideas.)

One night a week the children of choir members are cared for in our nursery. What is the best way to make sure our nursery policies are followed?

If there are regular caregivers for any programs using the nursery, meet with them at least once a year to communicate nursery policies and procedures. For other groups that use the nursery on a one-time basis, establish a handout that communicates guidelines the group needs to follow (ratio of caregivers to children, room maintenance, etc.). Give this handout to any group who has reserved use of the nursery (usually arranged through your church office) and post it in the room. A sample nursery guideline form is provided on page 41.

We are building a new facility, but until then we don't have a room just for the nursery. What can we do?

Store all nursery supplies in boxes or a cabinet in the room. Use portable cribs which can be quickly set up and taken down. In between sessions, boxes and cribs can be stored in a closet elsewhere in your facility. Schedule parent or other volunteers to set up and take down the nursery each week. If your nursery must meet in a kitchen or hallway on a short-term basis, check the room carefully before each session for safety hazards.

Our facility is quite old and our nursery appears outdated. How can we upgrade the appearance?

There are several ways to brighten up a nursery. Even more than the overall appearance, however, the first consideration should be safety. Evaluate your equipment, furniture and storage to be sure they meet health and safety standards. Then take a look to see if there are any unnecessary pieces of furniture that could be removed to create more space. Check to see if the lighting could be improved (consider asking a lighting expert to evaluate the light sources and recommend improvements). If your nursery does not have a water source, bring in a coffee urn filled with tap water, and a large plastic bowl. A fresh coat of paint, a wallpaper border, new carpet (with thick padding) or a few new pieces of nursery furniture will combine to make your nursery a welcoming place.

Outdoor Play Areas

An outdoor play area especially designed for babies and/or toddlers provides a special way to enrich the nursery experience of young children. Any outdoor area has two requirements: careful maintenance to remove items dangerous to children, and adequate supervision by adults who enjoy being outdoors with children. Even a simple wooden deck will help children experience a greater variety of sights and sounds.

More complex outdoor play areas can include:

❖ grassy areas which have good drainage and are well maintained.

❖ sand play areas surrounded with wooden borders. If sand is used to cushion falls, it needs to be 8 to 12 inches (20-30 cm) deep. If cats or other animals frequent the area, use a secure vinyl or wooden cover over the play area to keep it sanitary. It's best to rake sand weekly. Position sand areas away from hard surfaces or plan to frequently sweep hard surfaces so that children will not slip on the sand.

❖ asphalt areas for riding-toy and ball areas. Asphalt dries more quickly than sand or grass and is safer and softer than concrete.

❖ toddler wooden or plastic climbing and play structures with outdoor mats underneath. Check structures for splinters, rust, exposed bolts and nails, deterioration or any other defect which might lead to weakening of the structure, and sharp edges or gaps in which a child's arms and legs could become caught. Wide slides are safest.

❖ trees and plants that provide a variety of color throughout the year. Ask your local poison control center to be sure that no plants are toxic. Shrubs and low, flat boulders can create places for toddlers to walk around, hide behind, or even sit on. If trees do not provide enough shade, build an overhang over at least one play area.

❖ boundaries of wooden or chain-link fences. Wooden fences are more attractive, but require frequent maintenance. Adding wooden slats or fabric to chain-link fences can improve their appearance. Attaching a "cruise bar" to one area of the fence creates a place where beginning walkers can explore the outdoors.

Toys and Activity Supplies

Babies and toddlers are in a constant process of learning. They learn best through trial and error and repetition. Toys provide opportunities for children to experiment with how things work. The best toys make it possible for children to:

✓ see objects with a variety of colors, shapes and patterns;

✓ hear toys which jingle, squeak or rattle;

✓ touch objects with varied textures;

✓ manipulate items that can be stacked, taken apart and put together;

✓ figure out objects with zippers, snaps and clasps;

✓ pretend with items such as dolls, telephones, plastic dishes, cups, hats, toy animals and vehicles.

Provide two or more of children's favorite toys to prevent playtime disagreements. Store some of your nursery's toys in closed shelves or closets, rotating toys every month. Putting some toys away for a short time helps your room appear uncluttered and inviting. Too many toys at once can overwhelm children.

Note: All toys should be too large to be swallowed, with no sharp edges or points. All toys should be safe for mouthing and contain no small parts or pieces that could come loose. Choke testers can be purchased at educational supply stores. Check toys on a regular basis to be sure they are in good condition.

❖ **Assortment of tapes and/or CDs** appropriate for children, such as Gospel Light's *I Love to Sing!*

Toddler Notes: Provide rhythm instruments such as bells, shakers and drums with which toddlers may experiment.

❖ **Colorful, realistic picture books,** printed on stiff, coated paper, cardboard or fabric. Good topics for books include children and families, animals, familiar toys and activities and books about Jesus. Pictures should be simple and large with contrasting backgrounds. Avoid books featuring make-believe or fantasy characters which do not lend themselves to conversation about the real ways in which God expresses His love for us.

❖ **Gospel Light's** *I Love to Look!* Bible story picture cards **or a Bible story picture book**, printed on sturdy paper.

❖ **Posters** from Gospel Light's *Nursery Posters* or other posters purchased from educational supply stores or at your local Christian bookstore. Make your own posters by covering magazine pictures with clear Con-Tact paper. Tape posters to the wall at the child's eye level, or above changing tables. Depending on the type of wall surface, clear Con-Tact paper may be attached directly to the wall, covering the picture (see sketch a). Or screw sides and bottom of a large sheet of Plexiglas into the wall at the child's eye level. Slip posters or other pictures between Plexiglas and wall (see sketch b). (Note: Commercially made display centers are available from educational supply stores.)

❖ **Unbreakable mirror.** Hold mirror for child to view him- or herself, or mount on side of crib near baby's head. Toddlers will enjoy looking into full-length mirrors mounted on the wall.

❖ **Washable dolls** with molded heads (no hair). Doll clothing must be removable by teacher for washing.

   Toddler Notes: Doll bed, 28×14×11 inches (70×35×27.5 cm), sturdy enough for child to lie on. For other pretend "home experiences," provide washable doll blankets, plastic telephone that clicks or rings, unbreakable plastic dishes and cooking pans. Optional: round table (14 inches [35 cm] high, 36 inches [90 cm] in diameter).

❖ **Small, washable squeeze toys and teething toys.** Easy for child to handle and in a variety of textures.

❖ **Baby rattles** such as keys on a ring.

❖ **Mobile.** Hang mobiles from the ceiling over changing tables or cribs. Children should not be able to reach mobiles.

❖ **Balls.** A ball 5 to 9 inches (12.5 to 22.5 cm) in diameter for babies; 9 to 24 inches (22.5 to 60 cm) in diameter for crawlers and toddlers (good for rolling, bouncing, dropping). Also, clutch balls and texture balls too large to fit into child's mouth.

❖ **Washable fabric or vinyl blocks for babies; large cardboard, foam or plastic blocks for toddlers.**

❖ **Variety of nature items** (store out of reach of children and use only with teacher supervision): fish aquarium, leaves, flowers, nonpoisonous living plants, shells and rocks.

Additional Toddler Play Items:

❏ soft climbing steps/rocking boat (adult must be available to assist child)

❏ crawl-through tunnel (cardboard cartons, etc.)

❏ indoor gym with steps and slide

❏ push-and-pull toys

❏ quiet rocking horses

❏ fill-and-dump toys

❏ riding toys (if room area allows)

❏ wooden inlay puzzles (realistic, colorful pictures of familiar scenes, with no more than four or five pieces. Each puzzle piece should be a complete object. Pieces with small knobs make it easy for child to remove pieces.)

❏ flannel boards with art foam or fabric shapes to arrange

❏ stacking and nesting toys

❏ large pop beads

❏ small inflatable wading pool (can be filled with pillows, sat in, crawled over, etc. Also a good temporary sand box for outdoor play.)

❏ art materials (assorted sizes, shapes and colors of paper, jumbo crayons in basic colors, play dough made from water, salt and flour, paint brushes with ½-inch [1.25-cm] bristles, tempera paints—offer only one color at a time and provide paint smocks or discarded shirts, worn backwards.)

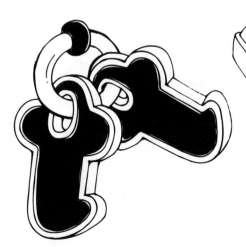

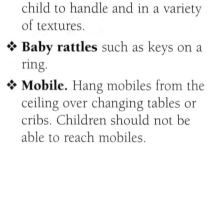

Getting and Maintaining Toys

The quality of nursery toys and activities can make all the difference in a child's view of the nursery. Anxious faces and cries are often calmed by the sight of a favorite, familiar toy. Parents, too, are reassured when they see an array of attractive toys for the child to enjoy. What are the overall guidelines that should be followed?

1. Is the toy safe, and can it be easily cleaned? In addition to regularly washing all the toys in the nursery, be sure to set up a system for washing and disinfecting all toys that have been in children's mouths or drooled upon. Washing toys can be a rotating job that is done by nursery staff, parents or other groups in the church. Establish a policy whereby nursery caregivers are constantly on the lookout for broken toys, small or sharp objects on the floor, loose parts or pieces on stuffed animals, etc. Many churches restrict the number of stuffed animals or do not provide them at all because of the difficulty of keeping them clean. Stuffed animals need to be regularly washed and replaced.

2. Is the toy visually interesting? Make sure the toys are attractive and will appeal to children.

3. Is the toy appropriate for the age level? Toys should encourage children to use a variety of skills. Think of the skills children are learning and experimenting with the most. The best toys give children more than one thing to do.

4. Is the toy durable? Look for well-made toys that will hold up under group use.

5. Is the toy enjoyable? Imagine a child's enjoyment while playing with the toy. Intriguing toys for children usually involve use of more than one sense.

Good toys can be purchased at educational supply stores, toy stores and second-hand stores. Some parents will want to donate toys and equipment that their own children have outgrown. Such generosity is a wonderful help—as long as the nursery doesn't become a dumping ground for broken toys, toys with missing parts or toys that can no longer be kept clean. Establish a donation policy in which only toys in good condition with no missing pieces are accepted.

Post a list of needed "outgrown" toys on the nursery bulletin board from time to time, along with a few guidelines as to what makes a toy useful in your nursery. This helps to avoid hurt feelings on the part of donors when they discover you cannot use the items they gave. Some donated toys may need to be redirected to a more appropriate age level, or occasionally not accepted if they don't meet the established guidelines.

Other sources for toys:
❖ Occasional "nursery showers" can be held at which specific items are requested to be given to the nursery program.

❖ Invite the congregation to participate in the nursery ministry by purchasing toys listed in a church newsletter or bulletin announcement.

❖ Plan an annual all-church open house in the nursery, conducting tours of the nursery, serving refreshments and listing items needed along with the prices. Ask participants to purchase or donate toward specific items.

Toys You Can Make

Many safe and attractive toys can be made with commonly available, low-cost materials. A senior citizen's group might enjoy making toys to your specifications, or invite each parent of a child in the nursery to make a toy or two. Provide the directions on separate sheets of paper for parents to take home. Find instructions for other homemade toys in books available at libraries or bookstores.

All homemade toys need to be frequently checked for safety hazards. Discard the toy if any construction appears less than durable. If your nursery often has many children supervised by few adults, do not use any homemade toys that contain or are made of small pieces.

Instant Toys

(Listed in order of age appropriateness.)

Most of these are easily obtained when kitchen cupboards and closets are cleaned out!

Bandannas or Hemmed Fabric Squares (4 to 24 months).

Place a clean, brightly-colored bandanna onto the floor so it "stands up" in the center. Younger babies will enjoy looking at it, crawlers will investigate it, toddlers will put it over their heads or dress a doll with it. Wash bandannas after each use.

Kitchenware (4 to 24 months).

Pots with fitted lids, sets of plastic measuring cups and spoons, plastic coasters, plastic cookie cutters, meat basters, plastic funnels and strainers, plastic ice-cube trays, wood or plastic napkin rings.

Lids (4 to 24 months).

Fill a sturdy plastic basket or box with flexible plastic lids in a variety of sizes and colors (coffee can lids, nut can lids, etc. Do not use lids from non-food products). Or punch holes in these lids with a hole punch and string on a new shoestring, knotting string securely.

Plastic Ware (4 to 24 months).

Provide clean margarine tubs, plastic jars, storage pieces that have lost their lids, plastic cups, etc. These toys are easily cleaned, and soft to chew on.

Instant Stackers (9 to 24 months).

Collect, sterilize and dry plastic spray-can caps in varying sizes. Caps may be both nested and stacked.

Carpet Squares (6 to 24 months).

Carpet samples in a variety of colors and textures should have bound edges. Lay them on the floor for crawlers to crawl over and walkers to walk over barefoot.

Simple Toys

(Listed in order of age appropriateness.)

Art Gallery
(Birth to 2 months).

Mount some of the following at baby's eye level, but out of reach, to create a unique art gallery: Black-and-white patterns, bull's-eyes, and checkers drawn on 5-inch (12.5-cm) squares of white poster board; brightly-colored animal stickers; large, clear magazine pictures; simple drawings of faces, emphasizing the eyes, nose and hair.

Texture Blanket
(6 weeks to 3 months).

Sew together 5-inch (12.5-cm) squares of five or six different-textured fabrics to make a small blanket.

Texture Mural
(6 weeks to 3 months).

Glue fabric pieces in a variety of colors, textures and shapes onto sturdy cardboard. Hang on the wall next to the changing table where baby can touch it.

Jingle Pillow
(6 weeks to 6 months).

Cut two donut shapes about 6 inches (15 cm) in diameter from washable fabric scraps (see sketch a). Sew shapes together, leaving seam partially open for stuffing. Sew several small jingle bells into a pocket of cotton fabric (see sketch b). Stuff the fabric donut with washable polyester fiberfill, wrapping fiberfill around the bell pocket before inserting it (see sketch c). Stitch seam completely closed (see sketch d). This shape is especially easy for young babies to grab.

Textured Glove
(3 to 12 months).

Sew a variety of textured fabric scraps to the fingers of a glove. Wear the glove as you play with a baby, allowing the baby to explore the textures.

Wave Bottle
(4 to 24 months).

Wash and thoroughly dry a clear plastic bottle and cap. Fill halfway with water, then add one or two drops of food coloring. Fill remainder of bottle with mineral oil. Drop in some glitter or sequins to accentuate the wave motion. Coat the inside of the cap with superglue; attach tightly to bottle. When the glue is dry, cover cap seam with duct tape. Babies will enjoy watching the movement of the water. Toddlers will have fun moving the bottle themselves, rolling, shaking or turning it.

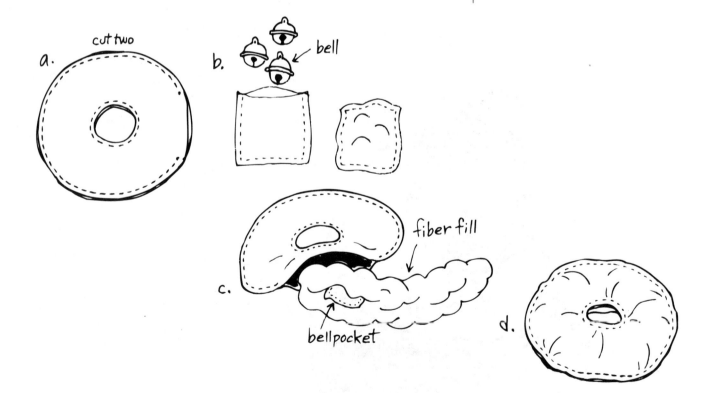

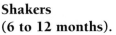
Shakers
(6 to 12 months).

Wash empty plastic soda bottles and caps thoroughly, inside and out. Pour a handful of macaroni, beans, hard candy, etc. into the bottle. Coat the inside of the cap with superglue and close tightly. When the cap is dry, cover cap seam completely with duct tape.

Milk Carton Blocks
(6 to 24 months).

Cut the tops off two cardboard milk cartons so that they are equal in height. Stuff one carton with newspaper for stability. Push the second carton completely into the first to form a cube. Cover blocks with decorative adhesive paper.

Washable Books
(6 to 24 months).

Place brightly-colored magazine pictures or photographs back-to-back inside heavy-duty clear plastic zipper-style bags. Staple the zipper ends together to form a book. Cover stapled end completely with duct tape.

Pictures may also be laid back-to-back inside a length of clear Con-Tact paper long and wide enough to fold over and cover pictures completely, leaving a margin of at least 1/2 inch (1.25 cm) on all sides of picture. Staple left margins together and cover stapled margin with duct tape.

Shake and Bang Toy
(6 to 24 months).

Thread clean, empty thread spools on a new shoestring. Securely tie ends of shoestring together.

Foam Box
(6 to 24 months).

Cut four equal-sized squares from 2-inch (5-cm) thick washable foam. (One square yard or meter is a good size.) Cover each square with washable fabric, leaving a 2- to 4-inch (5- to 10-cm) margin on two sides of each square (see sketch a). Sew squares together at margins to create a tunnel box for crawlers and toddlers (see sketch b). Wash and dry frequently.

This may also be done with other shapes (rectangles, triangles) and either used as play pillows or sewn together at the margins to make structures for resting on, crawling through, sitting in, hiding in, etc.

To make a foam donut ring, cut a donut of 4-inch (10-cm) thick foam, with the center hole large enough for a toddler to crawl through. Cover with washable fabric.

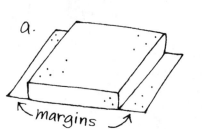

T-Shirt Pillows
(9 to 24 months).

Sew closed the sleeve and neck holes of a colorful T-shirt. Tightly stuff the shirt through the open bottom with polyester fiberfill or shredded foam that is machine washable and dryer safe. Sew the bottom closed.

Play Dough
(12 to 24 months).

Combine 1 cup flour, 1/2 cup salt and 2 teaspoons cream of tartar; mix thoroughly in a medium saucepan. Mix 1 tablespoon oil and a few drops of food coloring in 1 cup water. Add to dry ingredients and stir over low heat until mixture becomes thick and pulls away from sides of pan. Form into a ball and store in an airtight container.

Box Wagon
(12 to 24 months).

Cover a clean shoe box and lid with adhesive paper. Punch a hole in the end of box near the top. Slip a 2-foot (60-cm) length of sturdy cord through the hole; knot cord inside the box and also at pulling end. Outside may be decorated with other adhesive paper cutouts or pictures covered with clear adhesive paper.

An Eye-Catching Nursery

Your nursery environment will be enhanced by one or more special features that attract the attention of parents and children alike. Consider these ideas for the special touch that will truly say, "You're welcome here."

❖ Take advantage of windows. Hang mobiles or wind chimes near windows. Tape cellophane shapes to windows. If there are bushes or trees near the windows, hang one or more bird feeders in the branches. Bring a book about birds to look at with children.

❖ Make a fabric book pocket to hang on the wall. Books are placed in each pocket. Rotate the books every month or so.

❖ Cover a crib mattress with a sheet and place the mattress on the floor—perfect for experimenting crawlers.

❖ One or more large pillows will create a corner of coziness for reading books or talking. (Note: Safety experts recommend avoiding the use of beanbag chairs.)

❖ Wallpaper borders add a creative touch to nursery walls.

❖ Wading pool filled with small balls in which children may play.

❖ Stencil animal or nature scenes on walls. Do not hang pictures with frames or glass that would hurt a child if they fell off the wall. Avoid make-believe or fantasy scenes which convey a sense that the nursery is a place focused on pretending, rather than on discovering very real expressions of God's love.

Teacher Training Articles

This section contains dozens of concise, informative articles dealing with issues of concern to caregivers of babies and toddlers.

Articles include:

❖ Biting: Nightmare in the Nursery

❖ Communication with Nontalkers

❖ Understanding a Baby's Cry

❖ "Clean" Diaper Changes

❖ Discipline in the Nursery

❖ Teaching Babies About God

❖ Welcoming a Baby to the Nursery

❖ Toddler Tips

Use these articles in both preventive and prescriptive form: for staff training **before** problems occur, and as a remedy to problem situations **already** in place.

Just photocopy the articles of your choice and distribute; or use selected topics as the basis for nursery caregiver training sessions. Either way, it's a ready-made resource at your fingertips!

Meeting the Needs of Babies

What Are They Like?

When we say "baby," we may mean a newborn. Or we may be referring to a sitter or to the crawler who picks up, inspects and eats every crumb! Although babyhood is short, the changes from newborn to toddler are enormous!

Although a **newborn** baby is quite aware of and sensitive to surroundings, sleeping and eating are the order of the day. A newborn's optimal visual distance is 8 to 10 inches (20 to 25 cm), or about the distance from the baby's face to yours when you are holding the child in your arms.

Around six weeks of age, a baby begins to reach out to touch items that interest him or her, to control his or her head, and to notice and separate his or her fingers. The eyes are able to focus on a variety of distances. By the time a baby is able to roll over, he or she will be laughing and experimenting with making other sounds as well. The head is usually well controlled now, and the baby loves to kick and squirm.

A baby may become a **sitter** at around six months of age. Now that the baby's range of vision is broadened, he or she loves to reach (and perhaps even roll after) small objects, and drop, throw or bang them. Expect some anxiety when separating from a parent or other familiar person.

The **crawler** is now able to explore a brave new world! From the coffee cup to the full wastebasket, there is nothing that doesn't interest him or her. Once crawling is mastered, expect lots of pulling up, standing and attempts at climbing. This progresses into "cruising," walking a bit while holding onto something, and finally, into walking (and falling). What may seem to be random acts of discovery—banging, tasting and staring—serve to inform this little explorer of the nature of his or her world.

How Can I Help Them?

Newborns need a quiet place to sleep and nurse. An occasional change of scenery and the gentle talking, rocking and comforting that accompany feeding, changing and sleep preparation should keep them happy and content. Be sure to support the head of a baby this age. Remember that frequent burping is necessary when feeding a newborn.

Babies between six weeks and three months like to have objects placed within their view. A mirror mounted where babies can lie on their stomachs and look up at the reflection fascinates them. An infant seat or other device that puts the baby where he or she can see what's going on nearby is helpful.

Once a baby can sit up, try playing peek-a-boo with him or her, or pushing gently on the baby's feet so the child can push back. Provide a number of safe smaller toys (rattles, fabric or vinyl blocks) and other objects for discovering. As you interact with a baby, describe his or her actions or responses to your actions.

For the crawler, provide lots of space to roam without hazards. Crib mattresses and washable, firm pillows can provide a variety of safe crawling, climbing and sitting surfaces. Your calm and happy interaction with babies on the floor helps them learn ways to explore and communicate. When correcting or giving directions, speak in positive terms. Instead of, "Don't pull Jake's hair, Sam!" say, "Sam, pat Jake's hair. It feels soft. Here is a lamb you can pat, too."

A Smooth Schedule

There should be at least one caregiver for every three babies. This makes it possible to keep a close eye on every child's safety, as well as to give each child individual attention. If possible, the same caregiver should care for the same children from week to week. This continuity is especially important when babies begin to distinguish between strangers and friends!

When a baby arrives, give child and parents a friendly greeting! Talk to and watch the child; listen carefully to any comments the parents make. After check-in is complete, take a moment to talk to and sing to the child. To interest older babies in an activity, begin to do the activity yourself. If the baby cries, talk to and sing to the child first; hold the child if necessary.

When it's time to change or move a child, don't pick up the child without warning; rather, talk calmly about what's going to happen. Never underestimate the power of your calmness and relaxed attitude. It will likely "rub off" onto the babies you care for!

Remember to *watch*, *ask*, and *adapt* yourself to the children's changing interests and activities. Your enthusiasm for the theme-related activities suggested in your curriculum and your interest in each child are what make this a time of effective learning.

Biting: Nightmare in the Nursery

It's one of the worst moments in toddler care: a child screams; you see another child's jaws clamped shut like a pit bull's on the screamer! Babies and toddlers bite for a number of reasons. Sometimes they bite because they're teething and it feels good. Sometimes they bite because they want something and don't know how to get it, or someone wants their toy and they don't know another way to stop the child. Sometimes they bite because they are frustrated and their feelings overwhelm them, or they want to say something but don't know the words they need.

First Things First

Until all is calm again, separate the biter from the rest of the group. One adult should care for the bitten child while another adult deals with the biter.

Focus first on treating the injured child, offering comfort and first aid if needed. (All bites should be observed for infection: redness increases rather than fades.) Remove the bitten child from the area, talking calmly about what you are going to do ("We'll wash off your hurt place") and inspecting the wound. Even if the bite did not break the skin, cleanse the area with antiseptic. Offer a bandage or try a cold compress.

Helping the Biter

It may seem sometimes that a child has bitten out of pure meanness! But it's important to remember that toddlers still use their mouths for a great deal of exploration. The biting may have been motivated by exploration coupled with the enjoyable new sensation of biting down firmly! The biter may not have any idea that the biting caused the screams and excitement that followed!

What is needed is information, not punishment. Since you have already gently separated the biter from the group, help him or her understand what happened. "Timmy, your teeth hurt Jasmine. Teeth are for eating. I can't let you bite Jasmine." Then provide an alternative that will help the child remember that teeth are for chewing. "Here is a rubber ring. You may bite hard on that." By the time the biter has been instructed, the bitten child should also be calm and can be reintroduced to the group.

After the Bite

Now two things should happen: first, an adult needs to closely supervise the biter for the rest of the session, remaining available to intervene in case biting suddenly has become the biter's new "favorite activity"! If a child becomes enamored with biting for a period of time, the biter should have an adult assigned to him or her for the duration. If biting happens repeatedly, try to identify a pattern of circumstances that may lead to biting. Then intervene before biting occurs.

Secondly, a report should be made in writing to the parents of the child who was bitten. In your report, briefly describe the circumstances. Avoid naming the child who has bitten unless the parent asks. Simply say, "Another child wanted Emily's toy, so the child bit her on the arm." Include information about what treatment steps were taken and what was said to the biter. While reporting biting to parents may seem burdensome, it remedies the problem of forgetting to tell the parents the whole story due to the rush of child pick up. Add your phone number to the report so that parents may call you with any questions. See the sample form below.

Because biting is such a typical behavior in toddlers, it's helpful to let parents know when their child has bitten another only because they may see a developing pattern—not because an occasional bite is a sign of a serious problem. Let the parents know in a matter-of-fact manner, including a comment such as, "Most children bite at least once in their toddler years."

Biting is painful, but it is not the end of the world. Remember that adult calmness and kindness to *both* children is the key to quickly setting everyone at ease again!

Parent Note

Date: _____

_____ was bitten on the

_____ today in

the nursery when _____

_____.

The skin was
- ❑ not broken.
- ❑ broken.

We comforted and
- ❑ washed the bite.
- ❑ put an antiseptic ointment on the bite.
- ❑ placed a bandage on the bite.
- ❑ held a cold compress on the bite.

When a child is bitten in the nursery, we move the biter away from other children and gently but firmly instruct the child not to bite. While occasional biting is a typical toddler behavior, we closely observe the biter in order to prevent any future occurrences. Please call me if you have any questions or comments.

_____ (name)   _____ (phone)

Exploring Books Together

Exploring books with babies and toddlers will foster children's love of reading and appreciation for spoken language. But first, in using books effectively with very young children, put aside the expectation of reading aloud. Instead, plan to use books as a way of exploring with children the sounds and pictures offered.

Young babies' interest in books may seem limited to mouthing them! But even for crawlers, one or two cleanable vinyl books with large, clear pictures can catch the eye on the way to the mouth. A baby this age might even sit still for a moment while you point to and name a familiar object on the page. Or open the book and stand it up a short distance from a baby who is lying on his or her back. Periodically, turn the pages of the book.

What Books Should We Have in the Nursery?

Most older babies and toddlers enjoy exploring a book with an interested adult. Choose books with sturdy, cleanable pages (for health reasons) and large, clear, colorful pictures. The number of pages should be few and the subjects limited to objects and situations in a child's everyday life. Children especially enjoy books with small child-safe mirrors in them. Toddler Bibles may also be used in a nursery, or cover the picture pages of a children's Bible with clear adhesive-backed paper for extra durability.

What Makes a Good "Book Time"?

Use the book as a way to explore the world, rather than feeling bound to read the words on the page. Settle yourself comfortably in a large chair or on the floor where one child (or several) may sit in your lap or next to you. Making "book time" a caring and pleasurable experience is part of building a love for books and ultimately a love for God's Book.

The child will want to turn the pages, as much for the pleasure of turning the page as to see what's on another page. This page turning will go backwards and forwards, pages will be skipped, and some pages returned to again and again. Help the child turn the page only if he or she has difficulty doing so.

Point to and name the objects in the pictures ("Look! I see a dog!"). Ask questions to which a child can point to give the answers ("Where is the dog? Can you point to the dog?"). Talk about the action in the pictures ("The dog is carrying a bone. Where is the tree?"). Describe the picture, adding comments and asking simple questions that help children think of God's love ("That big green tree looks cool. God made big trees. Devon, do you have a tree in your yard?"). Books with repetitive rhymes are especially fun to read with children.

If you see that interest in a book is waning, select another book, shorten your comments or change the pace by doing a quick song or finger play. For most children, book time will not last long. Remember that baby and toddler attention spans are very short! A toddler may only be interested in one picture before sliding off your lap.

By providing a comfortable, loving time for busy babies and toddlers to settle in with a book, you are teaching them a great deal about God's love, His patience, and His world!

Take a Look at Babies

Birth to 6 Weeks

- ❖ Sleeps 20 to 23 hours a day
- ❖ Responds reflexively (sucking, grasping, startling)
- ❖ Is aware of surroundings for brief periods
- ❖ Changes mood easily; very sensitive
- ❖ Tracks slow-moving objects with eyes
- ❖ Brings hand to mouth

Provide for Enrichment:

- ❖ Mobiles with bold colors or black and white, hung from child's perspective
- ❖ Occasional changes of scenery
- ❖ Rocking while feeding and comforting
- ❖ Conversation directed to child

6 Weeks to 6 Months

- ❖ Shows curiosity by swiping, touching with hand
- ❖ Controls head while lying on back
- ❖ Relaxes fists, moves fingers
- ❖ Brings objects to mouth
- ❖ Focuses clearly at varying distances
- ❖ Stares at hand
- ❖ Smiles and laughs willingly

Provide for Enrichment:

- ❖ Time on stomach each day
- ❖ Mirror mounted seven inches (17.5 cm) from head
- ❖ Colorful toys or pictures to look at
- ❖ Conversation directed to child

3½ to 5½ Months

- ❖ Turns sideways and from back to stomach
- ❖ Kicks vigorously
- ❖ Experiments with making sounds
- ❖ Recognizes parent's voice and face
- ❖ Controls head while upright
- ❖ Laughs freely; giggles in response to brief, gentle tickling

Provide for Enrichment:

- ❖ Frequent one-to-one play times
- ❖ Variety of things to see, places to go
- ❖ Conversation directed to child
- ❖ Infant seat (for limited times)

6 to 8 Months

- ❖ Fascinated with small objects
- ❖ Pushes legs firmly when pressure applied
- ❖ Turns over from stomach to back
- ❖ Sits unaided
- ❖ May begin to show teeth
- ❖ Drops, throws, bangs objects
- ❖ Enjoys extended play with adult
- ❖ Shows anxiety toward strangers

Provide for Enrichment:

- ❖ Simple games to play with adults
- ❖ Words linked to actions and objects
- ❖ Brief, simple stories
- ❖ Freedom to move
- ❖ Variety of safe, small objects and containers
- ❖ Toys child can operate
- ❖ Balls
- ❖ Conversation directed to child

Take a Look at Toddlers

8 to 14 Months

❖ Is curious about everything

❖ Crawls and climbs

❖ Stands and cruises
(walks holding onto something)

❖ Walks—although clumsily

❖ Stares intently

❖ Responds to a variety of words and sentences

❖ Develops more teeth

❖ Explores objects, usually by mouthing them

❖ Actively uses small objects:
stacks, inserts, opens

❖ Shows affection for familiar people

❖ Continues to be shy with strangers

Provide for Enrichment:

❖ A safe environment for exploration

❖ Consistent, familiar people for interaction

❖ Conversation directed to child

❖ Books with stiff pages

❖ Balls 8 to 24 inches
(20 to 60 cm) in diameter

❖ Fill and dump toys

❖ Stacking and nesting toys

14 to 24 Months

❖ Uses objects with intent: stacking,
opening, throwing

❖ Walks well, often runs

❖ Shows frustration when his or her
desires are thwarted

❖ Enjoys conversation with adults, ranging
from single words to complete sentences

❖ Shows strong attachment to regular caregivers

❖ Demonstrates evidence of reasoning
in problem solving

Provide for Enrichment:

❖ Loving firmness with flexibility

❖ Natural conversation

❖ Conversation directed to child

❖ Push and pull toys

❖ Large, stable toys (rocking horses, etc.)
on which child can sit and move

❖ Plastic people and animals

❖ Plastic or rubber containers for pouring

❖ Household utensils and containers

❖ Paper and jumbo nontoxic crayons

...Next to Godliness

No, the Bible doesn't tell us cleanliness is next to godliness. But in the nursery, it's gospel! Nothing discourages parents more than having another earache or cold show up after each visit to the nursery! To provide effective ministry, the nursery must be a place where parents feel comfortable leaving their little ones. It's wise to know your church's own policy on these matters ahead of the time you are scheduled to work in the nursery.

Basic Training

What with giving babies personal attention, comforting criers, diapering, feeding and rocking, considering health and cleanliness may seem too much to ask! But one child who "catches" an illness in your nursery is one child too many. Listed below are some basic cleanliness procedures for any nursery.

❖ Don't work in the nursery if YOU are ill. Call another worker to substitute for you.

❖ Do NOT admit babies or toddlers who have symptoms of illness. Protect the healthy children. Follow your nursery's guidelines for maintaining a well-baby policy.

❖ Between sessions, the floors should be thoroughly cleaned. Wipe down furniture and frequently used surfaces with a bleach solution or disinfectant. At least once during the session, repeat this procedure on frequently used surfaces.

❖ Throughout the session, remove any toys that have been placed in a child's mouth or drooled on. Wash toys thoroughly in a disinfectant solution before returning them to use. (Rinse toys in hot water after disinfecting to remove disinfectant.)

❖ Replace a crib sheet with a clean sheet BEFORE use by another child.

❖ When placing a younger baby on floor or in a playpen, lay a washable blanket under child in case of spitting up. Use a fresh blanket with each child or use individual child's blanket (taken from and returned to diaper bag).

❖ Always wash your hands with soap and warm water before the children arrive, before feeding each child and after changing diapers or helping a child with the toilet.

Safe and Secure

At the beginning of your time in the nursery and during the session, keep an eye out for potentially unsafe circumstances or objects.

❖ Check to be sure no small or dangerous objects have been brought into the nursery.

❖ Confirm that all cleaning supplies have been put away out of the reach of children.

❖ Make sure that all cords are out of children's reach.

❖ Remove any broken toys.

Communication with Nontalkers

One of the joys of working with children who are too young to talk is rediscovering the wonderful ways of nonverbal communication! Some of the deepest and most important messages we send to each other are nonverbal ones. Learning to use these nonverbal modes of communication is the basis for getting in tune with babies and toddlers.

Watching, Responding

The observant caregiver finds that a great deal of communication goes on with even the youngest child. The first and most basic part of this process, however, is not to talk! It is simply to *watch* the child. One well-known psychologist has said, "If you want to know how a baby feels, watch his feet." That's good advice! Notice a baby's facial expressions, sounds, body posture and gestures, because these provide the foundation for your communication.

To begin communicating, always place yourself at the child's eye level. (Yes, this does mean you will spend a great deal of time bending, squatting, sitting or even lying on the floor!) While holding an infant in your arms, place your face 8 to 10 inches (20 to 25 cm) from the baby's face, the optimal visual distance for a young infant's visual focus.

To communicate with a young baby, begin by smiling and talking quietly with him or her. Your tone of voice is just as important as your choice of words. Sing songs and say rhymes that will catch a child's attention. Try imitating the baby's sounds and gestures. This can develop into a delightful game. As you imitate the child, try making one change in the pattern of sounds and gestures.

You can also communicate with your face. Eye contact, especially when doing something routine, like changing diapers, is a good way to express interest in a child. Use dramatic facial expressions and voice tones as you play with a child.

Toddler Talk

A toddler responds with verbal cues and words. As a toddler points, babbles or talks to indicate interest in something, use words to elaborate on the subject. "I see you want to throw the beanbag, Ryan. I see the blue beanbag." Use the words, "I see..." often. You will not only acknowledge your interest and attention, but also will encourage the child to respond.

With an older baby or toddler, first *watch*, then as you talk, be sure to *ask*. An older baby or toddler will nod (or give other visual cues) in response to a question. This will not only help you determine what the child wants, but it also helps the child to feel that you are trying to understand his or her attempt at communicating. Then as you continue to watch and ask, follow the child's lead in changing interests. *Adapt* what you are doing and saying to expand the child's activity. For example, "Oh! I see you want to throw the ball now. Do you want to throw it to me? I will roll it to you."

Talking Through

If you come to a child with a specific purpose in mind (such as changing a diaper) try to always "talk through" what you are doing. Begin by telling the child what you are going to do. Then describe what you are doing and describe the child's reaction. For instance, "Hello, Devon. I see you're chewing on your bear. I'm going to pick you up now. It's time to change your diaper." (Patting the diaper will reinforce this verbal message with a nonverbal cue.) "Let's walk to the changing table. Here we are. I'll strap you in. Where is your bag? Here it is. Now I'll take off the wet diaper. I see you like to stretch and kick! Devon is kicking." Continue this stream of conversation with lots of eye contact and smiles until you are finished with the task and the child is resettled and content.

Talking through an activity is an especially important technique for communicating with toddlers. Beginning a new activity with a toddler without talking about it first will often result in a "temper tantrum" or "no"-saying. This may be due not so much to a child's stubbornness as to the caregiver's lack of communication! For instance, "I see you've spilled your juice, Vanya. Your shirt is wet. I will bring you a dry shirt. Can you raise your arms? Here comes the dry shirt! There. Now it's over your head. Do you want more juice? If you do, bring me your cup."

By carefully observing and appropriately communicating with babies and toddlers, you help them to know that the caregivers around them are loving and considerate people who want to understand them, with or without words!

Understanding a Baby's Cry

Except for the moment of childbirth, no one likes to hear a baby cry! Whether you're a veteran caregiver or are relatively new to working with little ones, a crying baby gives rise to immediate tension in all of us. If the crying goes on and on, it may give rise to near panic! A crying baby makes nursery time difficult for the caretakers, for the other children and for the crying baby. Why do babies cry? Are they angry or spoiled? Or is it something more?

Why Do They Cry Like That?

Imagine you have had a stroke. Your mental faculties all function well but only a few muscles in your body will do what you tell them to do. Writing and walking are out of the question. And worst of all, you cannot talk. How would you communicate your needs and feelings? It wouldn't be easy, would it? In such a case, you might find yourself weeping out of sheer frustration!

For a baby, the situation is somewhat similar. With very little or no language, a baby must rely on nonverbal communication. Sometimes, these nonverbal attempts may go unnoticed or may be misunderstood. Crying is his or her first and most useful nonverbal way to communicate. As a baby grows, his or her cries will vary in tone, pitch and pattern to send varying messages. But it isn't always easy to tell what message a baby is sending by crying.

What to Do When You've Tried Everything!

Try walking the baby (going outdoors can be very calming). Rock or walk with the baby for a few more minutes. When you are so calm that you feel sleepy, you will probably find your little one is calm, too!

If the crying persists, call the parent. Some churches have found it helpful to establish a policy of when to call the parent. Be sure you know what your church's policy is. (Nonstop crying for up 5 to 10 minutes before calling the parent seems to be a safe norm.)

For many parents, leaving their baby in the nursery makes for a difficult day for all involved. The parents may be feeling rushed and may communicate their tension to the baby. The baby is also under some stress simply due to a change in schedule and to being in a strange place. As a caretaker who sees the child perhaps only once a week, it is wise to always respond to a child's cry. By quietly observing at first, you can often determine steps to take to bring the baby into a calmer frame of mind. You may not be able to bring peace on earth, but at least you may be able to bring peace to the nursery!

Here are some common reasons for, and cues to, the *kinds* of crying a baby may do:

❖ Is the baby hungry?

Look for a furrowed brow, chewing on the fist or fingers and drawing up the knees to the belly.

TRY feeding. When trying to calm a nursing baby, give the child to a person who is not a nursing mother. (The scent of milk on a nursing mother may make the baby even more aware of his or her hunger!)

❖ Is the baby in pain?

Look for drawing up of the knees (gas pains), tugging on or rubbing ears (earache) or a general thrashing and irritability (teething).

TRY burping or rubbing the baby's belly if it is distended from gas. If the baby seems warm, check temperature with a disposable forehead strip thermometer. Notify the parent if temperature is abnormal.

❖ Is the baby too warm or too cold?

Look to see if the baby is over- or underdressed. (A baby should be wearing about the same amount of clothing as you are.) Check for drafts or temperature differences that may affect the baby.

TRY adding or removing clothing as needed. Try moving the baby to a draft-free spot off the floor.

❖ Is the baby over-stimulated or bored?

Look at the room environment. Is it noisy and lively? Try a quiet, darkened room. Does a wide-awake baby need someone to interact with? (In such cases, babies may actually "call" first, then only cry if no one responds!)

TRY talking calmly to the baby. Move him or her to an appropriate room.

❖ Is the baby's diaper wet or dirty?

Look inside the diaper. Many babies are not bothered by wetness itself but may have rashes that are painful upon contact with urine or feces.

TRY changing the baby's diaper. Be sure to use any ointment for rashes included in the baby's diaper bag.

❖ Is the baby tired?

Look for rigid body posture, irregular crying patterns, other behaviors that may make the baby look like he or she has "lost it."

TRY placing the baby in a quiet place where he or she can stretch out. For some babies, crying is simply a way to release tension. Give the baby time to calm down. Slowly patting or rubbing the back may help. (Try patting or rubbing to the rhythm of your own heartbeat.)

Why Use Curriculum?

"Babies and toddlers simply need to be fed, changed, rocked...what can they possibly learn about God? Why would we need curriculum for them?"

First of all, our goal in using curriculum is not to get a baby to spout theological concepts! Instead, our goal is to individually (one-on-one) teach each baby through natural learning processes what he or she can begin to learn about God. Curriculum is designed to help you, the caregiver, use the time you spend with little ones in the nursery to build spiritual foundations.

Secondly, using curriculum also benefits you, the caregiver, as much as the child. Singing and talking about Jesus is a powerful reminder that what you are doing is not just custodial care, but ministry in its truest sense. The same is true for parents. Babies and toddlers may not NEED to hear about Jesus, but parents do need to begin talking comfortably about Him with their child. The model the church provides of how we care for and "teach"

babies and toddlers is intended to help parents catch on to the fact that they can and should do the same things at home.

Curriculum provides you with ideas and words that help make your natural teaching effective. Since the best kind of teaching for babies and toddlers is primarily one-on-one, don't expect that babies or toddlers will sit in a circle or have a group time, or even remain interested in what you are doing for very long. But as you sit on the floor talking and playing with two or three babies, make frequent use of the conversation ideas and songs suggested in your curriculum. Plan to provide at least one or two of the theme-related activities. Play portions of the cassette or CD, repeating the same songs frequently. The sounds, words, actions and most of all, the feelings that are created in this casual setting will flow into a natural pattern of teaching and

learning that will eventually build a young child's understanding of God, Jesus and the loving comfort found in the people around him or her at church. And using a curriculum with monthly themes helps provide continuity to the activities in the nursery, especially when caregivers change frequently.

In a large church nursery where there are many children and adults in the same room, designate certain activities for each adult to provide for children throughout the session. For example, one caregiver may position him- or herself near several books, looking and talking about them with interested children. Another adult may sit near an open area of the room with a cassette player nearby, playing one or two action songs and doing the suggested motions with children in that area of the room. However, as the session progresses, adults need to be ready to move to "where the action is." Flexibility is a key.

A baby's learning takes place all the time, as a natural part of living. So the teaching in your nursery is accomplished by your every look, word and act while you are in the presence of babies or toddlers. The nursery is ministry just as surely as teaching a theology class for adults would be. A nursery curriculum helps you to focus your playing, talking, caregiving, singing and finger plays in ways that familiarize a child with God's name and His love. Awareness of God's love for each child takes your time in the nursery far beyond the level of just singing "Itsy-Bitsy Spider" again!

Three stonemasons,
when asked what they were doing,
replied as follows:

"Laying a stone," said the first.

"Making a wall," said the second.

"Building a cathedral," said the third.

Three Sunday School teachers
were asked what they were doing:

"Baby-sitting these kids," said the first.

"Caring for the children," said the second.

"Sharing God's love," replied the third.

"Clean" Diaper Changes

Changing a diaper is no treat for anyone. But diapers are a fact of baby and toddler life. Beyond the fact that clean diapers are needed on a regular basis, babies and toddlers also need diapering time to be filled with gentle talk and loving interaction. Negative faces or comments should always be avoided. Health and safety procedures must be carefully carried out to insure the safety of both the child and the caregiver. To avoid any possible abuse allegations, it is accepted practice to always have two adults present in the room when diapers are changed.

Equipment

A well-equipped changing area needs access to running hot water and antibacterial soap, cleanable surfaces and good ventilation. Keep a bottle of bleach solution (one portion bleach to 10 portions water) or other disinfecting solution and a roll of paper towels within the caregiver's reach. Many nurseries use wax paper or form-feed computer paper as a disposable clean surface. Disposable gloves (available at drug and medical-supply stores) are also a standard part of diapering equipment. All caregivers should wear gloves while changing diapers. This eliminates worries about safety if the caregiver has cuts or open sores on hands or if a child has any communicable ailment (rashes, infections, etc.). Keep changing supplies (plastic bags, etc.) out of child's reach.

Changing Diapers

Use this quiet break from activity to focus on the child with your smiles, conversation and gentle care. Playing games with hands and feet, offering a book to look at and talking quietly about growing and about God's love can make changing time a valuable teaching time. Check diapers soon after arrival, once during the session and again near dismissal time—or whenever an odor is noticed!

Toddlers are increasingly aware of their abilities to control their own bodies. They are beginning to show an interest in the toilet and to have feelings about whether or not they like to have their diapers changed. If a toddler resists changing (kicking, trying to get down from the changing table), interest the child in a toy or sing a song while you change the diaper. As always, talking about what you are doing and about the child's reaction helps to keep the child focused on you rather than disliked aspects of the diaper change.

Toilet Training

Some toddlers in your care may have begun toilet training. While timing varies widely, toddlers who have older brothers and sisters often show an early interest. Some toddlers will indicate to you that they are aware of a need to use the toilet. For children this age, be sure to find out from parents whether or not it is necessary to take the child to the toilet or potty chair.

Request that toddlers who are being toilet trained always be brought to the nursery in diapers or in disposable training pants. If the child must be taken down the hall to the toilet, two adults should remain with the child to prevent any allegations of abuse. (If there is a bathroom attached to the nursery, simply leave the door open.)

A practical alternative may be to place a potty chair behind a screen in the nursery near the changing table. (Using a potty chair may be easier than trying to muster up an extra person for potty duty in a busy nursery.) After each use, clean out and disinfect the potty chair in the same way as the changing table. Pictures mounted at the eye level of the child seated on the potty chair can give you an opportunity for conversation as you and the child are together.

Ten Steps to Changing Diapers

1. Collect all necessary supplies (gloves, clean diapers, plastic bags, premoistened towelettes, etc.).

2. Wash hands and put on gloves.

3. Talk with the child about what you are going to do.

4. Place the child on a clean, disposable surface (wax paper or paper towels). Never turn away from a child on a changing table, not even if child is strapped onto the table.

5. Remove the wet or soiled diaper. Place in a plastic bag.

6. Use a premoistened towelette to clean the diaper area, wiping from front to back. Place towelette in plastic bag containing soiled diaper. Close and knot bag and throw it away. (For cloth diapers: dispose of wipes in wastebasket; tie shut plastic bag containing diaper and place in diaper bag).

7. Put clean diaper on child and remove child from changing table.

8. Remove disposable paper cover from changing table. Spray area thoroughly with bleach solution, wiping with paper towel.

9. Remove gloves and place in wastebasket.

10. Wash hands.

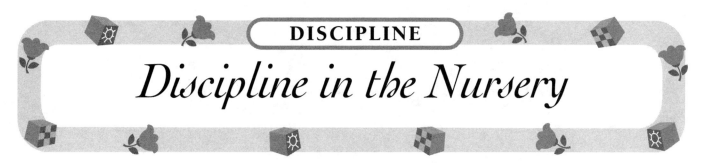

Discipline in the Nursery

What Is Discipline?

First, it is imperative to understand that "discipline" at any age level is NOT "punishment for bad behavior." Instead, the very word *discipline* means "teaching"—the very kind of teaching Jesus did with His disciples! Discipline is a door of opportunity: opportunity to teach children appropriate ways to meet their needs. Such teaching of these ways will be twofold: first, to immediately stop inappropriate behavior (behavior that might hurt a child, destroy materials or disrupt the group); second, to help the child find another, more appropriate way to behave.

Discipline of babies and toddlers should NEVER include any sort of negative physical touching (spanking, slapping, swatting, tapping, shaking, pulling, biting back, or the like). It also NEVER includes ridicule, sarcasm, threats or withholding any sort of care from a child.

Meeting Their Needs

Young children have a very small understanding of how the world works.

They have no idea of the consequences of their acts or how another child will respond to them. Part of the process of discipline is to help a child make sense of things even as you help the child understand appropriate ways to act. To meet the needs of very young children:

1. Prevent Problems. Be sure the environment is set up to be safe and "trouble-free." Young children need to be able to explore with as little restraint as possible; this helps a child develop his or her own internal controls and reduces stress on babies and adults alike. Also, having several identical toys can help when toddlers both want the same toy. Because toddlers are still too young to understand sharing, offering an identical toy can often avoid conflict.

2. Set Clear Limits. Use the word "no" as little as possible because it does not teach the child an appropriate way to act. Instead, give clear information about the situation. For example, "The truck is for rolling. We don't hit Jeremiah with it. It will hurt him. The truck rolls on the floor. See?"

Save use of the word "no" for dangerous situations in which the child must be immediately restrained.

3. Redirect Behavior. "Let's roll the truck. Look! I roll the truck to you. Can you roll it back to me?" Or offer another activity. "Here is a ball. We can roll the ball. Or you may roll the car. Jeremiah will roll the truck." Redirecting behavior does not mean trying to get a toddler to share or to apologize. This only results in adult frustration and toddler confusion! While your modeling of sharing and apologizing is an important part of your teaching, don't expect that toddlers will understand it—or imitate it—just yet!

4. Offer a Choice. When you offer, "You may play with the bear or the doll. Which one do you want?" you are giving the child a choice between two acceptable alternatives. You will often find that even the most resistant toddler is easily redirected!

5. Acknowledge Feelings. Use the words, "I see..." often. "Dana, I see you fell down. You hurt your knee. You feel sad." Acknowledging what you see shows the child you understand and helps the child begin to make sense of his or her emotions.

6. Talk Through Problems. If you are "talking through" as you watch children (describing what you see and how children are reacting) you are already in the perfect position to help solve any problem situation going on. "Ryan wants the car. Janna wants the car. What can we do? Here is another car. Here is a truck. Which one would you like, Ryan?"

Of course, the most important part of this opportunity to teach is found in the way you behave! As you model caring and respectful behavior and follow the above guidelines to meet children's needs in appropriate ways, you will find not only that the nursery is more peaceful, but also that you are naturally helping children make sense of their world and solve their own problems. This also shows children that their caregivers are loving and considerate people who want to help them. And that is the essence of showing God's love to little ones!

The View from Down Here

No one has yet surveyed babies to find out what they like or don't like about a nursery! But by carefully watching the behavior of little ones, we can begin to "think like a baby" about our nursery's environment and the ways in which it could better meet a baby or toddler's needs.

Sit Down!

An excellent place to begin is to sit on the floor of the nursery in several different spots. How does the toy shelf look from there—inviting or forbidding?

How does the carpet smell?
Is the floor clean?

Are the floor pillows
firm or squishy?

Are there interesting pictures
on the wall at a toddler's eye-level?

Keep looking around. The list on this page will help you think of the parts of a nursery environment that are important to a baby or toddler.

If I Were a Baby, I'd Ask:

❒ How many things are there for me to pull myself up on?
Climb over? Crawl in and out of? Rest on?
Is there space for me to crawl without being stepped on?
To walk without being knocked down?

❒ What places can I reach under (especially where the vacuum cleaner can't clean) or over? What can I climb up on?

❒ Are there different textures to touch?
A variety of sounds to hear?
Places to be quiet as well as places to be active and noisy?

❒ Are there interesting things to see on the walls at my eye level?
Are they safe for me to touch?
Are they free of pins or thumbtacks or staples
that I might put in my mouth?

❒ Are there different places (cribs, swings, bounce chairs, blanket on the floor) for me to be?
Will I have to stay in just one place for a long time?
May I move about freely when I want to?
Is the floor safe to explore?

❒ Do the toys offer lots of ways of exploring?
What things can I push? Pull? Stack? Manipulate?
Collect? Dump? Throw?
Can I get these things into my mouth and safely out again?
Will a grownup make sure the toy I put in my mouth is cleaned before another baby puts the toy in his or her mouth?

❒ Do I get to explore "messy" things like sand, dough or water?

❒ Do I have to wait to be changed or use the toilet?
Is there only one changing table for everyone?

❒ Will people here talk to me and look at me?
When I talk or cry, will they listen and respond to me?
Will someone sing to me? Read to me? Rock me?
Show me God's love with smiles, gentle talk and play?

Extending Your Nursery Ministry

In the nursery, the only member of a family we may often focus on is the baby! But each baby is part of a family to which we should minister, too; families with young children need the support and encouragement of others in the Body of Christ. So building solid relationships with the baby's family is a vital part of the nursery ministry.

Learn About the Family

While a baby's family may consist of two parents, be aware that you may also be dealing with other family types: single parent (mother or father), blended families (a stepparent), extended families with primary care-giving roles (grandparents, aunts), foster families, etc. Use your nursery's records to acquaint yourself with each child's family. Once you know the family, be alert for ways to build your relationship with them.

Building Relationships Every Week

When a parent brings an infant or toddler to the nursery, your friendly greeting and a personal comment to or about the child sends the message, "You and your baby are important to us. We care about you!" Parents feel comfortable when they know that the caregivers in the nursery see their child as an individual. When parents bring the child, ask a question or two to show your interest in the child's welfare ("What types of toys does he most enjoy? What new skill has she been working on this week?") When parents pick up the child, tell them about something the child enjoyed. If your church uses a form or note to communicate with parents about diaper changes, feedings, etc., read one aloud occasionally to the parents (if time permits) and add your observations.

Use informal moments around the church to talk with family members. You don't have to be outgoing, just caring!

"My Best Friends at Church"

"It's the best part of my week," said Kira about her church's service. "It's so refreshing to worship and learn when I can really relax. I don't have to worry about the baby. Some of my best friends are in the nursery. And they know just what to do!" For Kira, a solid relationship with the nursery staff helped make her growing walk with God a reality!

While it's wonderful to have solid human relationships with every family whose baby is in your care, your ultimate goal is to see each family develop a growing walk with Jesus Christ. Never forget that when parents brought their children to Him, He considered blessing those children to be such an important act that He became angry when He saw His disciples turn them away! May our attitude be that these little ones and their families are of prime importance! Never let anyone on your nursery staff think that his or her job is not important! The nursery may seem to be a "small" ministry, away from the public eye. But it can be one of the most vibrant and life-changing ministries of your church! Let the little ones come—and let Jesus' love flow to each family through your ministry!

Building Relationships During the Week

Often, time is limited to talk with parents before or after a session. Thus, take a few minutes during the week to strengthen the connections with each family. Consider ideas such as these, using those which fit best the situation in each family.

❖ If a child cried during the session, call and ask, "What suggestions do you have for helping Max feel more secure at the nursery?"

❖ If a child had a good time, call and tell parents about something you noticed.

❖ If a child bit, hit, or pulled hair of another child, call and ask for tips on redirecting the child's behavior.

NOTE: When dealing with a problem behavior, approach the parent with the understanding that the parent knows the child better than anyone else and is thus likely to be the best source of insight into the child's behavior. Be very cautious about seeming to criticize either the child or the parent.

The Nursery—an Amazing Ministry

Taking care of babies' and toddlers' physical and emotional needs is consuming and demanding; in retrospect, any given nursery session may often seem like one long period of chaos! A nursery worker may well wonder, "Is anything significant being accomplished?" It's important to keep in mind the "big picture." Tremendous ministry flows from an effective nursery program. The nursery can nurture not only young ones but their families as well!

First Goals of Ministry

Your ministry begins when a new family comes to drop off a baby or toddler off at the nursery. Your helpful attitude and warm friendliness convey a powerful first impression of what your church family is like. Remember that for first-time parents, giving their baby to a stranger for any reason can be stressful! If it's clear to them that your nursery is a clean, friendly and safe place, both parents and child are likely to have a positive experience that they will want to repeat! Parents are deeply influenced by their children's reaction to being at church. Young parents who are not deeply committed to church attendance are often influenced to continue by the caliber of care their baby receives and by their child's positive response. Parents are looking for caregivers who are reliable, trustworthy and responsive.

For the child, this may well be a first time away from mother or father. That's why it's so important that there be plenty of loving adult arms available in the nursery. Accept each little one in Jesus' name, just as if you could see Jesus standing right beside you! While holding a baby may seem a small thing, treat your relationship with each baby or toddler as seriously as relating to an adult! Watch each little one carefully for cues as to ways to best communicate. Show loving respect for each small person in your voice and your gentle actions. Such small, "unseen" acts of love may go unnoticed, but they build the invisible structure of the Kingdom of God even among the youngest!

Child development experts tell us that the first two years are among the most important in a person's life. These early years powerfully influence all of a child's subsequent development. Attitudes toward self and others are formed very early, and can be changed later only with great difficulty. The loving care given in the nursery builds wonderful foundations of trust, affection and security which will go a long way in helping children be receptive to instruction about God.

The Ultimate Goal of Ministry

As a visiting family begins to attend regularly, invite them to become involved in other ministries that are likely to be of interest to families with young children. Adult study groups and classes, including parenting classes, Parent's Night Out Programs, baby-sitting cooperatives and play groups, potlucks and volunteering in the nursery all draw the family into a deeper relationship with the Body of Christ.

Your job is powerful and important! Every interaction with a baby or toddler—and his or her family—counts for eternity.

Hungry Babies

Feeding is one of the most important activities of an infant's life! It's no wonder, then, that an infant can panic when his or her regular schedule and way of feeding are changed. This is one reason why feeding time in the nursery can create panic in adults, too—or it can become a time of genuine ministry to the "least" of these. These moments of comforting, undivided attention gently given to an infant help build confidence even in a very young child that this place is a safe, good place to be.

Feeding, Step by Step

As parents arrive, make sure bottles are labeled. During the session, before feeding an infant, first consult the information left by parent on a check-in sheet or information card. Some babies may need to have the bottle slightly warmed; some will not. If bottle has been warmed, before feeding the baby check with a few drops on back of your forearm to make sure milk or formula is not too hot. Never feed a baby from a bottle in which the milk or formula has warmed to room temperature—any bacteria in the milk or formula will rapidly multiply at room temperature.

Wash hands before feeding a baby. Then, taking baby and bottle in hand, seat yourself comfortably in a quiet place, preferably in a separate room that is not too brightly lit. This makes young infants feel comfortable to open their eyes and relate to the caregiver. Hold the child in a slightly upright position (thought to reduce ear infections) while holding him or her securely in your arm. Tilt the bottle so the nipple is always full. After a baby has satisfied his or her initial hunger, try to burp the baby, using a cloth (provided by the parent) on your shoulder, or a paper towel. Then go back to feeding.

As you feed the baby, talk or sing quietly to him or her. Use the baby's name often. Follow the baby's cues as to how firmly to hold him or her. Look into the baby's eyes. Touch, sound, sight and the relaxed quality of your care build a relationship with this very young person! After the feeding, note on the check-in sheet or report to the parent how much a baby drank.

When possible, it is helpful if the same person feeds the same child every time (especially for infants under six months of age). This continuity not only helps the child become comfortable with one caregiver, but also ensures that one person is familiar with a particular baby's feeding habits, burping patterns and so on.

Breast-Fed Babies

Know your church policy about how and when to call nursing mothers. Whenever possible, provide a quiet, private place or screened-off area where mothers may nurse without interruption.

Babies who are normally breastfed may have difficulty taking a bottle, even of breast milk. Different kinds of sucking are required for the two kinds of feeding, so it is especially important to observe the baby carefully. Follow his or her lead in finding out what works. Initiating feeding before the baby becomes extremely hungry may also be helpful.

Hungry Toddlers

There's no doubt about it—a hungry child is often a cranky child! For toddlers, however, food has now become something more than the comfort of bottle or breast. Toddlers are exploring the new tastes, textures, shapes, colors and sizes of the foods adults offer. Food is as much a medium for exploration as anything else! Expect toddlers to thoroughly enjoy every aspect of the food provided—from tasting to pinching, tossing or wearing it!

Bottles

While most toddlers will have a bottle packed into their diaper bags, don't simply hand it to them when they indicate hunger. Avoid letting a child wander about the room with a bottle: besides losing the bottle or exchanging it with someone else's, there is danger of the child falling and choking—it's difficult to watch one's path with a bottle in front of the eyes!

Use this time to maximize your one-on-one relationship just as you did when the child was an infant. Hold and rock the child. Talk to him or her, repeat a brief Bible story or verse, or sing a song (use the suggestions provided in your curriculum). Your warmth and loving care will teach volumes about God's love!

Snacks

Beyond the bottle, most toddlers love a snack! Snack time can be a welcome break that improves everyone's mood. Before providing snack foods, however, first talk to parents or read the information card on each child to check for possible allergies and other food preferences. Also check to be sure the food is fresh and free from obvious signs of deterioration. Consider spreading a sheet on the floor on which children sit while eating, or you may provide low tables and chairs where children sit.

Avoid giving children under the age of two raisins, nuts, popcorn, grapes, raw carrots, cherries or berries due to the possibility of choking. Avoid using honey, melon and chocolate, too. Some health officials are concerned about molds in honey that can affect very young children; children are often allergic to melon. Since chocolate is a high-sugar, high-fat food as well as a stimulant, it's best not to offer it to toddlers.

Some good finger foods for toddlers include: strips of dry toast, arrowroot cookies, unsalted pretzel sticks, low-salt saltines, graham crackers, mini rice cakes, fish-shaped crackers, dry cereal and pieces of fresh fruit. Provide only one simple, healthful snack item at a time rather than a smorgasbord. (This helps with pinpointing allergies as well as knowing what children really like.)

Small amounts of juice or water should be served with the food. Avoid sugared and colored "drinks"; instead, provide pure fruit juice, thinned with a little water if it is very sweet. Give just a few swallows at a time in a labeled sipper cup or sturdy paper cup. Offer more only if the first helping is gone. Treat spills in a matter-of-fact way, providing a wet sponge for children to use in helping to clean up spills.

When you offer a snack, first use premoistened towelettes to clean a child's hands before eating, or children may wash their own hands if a child-size sink is in the room. Sit with the toddlers and eat with them. Talk about God giving us the good food. Say a short prayer of thanks. However, don't expect toddlers to sit still and bow heads for this. Instead, simply pray while they eat. Your example is what teaches!

Teaching Babies About God

"Get serious," some may say. "We're dealing with babies here. They just need to be fed, changed, rocked—what can they possibly learn about God?"

The Style in Which It's Done

While no one thinks it's vital to post charts of major theological concepts on the nursery wall, it is vital to think about what babies can learn. The goal of the teaching in the nursery is not to get a baby to say, "God"! Rather, our goal is to individually (one-on-one) teach the baby what he or she can learn about God's love.

Such teaching is done by your every look, word and act while you are in the presence of a baby or toddler. (That should give some of us pause!) Work in the nursery is ministry just as surely as if you were teaching a theology class to adults—you represent Christ to each little person in your care. Using a curriculum with monthly themes will help bring consistency to your efforts to help little ones learn about God.

What do you communicate to that baby who seems to throw up on you every time you hold him or her? Do you tense as you pick up the child, steeling yourself against the inevitable? That baby senses your tension! A baby is very sensitive to even such subtle things. And it tells the child how you feel about him or her! Conversely, when your words, looks and actions are relaxed and gentle, loving and kind, you teach the baby not only that people at the church nursery can be trusted, you are also building a foundation for that little child's trust in God!

The attitude in which you meet a baby's needs greatly influences his or her developing personality. As a baby associates you with pleasant experiences and lovingly having his or her needs met, he or she also forms foundational opinions about trusting and about being loved that will affect his or her whole life. This is why it is important, whenever possible, to care for the same babies each time you are in the nursery. Continuity of care means the baby becomes familiar with one person, building the baby's trust and comfort.

Talking with babies and toddlers about God and Jesus is a reminder to yourself of your purpose in serving in the nursery. Your example in ministering to these little ones will help parents begin to develop these same skills in communicating spiritual truths to their children.

Individual Time with Babies

Play simple games lovingly with babies (such as gently pedaling a baby's legs and saying, "Jesse, God made your strong legs!"). Sing short, simple songs about God's love to even the youngest baby.

Remember that no baby cares about your vocal quality! Your low, gentle song relaxes, calms and teaches trust. As a baby often hears his or her name associated with God's love, he or she begins to associate song, self, God and love. No, it won't turn out a pint-sized theologian. But these experiences build a foundation for faith in the perfect Father who loves His little ones.

Each Little Child

(Tune: "Mary Had a Little Lamb"

Jesus loves each little child,

Little child, little child.

Jesus loves each little child,

He loves you, yes, He does.

Toddlers will enjoy hearing brief Bible stories and verses and short, simple songs about God and Jesus. Use toddlers' names often and show you enjoy them. Repeated, short, direct sentences are often quite well-understood by toddlers even if they don't make any verbal response.

Do a finger play as often as children seem interested. To interest children in an activity, do the finger play once or twice yourself. Never ask, "Would you like to do the finger play?" Simply launch into it once or twice and you will see interest on some faces by the third time!

Older babies and toddlers also enjoy looking at books with you. (Books for babies and toddlers need mainly pictures, not words.) With a picture book and a toddler in your lap, you are in position to look at the pictures and talk with the child about the pictures in the books. "Look, Elisa! There's a big, red apple. I like to eat apples. God made apples for us to eat."

Whether you interact with babies or toddlers, remember that letting God's love flow through you to each child is what makes your teaching in the nursery far more than just a baby-sitting experience!

God Cares for Me

God cares for me

When I sleep.

God cares for me

When I play.

God cares for me

All the time,

Every night and

Every day.

First Corinthians 13: The Caregiver's Version

Though I speak with the comforting tongue of a mother

(with all the right words in the sweetest tones)

and though I can sing like an angel

(on pitch)

the finest lullabies

(guaranteed to comfort the crankiest baby),

but have not love, I am a raucous noise in this peaceful place

(irritating babies, creating frustration and drawing attention to myself).

And though I may have the gift of prophecy

(singing doctrinally correct blessings over these babies),

and can fathom all mysteries

(even why the Hurley baby cries so)

and all knowledge

(having two degrees in early childhood studies),

and have a faith so that I can even move mountains

(mountains of unwilling adults, that is, into nursery volunteerism),

but have not love,

(even with all of my gifts)

I am nothing.

Love is patient

(it doesn't sigh or become tense);

Love is kind

(it stays relaxed when a baby spits up all over).

Love does not envy

(not even the people who are right this minute on the platform in the sanctuary, fully appreciated for their moving musical performances or their insightful words).

Love does not boast

(not even over seminars attended or degrees earned);

it is not proud

(not even of sensitivity to children gained by years of experience).

It is not rude

(ignoring babies or their sometimes irritatingly anxious parents);

it is not self-seeking

(not even for a little appreciation for such a demanding ministry).

It is not easily angered

(not even by that difficult Smith child or her parents who seem to present a new problem with every appearance);

it keeps no record of wrongs

(no matter how hard little Jonah may make that!). (It may, however, keep good records of diaper changes and feedings, of new discoveries and happy times, because)

love does not delight in evil

(though I may want to gossip about some mothers)

but rejoices with the truth

(God loves even the most finicky mom and her colicky baby).

Love always protects

(a copy of our safety policy is available),

always trusts

(I will rock you yet a little longer; if Jesus were here, He'd keep on rocking),

always hopes

(Mommy will be back!),

always perseveres

(I will keep loving you, Billy, even though you've bitten me three times.),

Love never fails

(I will love you, most difficult Monica — and your difficult parents, too.).

MALE CAREGIVERS

Men in the Nursery

It is enormously valuable for adults to take time to watch and understand little children. Jesus said that unless we become like them, we cannot enter His Kingdom. Watching and becoming sensitive to little ones teaches us well what heart-attitudes every child of God should have! But moms and grandmas often make up the staff of nursery ministries, and men are sometimes "left out in the cold" when it comes to this chance to watch, learn from and minister to little ones.

Using men in the nursery ministry benefits both the babies and the men involved. While some men may resist the idea of teaching babies or toddlers, little ones can greatly benefit from warm associations with male teachers. In fact, some babies respond better to men than to women! For a child without a strong or consistent male presence in the home, godly men in the nursery become important role models. Men are an essential part of a quality nursery staff.

Babies and toddlers need to know that they are loved and cared for by both women and men. And men who teach in the nursery ministry find that as they learn better how to play, to listen and watch little ones, they are growing in gentleness and sensitivity that pays dividends in every area of life. Fathers whose children are in the nursery can be made to feel more a part of the church by contributing their time and skills. And Jesus Himself set a strong example for men to be involved with little ones when He invited little children into His arms and blessed them.

Some churches are reluctant to involve men because they believe parents are comfortable only with women caregivers. But by using well-thought-out caregiving policies (such as having two adults present in each room at all times), there should be no problem with parent discomfort or possible abuse allegations. Adhering to clearly outlined policies eliminates confusion and frees adults to minister in the nursery by focusing their time and energy on the children.

Older Children in the Nursery

What do you do when there are babies, toddlers and children up through age five or six in the same nursery room? Sometimes, because of space limitations or the limited number of children in a small church, it is necessary to group children of several ages together. If the total number of children is small enough and the size of the room is adequate, children of a variety of ages can be adequately cared for and even enjoy being together! However, any time this situation occurs there are some guidelines that will help nursery caregivers oversee and guide the interaction of the children in their care.

How can I make sure infants and toddlers are safe?

Begin by making sure that you have enough adults for the number of children in the room. It works best to assign caregivers primary responsibility for either babies, toddlers or preschoolers, but retain flexibility so help can be directed where most needed at any moment.

Keep in mind the proper ratio of adults to children is important not only to be safe, but also to ensure that both adults and children will enjoy being together: 1 to 12 months—one teacher for two or three children; 1 to 2 years—one teacher for three or four children; 2 to 6 years—one teacher for four or five children. For example, if you have six children in the nursery ranging in age from a two-month-

old to a six-year-old with mostly three-year-olds, you will need a minimum of two adults. (A third adult may be needed to take a child to the bathroom if the bathroom is not nearby.)

If you have infants or crawlers in a room with older children, it's necessary to safeguard the toes and fingers of the younger ones. One way to ensure safety is to sit on the floor next to the youngest child, allowing the child the freedom to explore under your watchful eye. Be ready to gently steer an older walker away from the baby. Or you may provide a play pen or portable crib with mesh sides, providing a safe corner for the younger child while still allowing him or her to feel a part of the group. Another option is an inflatable pool or dense foam play pool in which young babies can roll and explore in safety (available from

educational supply stores). A sturdy 3-foot (.9-m) partition in a portion of the room will protect babies from those who can crawl and walk.

What kinds of toys should I provide?

If possible, bring older children into the younger child's environment. There is less chance that unsafe toys and equipment will be available for the curious toddler, and safety hazards such as electrical outlets should already be blocked.

If toddlers and preschoolers are together on a regular basis, provide toys that are enjoyed by both ages. Cardboard blocks, books, dolls, balls in a variety of sizes, stacking toys and plastic animals or people are examples of fun and safe toys. Wooden puzzles, with varying numbers of pieces (none of which

are small enough to be swallowed), are also good play alternatives.

Provide several toys for the older child, choosing only those toys which do not have small pieces. Some churches have a "Big Kids' Cupboard" or other enclosed shelf that has a variety of toys appropriate for older kids. Older children are encouraged to remove only one toy at a time from the shelf and to return it before choosing a different toy.

Sometimes playing quiet music throughout the session will create a restful atmosphere. Avoid any noisy group activities with toddlers or preschoolers that would awaken sleeping babies.

Carefully evaluate the furniture and toys in the room. Some toys may be easily damaged or even harmful if used by an older child. It may be necessary to remove some toys permanently.

How can I help younger and older children have fun together?

Many preschoolers will respond to your invitation to show a younger child how to roll a ball or count the number of blocks in a tower. Build the self-esteem of the older child by asking him or her to be your helper with a younger child. Thank the older child for his or her help. However, do not force an older child to play with a younger one. Often the best way to increase inter-action among children of differing ages is for you to begin an activity with a younger child, such as build-ing a farm with blocks and arrang-ing animals. As you have fun build-ing and making animal sounds, the older child will naturally want to participate with you.

Looking at books and talking about the pictures in the books is an excellent way to involve several chil-dren at once. A baby in the lap and a toddler or preschooler on each side can all enjoy a book with you. The baby will enjoy looking at the pictures, touching the pages and hearing everyone's voices. The older children can participate by answer-ing questions about the pictures such as, "How many baby animals do you see on this page?" or "Which animal on this page is your favorite?"

Another activity in which all can participate is music. Children of all ages will respond to songs. Sing a favorite action song yourself or play the song on a cassette player. Some children will enjoy listening, others will enjoy following your example of clapping, waving hands or nod-ding heads.

While children are playing in the room, encourage an atmosphere of "family" and friendship by using children's names frequently. Com-ment to an older child, "Ethan, I see you're really working hard on that puzzle. And look at Levi. He's just learned to roll over." Continue to talk with children about the activi-ties you observe they are enjoying.

Using Music in the Nursery

Music can be a wonderful gift to share with babies and toddlers. Music can create a mood, promote familiarity and comfort, make children familiar with concepts about God, increase language and listening skills, provide the basis for large muscle activities—the list is endless. Songs are fun for both children and caregivers! Here are some ways to effectively use music in your nursery rooms:

Repeatable Songs

If you sing the same "Hello" and "Good-bye" songs every week, children will become familiar with them. Repetition builds security for a young child. Such songs cue children about what comes next, and make the nursery seem a more comfortable place. A song to signal any new activity can make the transition easier.

Try singing a spontaneous song when you see a child is becoming upset. The song need not rhyme; it may only have two or three notes. For instance, "I see Jenny dropped her cracker. It's OK; I'll get another" sung to a simple tune (such as "Skip to My Lou") can refocus the child and head off tears. It acknowledges the situation, uses the child's name and tells the child that you will help. The same song may be used over and over, substituting another child's name and another situation.

Think about ways you will use music as you care for children. Your nursery curriculum may provide a song or two which reinforces each unit's theme. If the song is recorded on cassette or CD, play it for children. Learn it well enough to sing it spontaneously throughout the month at appropriate times during the session. Little ones love to hear you sing; your voice is fine to them!

Even though it is rare for most young children to sing with you, don't let that stop you from sharing music in the nursery.

Recorded Music

Some nurseries have a large collection of cassettes or CDs available for use. Take time to plan, considering the age and needs of the children as well as the activity and noise levels you want.

If you play recorded music in the background, turn it off before it becomes "background noise" and children are no longer interested. Even quiet music may increase the tension level if children must raise their voices to be heard above it.

Rather than playing the recorded song for the entire group, consider using a music tape with small groups of two to three children at a time. Provide adequate space for babies or toddlers to move, and seat yourself on the floor, with a CD player on a low table. Let children bounce or move in response to the music; when they lose interest, invite several more children to participate.

Using quiet songs to help a baby relax and go to sleep is as natural as breathing. These songs will not only comfort the little ones, they will communicate God's love and calm your spirit as well! Recorded quiet songs and lullabies may be played at a low level in the sleeping room. Always be observant to see if the music calms or enlivens the mood in the room and adjust accordingly.

Let's Eat

Tune: "Farmer in the Dell"

Now we're going to eat.
Now we're going to eat.
It's time to eat.
It's time to eat.
Now we're going to eat.

Substitute words such as "play" and "sleep" for the word "eat."

Hello

Tune: "Are You Sleeping?"

Hello to you.

How are you?

We are glad

You came today.

(Repeat)
Substitute child's name for the word "you."

Observation Guide

An open-door policy will help acquaint people with your nursery. Expectant parents, visitors to your church, and new or potential caregivers will all benefit from at least one observation session.

Plan for no more than two or three observers at a time in each room (the number will vary depending on the size of the room). Especially if you are using the observation time as a way of training caregivers, make use of the "Look and Learn" observation guide on this page. Reproduce a copy of the guide for each observer and ask him or her to take notes on what is seen. Seat the observers in a location where they can easily see the entire room. Do not expect observers to assist while observing. Explain to observers that if a child should approach them during the session, it's OK to briefly interact with the child. Ask nursery caregivers to gently redirect the child's attention away from the observers. If parents of a child in the room are observing, expect the parents' child to prefer being close to mommy and daddy while they are present. Accept this situation by not insisting the child do other things.

After the observation session, meet with the observers to talk about what they observed and to answer any questions about nursery procedures.

Look and Learn

What do you see that a baby enjoys doing?

What do you see about how a baby learns?

What do you see about the kind of toys provided?

How do you see a child's needs being met?

Other comments:

The Great Outdoors

Some time outdoors can be just the thing for calming a fussy baby or relaxing a tired, tense toddler. Some times the child (or caregiver!) just needs a change of scenery. Whenever your nursery has enough adults to carefully supervise young children and the weather is accommodating, consider a walk or playtime outdoors.

The Benefits

Watch a young baby outdoors and you'll see how quickly moving leaf shadows fascinate and soothe. The play of light and shadow, the change in sounds and air temperature, the feel of breeze on the cheek or the color and smell of grass are all rich sensory experiences for a baby or toddler. A sand box made from a small wading pool or a dishpan with a little water in it can expand the outdoor experience for toddlers.

The Place

Of course, it would be wonderful to have a quiet, grassy park just outside the nursery door! While some churches may have a play yard or mini-park, such a place may be only a distant dream for others. The first thing to do is to look at your resources. Is there a courtyard in your church complex that could be modified so babies could safely explore and enjoy? An unused corner of the parking lot that could be fenced and planted with grass? It doesn't take a large outdoor space, but that space should be quiet and able to be kept clean and safe. (Be sure to use fencing and a covering

that will keep animals out completely and babies inside safely.)

Safe Activities

Once you have an outdoor space that is clean and safe, consider the activities available. If your nursery is large, you may find it easier to bring babies out in similarly-aged groups for ten-minute rotations than to bring all ages outdoors together. If your group is small enough to warrant everyone being outdoors together, be sure to decide ahead of time which caregivers will be responsible for which babies.

Young babies may be laid on blankets in good weather, or placed covered up in infant seats when it is cooler. Simply walking a baby around in the outdoors to watch tree branches move in the breeze is fine entertainment. If you have space to store several strollers, take a baby for a brief walk.

Babies who are big enough to explore should be watched mainly

for the items from the sand box to the insects they will invariably pick up and place in their mouths. (This is where the benefit of keeping cats and dogs out of your play yard will be most obvious!)

Leave swings to the older children's playground to eliminate the danger of a toddler being kicked. Toddlers will enjoy sturdy climbing structures and other lightweight equipment. It is best to leave the "outside toys" outdoors and indoor toys indoors for cleanliness.

Talking About It

Time outdoors is a perfect opportunity to point out the details of God's creation. Make it a part of your natural teaching process to look around and describe what you see. "I see a big tree. It has green leaves. God made the tree!" Sing songs about God's creation and use appropriate finger plays provided in your curriculum. You and children alike will enjoy the great outdoors!

Play: Babies at Work

Born to Play!

Babies and toddlers don't have to be taught to play. Desire for play flows from the boundless curiosity with which children are born. As soon as they are able, babies play—first with hands and fingers, then with human faces and easy-to-grasp toys. They grow to play simple games with adults, manipulate every object from a rock to the family dog in an endless round of activity that may not seem to be especially valuable. But these play activities, the "messing around" that a baby or toddler does, are a baby's work! This is the way babies learn about and make sense of the world.

Play and exploration develop not only a baby's physical coordination but also the ability to think and reason, as well as language and social skills. When loving adults play with the baby, these skills are built even more effectively. Play with an interested adult provides a framework (such as a game of peekaboo) for teaching reasoning and language (as the adult describes his or her actions) and even prepares the child for an understanding of taking turns. Children who are played with regularly by caring adults generally have better mental, language and social development and are more responsive and confident.

How Do I Play, Too?

To play with babies and toddlers, you need not get out the checkerboard or bring along a specific activity outline! Play is part of the other forms of communication that naturally happen between babies and loving adults.

Unless you are playing with a baby in a crib, the first rule is: get down on the floor! There is no way to be with or play with babies when you tower over them like Jack's giant! On the floor, you are naturally at a baby's eye level. (This also means you get a baby's point of view on the world—be sure to take it in!)

Since play and communication are intertwined, be sure to talk with the baby as you play. To interest a child in an activity (such as rolling a ball, building a block tower or playing peekaboo), begin doing the activity yourself, talking about what you're doing. "Look, Jenny! Here is a blue block. I'm going to set it right here on this yellow block." If Jenny is interested (and she probably will be interested in the prospect of playing with you), she will come nearer, perhaps knocking the blue block off the yellow one. "I see you knocked the blue block off, Jenny! It fell down. I'm putting the blue one on the yellow one again...." You have just invented a game to play with Jenny—call it "Knock your block off!"

For an older baby or toddler, playing a game is also just that simple. You might expand the game by adding a red block, putting the blue block under the yellow one (telling what you are doing) or hiding a block under a beanbag to see if Jenny will move the beanbag to find the block.

In your conversation, occasionally make brief comments to build an interest in God or Jesus. For example, while building with blocks, you might say, "God made your eyes to see the blue and yellow blocks." Or while a child plays with pretend cars and people, you might say, "I see a mommy and a girl in the car. God made mommies and children. God made you."

As well as talking with (not at) Jenny and creating a game to play with her, give her space and time to do things herself. If you see she is interested in building the block tower on her own, don't interfere. "Let me help you" should be reserved only for times when you see the child is becoming frustrated. It may take Jenny ten tries to place the blue block on the yellow one, but if she is absorbed and content in the attempt, let her be. Talk about what you see her doing ("You're really working hard to stack those blocks!") and resist the urge to give advice or guide her hand.

It's important for a sensitive caregiver to know when not to interact or play with a baby. When the child is already occupied, exploring on his or her own, it's not necessary or even helpful to interrupt this valuable "playing alone" to interact. Most children (even very young ones) will call to you or let you know when they would like some company and a little play!

Play and exploration are the most basic parts of any baby's day. Your thoughtful participation in play activities will enhance not only the child's learning, but your relationship with the child as well.

To play with babies and toddlers:

For young babies:

❖ Create a safe space for exploring (eliminate hazards and provide a variety of simple objects to explore).

❖ Show and move interesting, colorful objects; talk to the baby about them as you do so. Use the baby's name often.

❖ Be sure there is enough for baby to do. Place objects to be explored nearby for hitting and grasping.

❖ If a baby seems bored, provide different objects to explore, move baby to a different location (moving outside often works wonders!), play a short game with him or her, etc.

❖ Try a hiding game (cover a ball with a blanket; ask, "Where's the ball?" then remove the blanket and say, "There's the ball!").

❖ Sing to babies, making up spontaneous songs.

❖ Let baby take the lead. Imitate his or her actions. Then add an action of your own to make it a game.

For older babies and toddlers:

❖ Talk to and play with puppets and dolls. Include the child in the conversation, using his or her name.

❖ Try more complex hiding games (invite the baby to point to the place where the hidden object is; play short, limited kinds of hide-and-seek games).

❖ Explain how things happen ("You rolled the ball. It went under the crib.")

❖ Share in block play, etc. Talk about what you do, describing your actions and the child's reactions. Occasionally provide sand and water play for children, too.

❖ Begin to ask questions such as "What do you think happened to the ball?" Give the child adequate time to respond, and look for nonverbal answers.

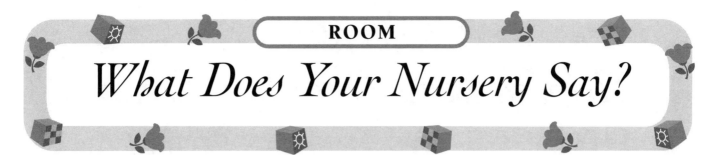

What Does Your Nursery Say?

When we've been working in (and looking at) the nursery for a long time, it is sometimes hard to think of how it might look to a visitor. But as an important part of any church's outreach, first impressions of the nursery really count for parents of young children! When a baby or toddler has a pleasant experience in the nursery, it builds good feelings in the child about being there. And the child's positive reactions deeply influence the parent. Conversely, a family may be reluctant to return to a church if the nursery appeared unwelcoming.

A Safe Place

What do parents see when they leave their child in your care? Cheerful room decoration is an important part of a first impression. Decorate walls by displaying appropriate pictures and art at toddlers' eye level on the wall. But remember that safety, space, warmth and comfort are more important than the latest fashion in decor. The room should look inviting and uncluttered.

Of course, your nursery has already been prepared with safe flooring surface, adequate ventilation, safe supply storage and the like. But on arrival for any session, always inspect for safety hazards before children arrive. Check the floor for dangerous objects, the outlets for secure covers, and the toy shelves for dirty, broken or dangerous toys. Be sure furniture is stable and smooth and that any cords or heaters are out of tod-

dlers' reach. Make sure cribs are in working order and clean.

A Happy Place

When visitors bring their child to you, your friendly interest in them and their children is another important factor. When parents see that you love babies and are glad to care for their child, they begin to relax and feel that this is a good place to be.

Of course, every nursery worker needs to be instructed in and able to follow the health and safety procedures listed where all can see. But the most important

part of making this a happy experience for any baby or toddler is to remember this: you are here to pay attention to the children. It's easy to forget and begin to converse with other adults, but as natural as that may be, your conversation should be directed to the children most of the time.

When the message your nursery sends is "Come in! We are clean, competent and caring," you are well on the road to building a strong relationship with visiting families. When that message is reinforced by the quality of care you give to children, families want to return!

Helping Little Ones Feel Secure

Imagine disembarking from a ship onto an uncharted island. You know nothing of the people there. You cannot speak their language. Fearful, nervous and full of anticipation, you wonder, *How will I know if the natives are friendly?* A very similar scenario is played out weekly in your nursery!

In a world as new and untried as that uncharted island, the small people who come to us need our help to feel that this place is a safe one. We need to be sure that they know that the "natives" are indeed friendly!

Limited Responders, Active Observers

Between feeding, changing, rocking and burping, it's easy to forget that babies and toddlers have deeper needs than physical ones. The way in which a baby's immediate needs are met teaches a child that adults are (or are not) trustworthy. From these responses, he or she learns that relationships with others can—or cannot—be trusted. Repeated acts that teach mistrust in infancy cripple a person's ability to trust others—including God—throughout life. God intends for us to help lay this foundation of trust in even the youngest child.

When a baby calls or cries, respond. Even if your arms are already full, go to that baby and talk quietly to him or her; stroke the baby's head to let the child know that you are there. You have sent the important message that, "In this place, people care if I cry. They want to help me."

Laying the Foundation

A feeling of trust and security in the nursery becomes the basis for a child's learning to trust God and beginning to feel His love. Nursery staff cannot make up for experiences that have taught a child not to trust, but we can make sure the child understands that this place is safe and that the people here are caring ones.

Here are some specific ways to lay a foundation of secure feelings in babies and toddlers:

❖ Respond. Don't ignore a baby or toddler or dismiss his or her crying or other behavior as "just crankiness." Make the effort to understand and help.

❖ Provide interesting things to do, to look at, to listen to.

❖ Talk in a quiet, respectful and soothing way. Never respond in anger.

❖ Be observant. When you see trouble coming, distract a child with another activity or toy.

❖ Remove a child from danger or potential problems, talking to him or her as you do so to help the child understand what you are doing.

❖ Allow a child who brings a "security" blanket or toy to keep it. Protect the child's possession of that item from other children who might try to take it. When the child seems to be comfortable, try removing the item with the child's permission. Whenever the child needs the item, return it.

❖ Be fair and consistent in the way you treat children.

❖ Take time to watch each child, and to respond in appropriate ways to the child. This tells the child he or she is important to you—and to God.

Welcoming a Baby to the Nursery

It's a familiar scenario: a parent, hurrying to get into the church service on time, hands a baby to you. At that moment, the baby begins to scream! You are in the nursery to minister not only to babies but their families as well. What can you do to improve the situation?

Time to Separate

By around 6 or 7 months, babies begin to very clearly distinguish who they know well and who is a stranger. In most children, this brings on a mild anxiety that is fairly easily dealt with by your gentle smiles and a few distractions. But some children appear to have feelings of screaming panic that just won't quit!

Always remember (and gently remind parents) that when a child cries at separation time, it is normal. It is part of the child's growing ability to distinguish between parents and strangers (and to prefer parents)! Your calm reassurance of both parents and child will make the separation easier all around. Words such as, "I know you are having a hard time...I know you miss your daddy...I know it's hard...he will be back soon" help both child and parents know that you recognize and accept their feelings. Some babies have a hard time with transitions and are likely to cry upon arriving and departing from the nursery.

Acknowledge Feelings

Always encourage a parent to say a brief good-bye before leaving the nursery, telling the child that he or she will return: "I'll be back after you've played with toys for awhile." Then be ready to help the child become involved in an interesting activity. When good-bye routines are established, children and parents get to know what to expect, and separation should become less difficult.

Expect, too, that a baby's anxiety may vary from week to week. Just when it seems that little Zack is comfortable with separation, he'll "slide back" into anxiety. Remember that this, too, is not a failure on anyone's part! It's simply a normal part of a baby's growth and is best dealt with calmly.

For most children, the crying will not last for long (although it may seem like a long time to you!). Usually, the child will soon calm down and become absorbed in an activity. But remember that you communicate love, relaxation and comfort by your words, your voice and your relaxed body posture, patting or stroking. If you are relaxed, the baby will likely follow your lead.

Crying It Out

Babies have legitimate reasons to cry! Don't leave them alone to "cry it out"—this sends the opposite message from what you want the child to remember. Because babies often have little experience with adults other than parents and little memory about past experience, it's legitimate for them to wonder if their parents are ever going to return!

Here are some tips to try:

❖ Sing the same welcoming song every week or use other "welcoming rituals." It's also helpful for the same person to greet the child and settle him or her into the new surroundings each time.

❖ Talk calmly to the child, even if he or she is crying loudly. Your gentle, soothing voice will help the child begin to relax.

❖ For some children, too much contact too soon with a stranger results in more fear. Take time instead to talk further with the parent so the child sees that the parent trusts and accepts you. With children who are obviously frightened by your attention, try indirect interaction, playing with a toy that interests a child and talking to the toy to draw the child's interest.

❖ As you go through your greeting ritual and attempt to interest the child in a toy or activity, time the length of the child's crying. If the child cries for an extended period of time (no more than 5 to 10 minutes), send for a parent. Many churches have a "crying policy" limiting how long a baby may cry before parents are summoned.

❖ Try blowing bubbles. Most babies find bubbles fascinating! Taking a baby outdoors briefly may have the same effect.

❖ Invite the parent to stay for a while or even to help in the nursery for a month. If the parent stays, try having him or her leave for five minutes, then come back. Increase the length of time with each absence until the child (and parent) are comfortable.

❖ Invite families of infants who are having difficulty separating from parents to visit the room when no other children are present (after a church service, a weekday morning, etc.). Familiarity with the room can boost the child's comfort level.

❖ Visit the home of a child who is experiencing strong anxiety. Take time to let the child begin to feel comfortable with you.

❖ If a child brings a "comfort object" such as a blanket, toy or pacifier, use it!

Remind parents that repetition and familiarity help to keep separation from becoming a weekly problem. Sending pictures of the caregivers home with the child or visiting the family can also increase familiarity. Keep pictures of the parents and children at the nursery, too.

Sleeping in the Nursery

During each session, there will invariably be babies and toddlers who need a rest. Be sensitive to the signs of a baby in need of sleep: rubbing of eyes, pulling at ears or crying. (Some babies seem to cry as a way to release tension before falling asleep.) If you are a child's consistent caregiver, you will discover other signs unique to the child. Before the symptoms escalate into full-scale crankiness, check the parent's instructions about a possible nap time. Even if it is not a stated nap time, however, take your cue from the child.

The extra stimulus of the nursery often makes it difficult for a child to relax; for rest or sleep, it is best to take the child to a quiet place or to the "sleeping room" of the nursery. Some children willingly lie down in a crib and calmly go to sleep. Others may need to be patted, rocked or sung to until they are drowsy.

Time Out for Resting

If the child does not seem interested in lying down and sleeping, he or she may benefit from a brief "time out" of rocking with a caregiver or listening to a soothing song sung by you or played on a cassette player. Or the child may feel rested after simply lying in a quiet corner of the nursery (such as a large pillow) with a favorite blanket or toy. A comfort item (a blanket or toy) brought from home may help the child to relax and fall asleep.

When a child awakens, don't necessarily rush to pick up the child but look for clues to indicate the child's preference. Some babies need time to awaken fully and be ready to face the bright and active area of the nursery again. Others are ready to go immediately.

Small Babies

A parent may indicate a baby's preferred sleeping position—side or back. This may be especially important for a young baby's comfort and security. Health specialists who have studied crib death, however, now recommend that babies be placed on their backs to sleep and not be wrapped too tightly.

For young babies, use firm bedding materials to avoid suffocation. Always check the crib for hazards and sharp edges before leaving a baby to sleep there. Avoid placing pillows or large stuffed animals in cribs and always raise crib rails fully, being certain they are securely locked into position.

Caring for Special Children

When Dana and Andrew brought their young son to the nursery, they saw a ripple of panic pass over the caregivers' faces. Their son has Down's syndrome—and it was clear that the caregivers didn't know how to comfortably include their son in the nursery activities.

To be ready to minister to the special-needs child and his or her family, we need to be prepared. Start with complete information. First, be sure that at least one nursery staff member (or someone on the premises of your facility) is current in his or her CPR skills. Knowing CPR for infants and toddlers is a vital part of caregiving for all children, but keeping current on these skills may be even more important when dealing with a special-needs child. CPR classes are available through any Red Cross chapter and are of minimal cost.

Second, be sure parents give you all the needed information for you to be comfortable and effective as a caregiver. As parents fill out the child's information card, they will need to include detailed instructions. If medication is to be given, ask the parent to return to the nursery to give it. This eliminates the likelihood of forgetting in the midst of a busy time or of giving an improper dosage. Do not give the child snacks unless the parent instructs you to do so, especially in the cases of children with allergies or problems in eating or swallowing.

To familiarize you with the child's schedule, needs and signals, invite the parent to spend some time in the nursery with you. He or she can observe the child along with you and interpret what the child does so you better understand the child's needs and behavior. When the same caregiver cares for the same child every time, he or she will soon be able to understand and interpret the child's needs.

Physical Disabilities

Children whose bodies are disabled quite often have bright minds and always need the same kind of smiling, loving attention as an able-bodied child. Watch for times when such a child may not be able to get up after falling, or seems to have difficulty moving from place to place. While it is best not to "do it for them," the caregiver who knows the child through consistent time with him or her will soon know when to intervene.

Down's Syndrome

Down's syndrome comes in varying degrees of severity. Be sure to ask parents if the child has any associated problems such as hearing loss (some Down's syndrome children are hard of hearing). Since a Down's syndrome child may find it harder to communicate, he or she may seem more aggressive. Knowing this, watch for ways you can help the child break down barriers and communicate more effectively. (Sign language may be helpful for some children. Ask the parent for a few commonly used signs.) Designate one caregiver to work consistently with the special-needs child. This caregiver can then help both the child and the group enjoy better communication.

Hearing or Visual Impairment

Be sure to get complete information on the child's disability. A child with a hearing or visual impairment is often of normal intellectual ability. Speak naturally to a deaf child; it doesn't help his or her learning of language for you to exaggerate your words. It will help, however, if you stand in front of a hearing-impaired child as you speak or sing. Involve a visually impaired child by providing experiences that involve other senses, such as music and sensory stimulation. Describe your actions aloud. And remember that every child responds to positive body language, facial expression and touch!

Asthma and Allergies

Asthma and allergies are often diagnosed later in childhood; however, if any child in your group is known to have allergies or asthma, be aware of the child's normal breathing patterns. If a child seems listless or has shortness of breath, difficulty in breathing, unusually rapid heartbeat, call the parent. For toddlers who have food allergies, be sure parents know and approve the snack you will be serving. Parents may want to provide their own child's snacks. (For children with life-threatening allergies, note the forbidden foods directly on the child's name tag.)

Toddler Tips

What are they like?

The operative word for toddlers is **mobile**. No longer must these babies sit still and gaze at the world around them. They can get up and experience it—and that's just what they do! With their eyes and noses, their hands and feet, and especially with their mouths, toddlers' lives are a constant quest to satisfy their boundless curiosity. Watch a toddler for long and you will see constant seeking for answers to: *What is it? How does it taste? How does it feel? What can it do?*

The other descriptive word for toddlers is **me**. Toddlers are still largely fascinated with their own abilities and unaware of other's needs. So while they are now placed in a social situation—a group of other babies—they have no social skills. They engage in parallel play—alongside others but not interacting with them. Their behavior reflects the toddler truth: *If I want it, it's mine. If you want it, it's mine. If I ever had it, it's mine.* They are natural grabbers and can cling to an object (or to your leg) with the strength of Hercules! Some children may also have learned that biting or hitting can get them what they want. Words used to express anything at this age are very limited!

How can I help them?

Toddlers need freedom to explore within safe limits. Provide lots of space without hazards for them to roam. Crib mattresses or large, washable pillows can provide a variety of safe crawling, climbing and sitting surfaces. Carpet-sample squares can provide interesting textures to crawl or walk across. Of course, a variety of age-appropriate toys and books is also important.

As well as space, toddlers need your calm and happy interaction with them. Since toddlers have few social skills and a small vocabulary, it's important for loving adults to be on the floor with them to help them solve problems and say the words that they cannot say. As you talk, you may include a brief Bible story, a short song, a Bible verse or a finger play in your natural conversation. Rather than blocking out time for toddlers to sit while you teach them, they learn best by your frequent repetition of the above elements. You are teaching them naturally—and literally, right where they are!

When you see conflict arising, intervene by refocusing a toddler's attention. Offer another toy, ask a question or interest the child in a new activity. (This might be a good time to repeat a finger play!) You may use words about sharing as you describe what you are seeing, but don't expect the words to change the child's behavior. Toddlers simply aren't developed to that point yet! Never shame or berate a toddler for "being selfish." At this stage of life, selfish is the only way he or she *knows* how to be. For instance, when you see Sam is about to go into an all-out tug-of-war with Danila over a teddy bear say, "Here, Sam. Here is another bear. We'll share this bear with Danila. See this bear? It has a red nose!"

When correcting or giving directions, speak in positive terms. Instead of, "Don't throw the blocks, Sam!" say, "Sam, we build with the blocks. You can put your block on top of mine. Let's build a tower."

A Smooth Schedule

There should be at least one caregiver for every three to four toddlers, with two caregivers in each room even if there are only two or three toddlers. This ratio of adults to children makes it possible to keep a close eye on every child's safety as well as to give each child individual attention. When a toddler arrives, give child and parents a friendly greeting! Talk to and watch the child; listen carefully to any comments the parents make. After check-in is complete, take a moment to sing a welcome song to the child. Repeating the same song each week builds familiarity and makes the toddler feel more secure. To interest the child in an activity, begin to do the activity yourself. If the child is crying, talk to him or her; hold the child if necessary and if welcomed by the child. Repeat this process with each child. But once everyone is playing on the floor, your job has only begun!

As you seat yourself on the floor to play with and talk with one or more children, repeat the Bible verse, sing the songs and do the finger play suggested in your curriculum. Repeat them as often as you see children are interested. However, don't expect toddlers to join you in singing, or in more than one or two gestures of the finger play. For children this age, watching is participation! Remember to *watch*, *ask*, and *adapt* yourself to the children's changing interests and activities. Your enthusiasm for the learning activities and your interest in each child make this a time of effective natural learning.

When it's time for another activity (such as reading a book, showing a nature object or having a snack), begin the transition by singing a song to signal children that a change is coming. Again, repeat the same song from week to week to help children feel secure in knowing what comes next.

When it's time to change or move a child, don't pick up the child without warning; rather, talk calmly to him or her so the child understands what's going to happen. Never underestimate the power of your calmness and relaxed attitude. It will likely "rub off" on the toddlers you care for!

When parents begin to arrive, sing a "good-bye" or "picking up toys" song as an auditory cue to children that it's time to pick up toys and prepare to leave. Watch toddlers' attempts to help pick up; comment on what you see and thank them! Even a child this young likes to feel competent and able to help.

Now It's Time
Tune: "London Bridge"

Now it's time
To say "good-bye"
Say "good-bye"
Say "good-bye."
Now it's time
To say "good-bye,"
See you later!

Look and See
Tune: "Twinkle, Twinkle, Little Star"

Look and see around your room.

Find a toy to put away.

When you visit us to play,

You will have a happy day.

Welcome, Visitors!

Ministry!

When a visitor with baby in arms appears at the nursery door, we should see not only another baby to care for, but also a tremendous opportunity to minister! For visiting parents, you are now an important point of contact—perhaps the first person they meet at your church and also the person who will care for their child. Your genuine friendliness and interest in them during this first contact may communicate Christ's love more effectively than anything else. Don't take the value of your work lightly; be prepared for effective ministry! It may help you to keep in mind the following:

Attention!

❖ It does take time and care to properly check in a visitor's child. Allow for this by having an extra person ready to check in other babies while one concentrates on the visitors. Provide your church's information sheet or brochure and explain nursery procedures. Take time to answer visitors' questions and gauge the visitors' comfort level. Ideally, a registration area away from the nursery door will help avoid congestion at the entrance.

❖ Understand that some parents may be reluctant to leave their children in a strange place. Accept their feelings. Reassure them that they will be called if their child needs them. But if the parent still seems unsure, invite him or her to remain in the nursery for awhile. And wisely use this time with the visiting parent to get to know the family and begin building a loving relationship!

Crisis!

During the busiest nursery sessions (holidays, special church events), several visitors often arrive at one time. Plan for these possibilities ahead of time so that this experience is still a positive one for the visiting child and his or her family.

❖ When your church is sponsoring a special event, or when holidays come around, call for help in advance! Arrange for extra staff to be present.

❖ When it looks as if your child-to-caregiver ratio is going to be lopsided, request several parents of regular nursery attendees to help out temporarily, or consult an already-compiled list of people willing to be called for work in the nursery on an occasional basis.

Remember, your goal is to see that every child and parent who comes to your church nursery sees and experiences the love of God. With a "ministry mentality" and a little planning, this blessing of love can be a reality for all involved!

Parent's Home Pages

The Parent's Home Pages provide specific plans for ways parents can continue at home the teaching that has taken place at church. Each Parent's Home Page emphasizes a monthly Bible-based theme—the same theme that is described in the Teacher's Home Page.

These Parent's Home Pages are wonderful ways to:

❖ help parents in their important task of parenting;
❖ encourage parents to participate in the spiritual nurture of their children;
❖ acquaint parents with the nursery ministry offered by your church.

Here's how to do it:

❖ Photocopy and distribute each page at the beginning of each month. (The first time a parent receives a Parent's Home Page, include the Introductory Parent's Home Page on the next page.)
❖ Distribute pages by mailing them, setting them out on your nursery check-in counter or in a pocket on your nursery bulletin board for parents to take, or caregivers may place them in diaper bags.
❖ For two full years of parent tips and activities, alternate Years A and B Parent's Home Pages. Store the Parent's Home Pages in a binder or folder for reuse.
  Tips for mailing: Be sure to put the church's return address on each page. Ask your church office staff to print out several sets of mailing labels. Add new names as needed.

Attract interest in the Parent's Home Pages by:

❖ Asking caregivers to sign their names to the pages, perhaps writing personal notes to different parents each month (thanking them for bringing child to the nursery or describing something the child enjoys in the nursery).
❖ Posting the current month's page on a nursery bulletin board with a caption such as "Don't miss out on this month's suggestions for helping toddlers play together!"
❖ Occasionally adding a page describing your nursery's policies and procedures.
   ❖ Adding a note to the page that says, "Our church welcomes babies and their parents!" Include information about your nursery as well as programs of interest to young families.
   ❖ Sending a sample Parent's Home Page to recent visitors to the nursery as a way of introducing the nursery ministry.

Nursery Smart Pages • 139

Good Things Come in Small Packages

"I thought I was ready to be a father. But the first week after the baby came home from the hospital was amazing! I never knew anything so little could make such a big difference in our lives."

This father's story could be repeated in almost every home where a tiny bundle, weighing in the neighborhood of eight pounds, literally turns all daily routines upside down. The baby's size has nothing to do with the impact made on parents and their households!

Neither does the size of this little news sheet have anything to do with the impact it can produce in your home. The Parent's Home Page will never compete with the *New York Times* or even the Internet, but it can make a big difference in the quality of your family's life.

Each month until your child is promoted out of the nursery at our church, the people who care for your child there will give you a Parent's Home Page.

As you read each page, you will receive these benefits:

1. Fresh insights into your child's developments in the first two years. Did you know that's when more learning occurs than in any other two-year period of life?

2. A variety of activities to enjoy with your child—designed to help you know each other better and to stimulate your child's intellectual, social, physical and spiritual growth.

3. An increased understanding of the goals of the nursery in your church. The activities suggested in this page are also used with your child when he or she is cared for at church.

If this sounds like a tall order for such a small paper, just keep reading. You will find it full of surprises and delights, well worth a few minutes of your time every month.

If you have any questions or comments about the nursery, please call

_____

_____

at

_____

_____

We're looking forward to participating with you in the care of your child.

Parent's Home Page

TIPS AND ACTIVITIES FOR PARENTS OF CHILDREN UNDER TWO

Do these activities with your child to continue the learning your child has experienced at church.

September

I See God's Love at Church

"I like to come to church." (See Psalm 122:1.)

This month we will help your child:

❖ feel secure and comfortable at church as we demonstrate God's love to him or her;

❖ begin to associate God and Jesus with loving people and enjoyable activities.

Say and do this finger play with your child as you prepare to go to church. Use the child's name instead of "I" and "my." Infants and toddlers will enjoy the sounds and actions, although they will not yet be able to do the finger play with you.

Little Activities for Little People

Babies

❖ Hold a hand mirror or stand in front of a mirror, holding your baby so your child can see his or her face and hands. Talk about and touch each part of your child's face while he or she looks in the mirror. Sing a lullaby to show your pleasure in your child.

❖ While your baby is lying in a crib or sitting in your lap, offer a finger for him or her to grasp. An older baby may pull him- or herself to a sitting or standing position. Younger babies will simply enjoy pulling on your finger. Talk to your baby about what he or she is doing, commenting on the baby's strong hands.

Toddlers

❖ Provide a favorite toy for your child to hold while being changed. Talk with your child about the diaper change. Sing to him or her and imitate your child's sounds. Think of changing time as an ideal setting for enjoyable one-to-one interaction, and not as an unpleasant chore.

❖ Place a few fresh flowers or leaves in an unbreakable container without water. Invite your child to touch and smell the nature items. Talk about what your child is doing. Say, **We are glad God made pretty flowers! Thank You, God, for the flowers.**

SiNG iT!

It's Fun to Go to Church

(Tune: "Farmer in the Dell")

It's fun to go to church!

It's fun to go to church!

With all the other boys and girls,

it's fun to go to church!

Sing this song as you rock, feed or play with your child. Young children like to hear the same song over and over. They look forward to the familiar and happy sounds of a song sung many times. Children will experience God's love at church when they are having enjoyable experiences with loving caregivers.

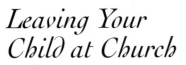

Leaving Your Child at Church

Separation anxiety may begin with a look of uncertainty as a child's eyes dart around the room, absorbing each detail of this strange place. Then the arms desperately clutch at Mommy or Daddy and the head presses firmly against the familiar shoulder. Finally, tears mix with loud wails that seem to ask, "How could you leave me in this place?!"

Vigorous protests are common when young children sense they will be separated from Mommy or Daddy. Anxiety at being left with strangers usually begins at around six to eight months of age. But such an upset is actually a healthy sign that the child has built a strong attachment to parents. However, learning to accept and trust other adults is a necessary step in every child's growth.

When your child begins objecting to leaving you, consider these suggestions:

❖ On the way to church, talk with your child about enjoyable activities or people he or she will encounter at church. Even if your child does not understand your words, your loving, focused attention will strengthen feelings of security.

❖ When your child is staying in the nursery for the first time, you may choose to remain through the beginning of the first session to help your child relax and become comfortable with the new surroundings.

❖ When leaving your child, move at a relaxed pace, but don't linger. It may help to establish a "good-bye ritual" of a hug, a kiss and a wave good-bye. Do this every time you separate. Then make a quick exit, even if your child cries. Tears are normal—and prolonged departures often make matters worse. Be sure the caregivers know where you will be in case they need you.

❖ Return to check on your child only if you intend to stay for the remainder of the session. One tearful good-bye is all a little one should be expected to endure in a morning!

❖ If your child cried when you left, seeing other parents come for their children may stimulate more tears. So return quickly to the nursery after church has concluded. During the time your child is adjusting to being left at church, limit your separation to one hour at a time.

❖ If possible, invite a regular caregiver from the nursery to visit your child at home. Seeing a familiar face at church also eases separation.

❖ Be as regular as possible in attending church. Even one absence may make your child feel like a stranger again.

Stacking Toys

❖ Collect a variety of colorful plastic spray-can caps from items you use around the house (shaving cream, cooking spray, dusting spray, etc.). Try to find caps of varying sizes, making sure not to use caps that are small enough to fit into a child's mouth. Sterilize and dry each cap.

❖ Children will enjoy stacking the caps, knocking down the cap towers you have built, or nesting the caps inside each other. Help children learn colors by naming the color of each cap a child holds.

"Who of us is mature enough for offspring before the offspring themselves arrive? The value of marriage is not that adults produce children but that children produce adults."
Peter DeVries

Return Address:

Postage Stamp

TO: _____

_____

_____

Parent's Home Page

TIPS AND ACTIVITIES FOR PARENTS OF CHILDREN UNDER TWO

Do these activities with your child to continue the learning your child has experienced at church.

October

Jesus Loves Children

"Jesus loves the children." (See Mark 10:16.)

This month we will help your child:

❖

develop an awareness of the name of Jesus and associate Him with being loved;

❖

enjoy the activities provided.

Little Activities for Little People

Babies

❖ Even the youngest baby usually responds positively to soft, quiet singing. Hearing simple yet rhythmic melodies again and again will give your baby great pleasure. Sing the song for this month to your baby many times. Even if you're not comfortable singing, simply repeat the words of familiar songs as poems. Your voice is the sweetest sound in the world to your baby!

❖ Give your baby an intriguing toy with which to play. Talk to your baby, describing the toy and the baby's actions. Occasionally play with the toy yourself, moving the cradle gym, turning a dial or shaking a rattle. Respond to your baby with a smile and an encouraging nod when he or she attempts to imitate your actions. Play music on a cassette or sing a song and shake a rattle. Give your baby a rattle to shake to the song, too.

Toddlers

❖ Hold a sturdy cardboard book and sit on the floor near your toddler. Show the first picture to the child. Point to something familiar in the picture and say its name. If your child is interested in looking at the book, he or she may want to turn the pages and point to things of interest. Little children like to look at the same book many times. Each time, they recognize more of the things in the book.

❖ Children enjoy the feeling of different textures. Take your child outside and invite him or her to feel the bark on a tree, the fur of a dog, the water from the hose, a feather, flower or rock. Let your child touch the back of your hand and the side of your face with his or her fingers. Talk about what these things feel like. Say, **God made your hands so that you can feel (a rough rock).**

DO iT!

Jesus Loves Us All

Who are the children Jesus loves?

Jesus loves us all!

He loves us when we clap;

He loves us when we crawl.

He loves us when we walk;

He loves us when we fall.

Who are the children Jesus loves?

Jesus loves us all.

Jesus loves you!

Show your child a picture of Jesus from a child's Bible story book (available at most bookstores). Point to Jesus and say His name. Tell your child that Jesus loves every child. Say the finger play, making the motions with your fingers. If your child is interested, repeat the finger play slowly and encourage him or her to act out the actions with you by clapping, crawling, walking and plopping down on the floor. Say your child's name in the last line of the finger play.

SiNG iT!

Each Little Child

(Tune: "Mary Had a Little Lamb")

Jesus loves each little child,
little child, little child.
Jesus loves each little child.
He loves you, yes, He does.

Sing this song to your child, inserting your child's name in place of "each little child." Show your child a picture of Jesus. Say, **Jesus loves you!** Sing the song. Point to Jesus when you sing His name. Point to your child when you sing his or her name.

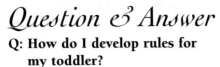

Question & Answer

Q: How do I develop rules for my toddler?

A: It's easy to find oneself saying, "No!" to nearly everything a toddler does! But rather than fall into a "no" pattern that makes little sense to your child and creates constant irritation for you, take some time to determine what your essential house rules should be. It may help to write them down and discuss them with other family members so that everyone can help your toddler understand what rules apply around the house.

❖ Physical safety issues (staying in the yard) and family routines (bedtimes) need a few basic rules. For instance, "We play in the yard. We keep the gate closed." "We are going to take a nap now. It's nap time."

❖ When you state a rule to your toddler, do your best to state it positively. (Children often *don't* hear the "don't" part of a rule and instead act on what they *did* hear, thus doing just what you said not to do!) Help a child understand *why*, even at this age. (It's good practice for later years when your child will ask, "Why?" constantly!) For example, rather than, "Don't touch the cord!" try, "The cord stays in the wall. It can hurt your hand if you touch it. Owie!"

❖ Toddlers will test you. This does not mean you need to change the house rules! A child needs to know that you (and your rules) are a sure thing. A child gains comfort and security in knowing what you expect and what comes next. Rules help a child make sense of his or her world.

And remember! A few rules, consistently enforced, are far more effective than many rules (and you will not have to wear yourself out playing "police"!).

Play Dough

❖ Mix 1 cup of flour with 1 cup of salt in a bowl. Put half of this mixture in another bowl. Put 2 to 3 drops blue food coloring in ½ cup of water and mix the colored water into one bowl of flour/salt mixture. In another ½ cup of water put 2 to 3 drops of yellow food coloring and mix into second bowl of flour/salt mixture.

❖ Give your child a lump of blue and a lump of yellow dough to play with. Sit down and play with some dough too, demonstrating how to roll, squeeze or mold it. Your child may try to taste the dough, but it will taste so salty that he or she will stop (and it will not hurt your child, should he or she swallow a small amount). Your child will want to see how play dough feels and to experiment with it.

❖ Let your child mix the two colors of dough together to discover the new color it makes. Store the dough in an airtight container for use on another day. Children enjoy repeating this activity. Repetition allows them to build on the knowledge they have previously gained.

Little children remind us not to take ourselves so seriously.

Return Address:

Postage Stamp

TO: _____

_____

_____

Parent's Home Page

TIPS AND ACTIVITIES FOR PARENTS OF CHILDREN UNDER TWO

Do these activities with your child to continue the learning your child has experienced at church.

November

God Gives Me Food

"God gives us food." (See Genesis 1:29.)

This month we will help your child:

❖

develop an awareness that God made food;

❖

enjoy eating food with teachers and other children.
(Alert nursery staff of any food allergies your child has.)

Little Activities for Little People

Babies

❖ Babies like toys that can be held easily in their hands and chewed upon. (Toys that are too big to be manipulated by small hands are frustrating.) A baby cannot really experience something unless the baby can get it into his or her mouth. Make sure the small toys you provide are safe: too big to be swallowed, no sharp or rough edges, no pieces that can come off.

❖ Your baby likes toys that respond to his or her actions, not ones that he or she must passively observe. A ball that your baby can roll, or a toy that bounces back when hit are great favorites. Perhaps most fun of all are your responses when your baby does something. A parent who laughs, squeals and claps when a baby does something is the best of all possible playmates.

Toddlers

❖ A toddler seldom comes to you and announces, "I'm tired!" However, each child has his or her own signals to let everyone know when a brief rest is needed. Be alert to provide a few quiet minutes for sitting in your lap, looking at a book or singing a quiet song.

❖ When a playmate visits your child, expect your child to be reluctant to let the intruder use his or her toys. A ball is an excellent toy to begin helping a child have fun taking turns. Roll it first to your child, then to the visitor. Continue alternating, talking about who has the ball now. Provide several similar toys for the children to share. However, if a conflict arises, avoid scolding your child for being selfish. That will only make your child feel more insecure and reluctant to take turns.

DO iT!

My Food

This is my nose
to smell my cracker.
These are my eyes
to see my cracker.
These are my hands
to hold my cracker.
This is my tongue
to taste my cracker.
Thank You, God,
for my cracker.

Do this finger play with your child before giving him or her a snack. If your child is interested in what you are doing, ask, **Where is your nose? Where is my nose?** Watch your child point to the noses. Then do the whole finger play, encouraging your child to do it with you. While your child is eating his or her snack, do the finger play again. (If you are having a different snack than crackers, use the name of your snack in the finger play instead of crackers.)

SiNG iT!

I Thank God

(Tune: "Mulberry Bush")

Apples taste so good to me,
so good to me, so good to me.
Apples taste so good to me.
I thank God for my food.

Show your toddler an apple. Say, **Is this an apple or a banana?** Wait for his or her answer. **Are apples red or blue?** Give your child a chance to respond, then say, **These apples are red!** Sing this song with your toddler. Do the motion of rubbing the tummy when saying the words "so good to me." Serve your child an apple. (When having a different snack than apples, sing this song about the snack you are having—bananas, pears, crackers, etc.)

Get Ready! Holidays Are Coming

Thanksgiving and Christmas are traditional times for families to gather. And your baby is bound to be one of the main points of interest for everyone from the youngest cousin to the oldest grandparent. All this togetherness is great fun for the cousins and grandparents, but it can produce real stress for your child and you.

To reduce the chances of your child (not to mention his or her parents!) getting overstimulated, tired and fussy during holiday celebrations, remember these five hints:

❖ Avoid overscheduling through the holiday season. Turn down a few invitations if necessary. When visiting at someone's home who doesn't have children, don't expect that your host will necessarily have appropriate food or toys for your child. Bring a favorite snack and several favorite toys along with you.

❖ Plan time each day when you can be alone with your child—and with your spouse when possible!

❖ Plan a time of prayer every day— even when taking a walk with your child, driving on an errand or in the shower!

❖ Protect your child's nap time as much as possible.

❖ Understand and accept your child's times of upset. The holiday excitement is bound to take its toll sooner or later. Offer calm words of understanding, a hug of comfort and a short break from a crowded room.

Feely Sock Game

❖ Put an object (baby's brush, a toy car, a block, a piece of fruit) inside a clean adult sock. Stick your hand in the sock and feel the object. Let your child do the same. Say, **What do you think it is? Is it a blanket? an apple? a car?** (If child is reluctant to put a hand in the sock, show the object before putting it in.)

❖ Let your child feel the object and, if interested, guess the object's name. Then let your child take the object out and look at it. Say the object's name.

❖ Then, without letting your child see, put a different object in the sock. Let your child feel this object, too. Say, **What do you feel? Is it hard or is it soft? Is it smooth or rough? Is it hot or cold?**

❖ Continue letting your child feel different objects in the sock as long as he or she is interested. Name and talk about each object as your child takes it out of the sock.

❖ As your child gets better at this game, try placing an item with an easily defined shape (such as a toy airplane) into the sock and invite your child to feel the object from the outside to guess what the item is. Then let the child place his or her hand in the sock and pull out the item.

❖ For very young toddlers, simply use the sock to play a peekaboo game. **Here is a car. Here is a sock.** Place the car inside the sock. **Oh. Where did the car go?** (A child may or may not realize that the car is inside the sock, even if he or she saw you place it there. Every child moves beyond the "out of sight, out of mind" stage of development at an individual rate.) **Look! Peekaboo! Here is the car!** If child is interested, repeat the game. Invite him or her to pull the item out of the sock.

"Before I got married I had six theories about bringing up children; now I have six children and no theories."
**John Wilmot
(1647-1680)**

Return Address:

Postage
Stamp

TO: _____

_____

_____

Parent's Home Page

TIPS AND ACTIVITIES FOR PARENTS OF CHILDREN UNDER TWO

Do these activities with your child to continue the learning your child has experienced at church.

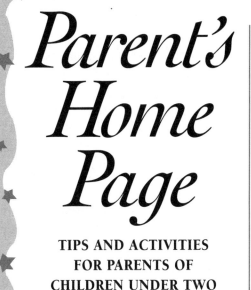

Jesus Was a Baby

"His name is Jesus." (See Luke 1:31.)

This month we will help your child:

❖

show interest in pictures, conversation and songs about baby Jesus;

❖

receive personal attention and love as teachers seek to show Jesus' love in ways a child understands.

December

DO iT!

Look into the Stable

Look into the stable now.
Who do you see?
I see baby Jesus
sleeping in Mary's arms.

Look into the stable now.
What do you hear?
I hear baby Jesus laughing
in Joseph's arms.

Before doing this finger play, show your child a picture of baby Jesus in the manger from a story book or Christmas card. Or purchase a nativity scene (be certain it is unbreakable and has large pieces) for your child to look at and handle. Then do the finger play with your child. If your child is interested in what you are doing, ask, **How do you rock a baby?** Let your child show you how by pretending to rock a baby. **Show me how a baby laughs.** Enjoy and imitate your child's sounds. **It's fun to laugh together. We're happy because Jesus was born. We love Jesus.**

SiNG iT!

Happy Birthday, Jesus!

(Tune: "Jesus Loves Me")

It's Jesus' birthday, time to sing!
Shake the bells and make them ring.
Let's all sing a happy song.
Bring your drums and march along.

Happy birthday, Jesus,
Happy birthday, Jesus,
Happy birthday, Jesus.
We sing this happy song.

Sing this song and shake jingle bells. When your child shows interest, give him or her a child-safe rhythm instrument to play as you sing. Say, **It's fun to sing about Jesus! I'm glad Jesus was born.**

Little Activities for Little People

Babies

❖ Recorded Christmas carols played at a low volume help create a cheerful atmosphere for your baby. Sing along with the records. Even though your baby will not understand the words, he or she will respond to your voice and smile. Use your baby's name wherever appropriate in the songs.

❖ Hold your baby in your lap to look at picture books. Hold the book steady. As you point to the dominant items in each picture, describe what you see. When your baby's interest wanes, provide another activity.

Toddlers

❖ The name Jesus can become a name your toddler associates with feelings of love and warmth. For example, when you show interest in a picture of Jesus, your toddler will probably mirror your actions. Be alert for opportunities to show your child pictures of Jesus from a child's Bible story book or Christmas cards. Talk about Jesus' birth. Your attitude and example powerfully influence your child's feelings and behavior. Long before your child understands all your words, he or she senses your emotions. Repeated use of songs, short Bible stories and loving conversation about Jesus helps your child gradually become familiar with these words and phrases.

❖ December is a time when your child may be offered a variety of seasonal treats, so keep the foods you serve at home simple and familiar.

Question & Answer

Q: How can I build good relationships with my child's grandparents and minimize some of the inevitable problems?

A: Here are a few suggestions:

❖ Remember that grandparents are not automatic baby-sitters. Respect their time and privacy.

❖ Communicate regularly and openly with grandparents. While some grandparents may give you more advice than you want, the important thing is that you both talk and listen to each other.

❖ Accept differences that arise about ways to manage your child. It is not necessary for parents and grandparents to agree. However, it is essential that they respect each other's ideas.

❖ Remember that while you are learning to be a parent, your parents are having just as many challenges learning to be grandparents. Allow them to make as many mistakes in their new role as you are making in learning yours. Ask God's help for both of you as you guide and care for your child.

❖ Include grandparents in the life of your child by taking time to share with them milestones of development or humorous things your child says and does. Long-distance grandparents will especially appreciate photos or videos!

Christmas Collage

❖ Your child will want to play with your gift-wrapping supplies. Give your child a safe and fun time exploring gift-wrap materials. Your extra effort to provide this activity will be well worth it!

❖ Squeeze a small line of glue onto a sheet of construction paper or piece of grocery bag. Tear off a small piece of wrapping paper. Encourage your child to do the same. Stick your piece of wrapping paper onto the glue and let your child do the same.

❖ Crumble a small piece of wrapping paper into a ball and stick it to the glue. As your child puts pieces of paper and ribbon onto the construction paper, add glue as needed.

❖ Your child will want to touch the glue. Talk about how glue helps things stick. Say, **Now there is glue on your fingers. Papers are sticking to your fingers. Let's wash the glue off your fingers so you can stick the papers to the picture again.** Then clean your child's fingers.

❖ Hang the collage up where your child can see it (but not touch it if small pieces could be removed). Talk about the collage in the days to come.

"In bringing up children, spend on them half as much money and twice as much time."
Laurence Peter

Return Address:

Postage Stamp

TO: _____

_____

_____

Parent's Home Page

TIPS AND ACTIVITIES FOR PARENTS OF CHILDREN UNDER TWO

Do these activities with your child to continue the learning your child has experienced at church.

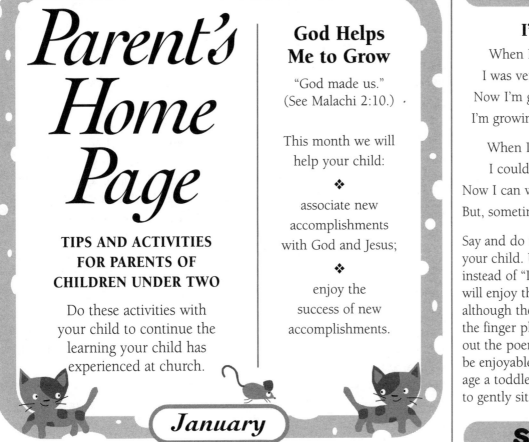

January

God Helps Me to Grow

"God made us."
(See Malachi 2:10.)

This month we will help your child:

❖

associate new accomplishments with God and Jesus;

❖

enjoy the success of new accomplishments.

DO iT!

I'm Growing

When I was a baby,
I was very, very small.
Now I'm growing older.
I'm growing big and tall.

When I was a baby,
I could only crawl.
Now I can walk, and I can jump.
But, sometimes, down I fall!

Say and do this finger play with your child. Use your child's name instead of "I." Infants and toddlers will enjoy the sounds and actions, although they will not be able to do the finger play with you yet. Acting out the poem as you say it will also be enjoyable for your child. Encourage a toddler to crawl with you or to gently sit down.

SiNG iT!

I Am Growing

(Tune: "Are You Sleeping?")

I am growing.
I am growing.
Yes, I am.
Yes, I am.
One time I was smaller.
Now I am much taller.
Watch me grow.
Watch me grow.

Sing this song to your child as you rock, feed, dress or play with him or her. Show your child a picture of him- or herself when younger and smaller. Talk about how much bigger he or she has grown. **Lindsay, you're growing! You've learned to sit up, and now you're learning to crawl. God made you, and He helps you grow.** Children will begin to associate God's care with their growth and new accomplishments.

Little Activities for Little People

Babies

❖ While feeding your baby, talk about the parts of the child's body. Say, **God made you. God made your mouth so you can eat.** Touch the child's mouth when you mention it. Repeat the word "mouth." Continue similarly, naming and touching fingers, toes, nose, ears, etc.

❖ What would it feel like to have someone much bigger than you suddenly take your arms and push them into the sleeves of your coat when you had no idea you were going anywhere requiring a coat? Talk to your baby about what you are going to do with him or her. Babies understand much more of your speech than you may imagine. And the tone of your voice calms and helps your child move with ease into the next activity.

Toddlers

❖ Point to facial and body features of people pictured in magazines and books. Ask the child to touch his or her own nose, ears, chin, etc.

❖ As your child plays with toys, comment on the parts of his or her body being used in play. Show pleasure in your child's developing skills. Say, **God made you so you can do so many things. You're growing just as God planned!**

❖ Rocking a crying child and acknowledging the child's feelings ("You're feeling sad right now") are time-proven methods for soothing upset feelings. However, sometimes an unhappy child will object strenuously to merely being rocked. So, you will need to gently draw your child's attention to a colorful toy, book or picture. Your quiet voice and interesting movements will help your child relax and calm down.

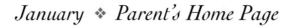

Praying with Your Child

I stood over the tiny bundle lying in the bassinet and decided she was starting to look less like a prune. But she was still so helpless and I felt so inadequate. So I did the only thing I thought might help. I prayed.

"Lord, you know I've never been a father before. The idea used to sound like fun, but now I'm scared. I really need your help."

That was the first of many similarly inelegant prayers I whispered late at night, standing beside my sleeping baby's crib. I knew she could neither hear nor understand me. But I began to feel these moments of prayer were bonding me to her in a way I found very special.

Gradually, a brief prayer became part of our bedtime ritual, mixed in with the tummy rubbing, forehead stroking, chin tickling and cheek kissing that helped Kari relax and go to sleep.

Through this process, I stumbled onto a key that continued to make our prayer time meaningful, even as Kari entered adolescence. I found myself talking to God about the experiences Kari and I had shared each evening. As Kari grew and began to contribute her own prayers, she followed the same pattern of thanking God for herself and me and for the good times we shared, and of asking God's forgiveness for failures.

Over the years our father-daughter prayer times have been among the strongest experiences in building our relationship. I have often wondered if the pattern would have been so consistent and meaningful if I had not begun practicing in those nights beside her crib. If I had waited until she was two or four and could have understood what I was saying, would I have persevered through my awkwardness or simply given it up as inappropriate for a young child?

Wes Haystead, Parent and Author

Have a Snowy Day Indoors

❖ Sit with an older toddler at a kitchen table or counter. Put a small amount of non-mentholated shaving cream in your child's hand to feel. Say, **This shaving cream feels and smells good, but it isn't good to eat.**

❖ Spray a 1-inch (2.5-cm) layer of shaving cream on a cookie sheet (or directly on the table top, if you prefer). Show your child how you can "walk" a plastic animal through the shaving cream "snow," making prints. Then "drive" a play car through the snow or use a paper cup to clear a road.

❖ Let your child experiment with moving things in the shaving cream. He or she may enjoy simply moving fingers in a sensory experience.

❖ If your child remains interested in playing with the shaving cream for a length of time, refresh the snow by smoothing over the previous marks or by spraying more shaving cream onto the cookie sheet.

"You can talk to God about your children. You can tell Him everything, ask Him anything. You can even laugh with Him about the funnier things. I believe He understands laughter, for He is the One who made your child so funny in the first place."
Ethel Barrett

Return Address:

Postage Stamp

TO: _____

_____

_____

Parent's Home Page

TIPS AND ACTIVITIES FOR PARENTS OF CHILDREN UNDER TWO

Do these activities with your child to continue the learning your child has experienced at church.

February

My Family Loves Me

"God gives us families."
(See Psalm 68:6.)

This month we will help your child:

❖

begin to associate God and Jesus with loving people at home and at church;

❖

respond to demonstrations of affection.

DO iT!

Families

We all live in families,
you and me.
What kinds of families?
Let me see!
Tall ones and short ones;
big ones and small ones.
We all live in families,
you and me.

Say and do this finger play with your child. Use your child's name instead of "you." Draw your child's attention to a photo of your family and other pictures of families as you say and do this finger play.

SiNG iT!

My Family
(Tune: "Row, Row, Row Your Boat")

Thank, thank, thank You, God,
for my family!
God made families to love
and care for you and me!

Sing this song to your child as he or she plays with a doll, toy dishes or household items. Talk about ways you show love to your child. Say, **I give you good things to eat because I love you. I play with you because I love you. I'm glad we're a family together. God gives us families.** Your child will begin to develop an awareness of God being associated with the love he or she experiences with you at home.

Little Activities for Little People

Babies

❖ Convey your love and acceptance of your child with smiles, hugs and caresses. Make feeding and changing activities times of relaxed personal attention, not just tasks to be completed as quickly as possible.

❖ Provide your baby with as much freedom to move as possible, whether in a crib, playpen or on the floor. Remove unnecessary clothing and blankets and avoid cluttering the area with an abundance of toys.

Toddlers

❖ Provide a favorite doll or stuffed animal for yourself and your child to pretend to care for. Rock the doll and sing to it. Pretend to feed it and help it to sleep. Wrap it in a nice warm blanket. Boys enjoy this kind of play as much as girls do, and the nurturing behavior they practice will help them be good fathers one day.

❖ Doll play can be extended to include use of some familiar home materials. Your little one will enjoy loading and unloading a plastic dishpan with a few unbreakable dishes, pots and pans. As you and your child play together, sing "My Family."

Question & Answer

Q: What can I do about my child's whining?

A: A very young child needs to communicate a need for attention. What we call whining (fussing, moaning, refusing to play with a toy, crying) is a normal way for a child to say he or she is hungry, tired, uncomfortable or frustrated. Here are some suggestions to help minimize your child's whining.

❖ Respond to any obvious problems that require your attention, such as hunger, ear infection or frustration.

❖ Consider the time of day. Is it nap time? Time for a change of scenery? Is it time for a snack or a drink? Experienced parents say that in the late afternoon from around four until dinner time, some children (and adults) seem to be at a low ebb emotionally and physically. Plan ahead to take a few minutes' break during this time (or any other part of the day when your child seems to whine consistently). Sit on the floor with your child, rock him or her, read a story together or take him or her for a walk.

❖ Be sure to give your child age-appropriate toys. Toys that are intended for older children will provoke frustration. Toys that are intended for younger children will lead to boredom.

❖ Respond verbally to your child immediately. ("I hear you calling me, Justin.") A lack of response simply encourages the child to keep trying to gain your attention.

❖ If you must say no to a child's request, give a clear, simple reason, and then provide an appropriate substitute.

Every child whines sometimes. However, if you don't whine, but talk calmly to your child, helping your child put his or her feelings into words as he or she grows, your child will likely outgrow whining.

Wave Bottle

❖ Wash and dry a clear plastic bottle and lid. Fill halfway with water, then add one or two drops of food coloring. Fill remainder of bottle with mineral oil. Drop in some glitter or sequins to accentuate the wave motion. Coat the inside of the lid with superglue; seal tightly. When the lid is dry, cover lid seam with duct tape. (Check bottle often for leaks.)

❖ Babies will enjoy watching the movement of the water. Toddlers will have fun moving the bottle themselves, rolling, shaking or turning it.

"We are apt to forget that children watch examples better than they listen to preaching."
Roy L. Smith

Return Address:

Postage Stamp

TO: _____

_____

_____

Parent's Home Page

TIPS AND ACTIVITIES FOR PARENTS OF CHILDREN UNDER TWO

Do these activities with your child to continue the learning your child has experienced at church.

Jesus Loves Me

"Jesus loves us." (See Revelation 1:5.)

This month we will help your child:

❖

enjoy activities in which teachers talk lovingly of Jesus;

❖

frequently hear the words "Jesus loves us."

March

Little Activities for Little People

Babies

❖ Talk simply to your baby about a picture of Jesus and the children. Point to Jesus and say, **This is Jesus.** Point to the baby in the picture and say, **Here is a baby. Jesus loves babies. Jesus loves you. I love you, too.** Use your child's name in the conversation.

❖ Babies that are able to sit seem to have an insatiable curiosity about small objects which they can pick up, hold, examine and then drop, only to repeat the process. Suitable objects must be too large for swallowing, but small enough for easy handling.

Toddlers

❖ Toddlers are beginning to associate words with real objects, people, actions and feelings. Your child's understanding of words and sentences comes at least several months before the ability to use those words. When you talk lovingly about Jesus while looking at a picture of Jesus or while participating in enjoyable activities with your child, you are building a positive feeling in your child toward Jesus.

❖ Collect a variety of textured fabrics or materials for your child to feel: silk, towel, plastic mat, wool, corduroy, etc. Remove your child's shoes and socks so he or she can walk barefoot on the fabrics. Encourage your child to feel the differences in the fabrics. Comment, **I'm glad to feel this shiny cloth. And I'm glad that Jesus loves you, Julie.**

DO IT!

Day and Night

When the sun is in the sky,

Jesus loves me.

When the stars are way up high,

Jesus loves me.

In the day and in the night,

while I play and then sleep tight,

Jesus loves me.

Say and do this finger play with your child. Use the child's name instead of "I" and "me." Take your child outside on a sunny day and again on a starry evening and do this finger play each time. Do this finger play with your child at nap time or bedtime or when he or she is having fun playing.

SING IT!

Yes, Jesus Loves You

(Tune: Refrain to "Jesus Loves Me")

Yes, Jesus loves you.
Yes, Jesus loves you.
Yes, Jesus loves you!
The Bible tells us so.

Show your child a Bible. Say, **This book is called the Bible. The Bible tells us that Jesus loves us. Jesus loves you.** Then sing the song with your child. Use your child's name instead of "you." This song can be sung while you rock or bounce your child or hold hands. Finish each song by reminding your child of your love for him or her.

How Do I Get Time for Myself?

No doubt the birth of a child is one of life's most completely altering experiences! People often think that one can just "work the baby into the schedule." But although the scheduling of naps and feedings improves with time, nobody schedules an earache! But realize that what may feel like slavery to an unpredictable life neither means you are a "bad parent" nor that your baby is a "difficult child." It's simply a normal feature of early parenthood!

You and your spouse need extra patience with yourselves and each other as you adjust to this tremendous change. As a new mother, your body systems go through great hormonal change during the first months of parenthood, causing mood swings and crying jags. And if you face a return to work (with the stress of finding day care and performing perfectly at work), stress can go through the roof!

As a new father, you may find plenty of stress, too. It's soon apparent that weariness due to three o'clock feedings doesn't get much sympathy at work! And your wife is not only tired, but often focused on the baby. Interest in physical intimacy with you seems to disappear. But take heart: It happens to every new dad.

Decide what's really important for your new family. Remember that while errands and chores will forever be there, your baby is already closer to starting kindergarten than you can imagine!

❖ Schedule individual renewal time during your baby's most reliable nap time. Whether reading the Bible, listening to soothing music, talking on the phone or just sitting quietly, DON'T use that time for chores.

❖ Plan a night out at least once a week. Knowing that you WILL spend some time with each other or with other adults can help you through a difficult time with your baby. A single parent might ask close friends to take turns planning a night out. If you cannot afford child care or have no one to baby-sit, consider inviting one or two friends over to play a board game or watch a video. And don't wear yourselves out cleaning before they come!

❖ Remember that tiny bits of "adult time" will help you feel connected to the grown-up world. Even a few minutes of reading a thought-provoking article can help—even if the magazine lies open on your kitchen counter for days at a time and you read standing up!

Because your baby is extremely sensitive to your stress level and moods, your tension can make him or her irritable and cranky. By reducing your stress, you are actually calming your baby. Take a deep breath, let it out and smile. *Then* pick up the baby!

Picture Puzzle

❖ Glue a 5×7-inch (12.5×17.5-cm) photo of your child to a piece of cardboard. Then cut the cardboard-backed photo in half to create two pieces. (Optional: For an older child, cut the photo in half each direction, creating four equal pieces.)

❖ Show your child the picture puzzle put together. Then take the puzzle apart. Let your child explore how he or she can put the puzzle together. If needed, help your child put the puzzle together again.

❖ Talk about the picture. Point to the picture of your child and say, **Do you see a picture of Nadia? There's Nadia! I can see her eyes and her nose and her mouth. I love Nadia. Jesus loves Nadia, too.**

"You can learn many things from children— how much patience you have, for instance."

Franklin P. Jones

Return Address:

Postage Stamp

TO: _____

_____

_____

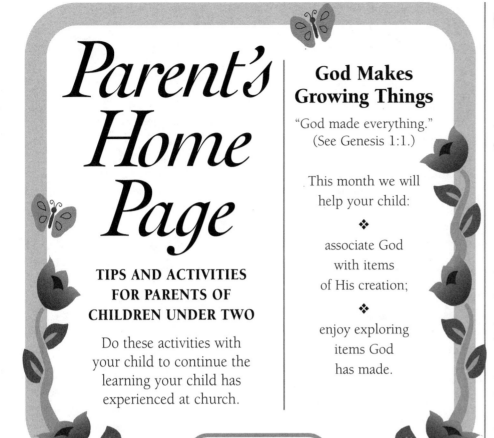

Parent's Home Page

TIPS AND ACTIVITIES FOR PARENTS OF CHILDREN UNDER TWO

Do these activities with your child to continue the learning your child has experienced at church.

God Makes Growing Things

"God made everything." (See Genesis 1:1.)

This month we will help your child:

❖

associate God with items of His creation;

❖

enjoy exploring items God has made.

April

Little Activities for Little People

Babies

❖ Collect magazine pictures of growing things. On each picture, glue several fabric scraps in a variety of textures to make a touch-and-feel picture. As you talk about the pictured items, rub your baby's hand gently on the fabric.

❖ Provide texture cubes or balls for play with your baby. These learning tools can be purchased or made by stitching a variety of textured fabric scraps around a foam ball or cube. Hold the ball in front of your baby, moving it slightly to gain his or her attention. Slowly move the ball toward your baby's stomach. Say, **Here comes the ball, right to Mario's tummy!** Repeat several times until your baby attempts to hold the ball. Help your baby feel the various textures. Say, **God gave you hands to touch and hold. God made everything!**

Toddlers

❖ Take your child outside and let him or her touch leaves and the bark of trees. Show your child birds and bugs and other living things around your home.

❖ Put out some large pillows and a small step stool for your child to climb on. You may want to remove other items in the area to provide space for climbing, crawling and jumping. Encourage your child's attempts at moving in new ways. Say, **Veronica, you are learning to climb! God made your legs to climb with. Thank You, God, for Veronica's strong legs.** Touch your child's legs as you say the word "legs" to help develop word-object associations.

DO iT!

I'm a Little Seed

I'm a little, tiny seed
in the earth so low.
God sends sun and rain,
then I start to grow.
Up, up, up,
slowly I grow,
then my leaves
and flowers show!

Say and do this finger play with your child. Use the child's name instead of "I" and "I'm." To act out the poem in another way, sit on your knees with your head down to be the seed. As you say "Then I start to grow," begin to stretch your head up, then your arms, and then stand up. As you say the words "Then my leaves and flowers show!" stretch your arms out and wiggle your fingers or cup your hands to represent leaves or flowers.

SiNG iT!

Animal Friends

(Tune: "Jingle Bells" chorus)

Oh, God made ducks
and rabbits and squirrels
and little birds to sing.
God made you and God made me.
Yes, God made everything!
(Repeat.)

Show your child books picturing ducks, rabbits, squirrels and birds. Ask your child, **What does the duck say? Show me how a squirrel runs. I can wiggle my nose like a rabbit. Can you? Can you flap your arms like a bird flaps its wings?** Then sing the song with your child. Your child may enjoy pretending to be a bird by flapping his or her arms, chirping and moving around while you sing and pretend to be a bird, too.

Question & Answer

Q: How should I talk to my child and help my child learn to talk?

A: Magda Gerber, an expert on the development of the very young says, "Rather than purposefully teaching language to infants and toddlers as such, communicate, listen, and read babies' cues. Then simply talk to them as though they understand." Here are some examples of ways to talk to the very young:

❖ Help your child begin to understand what is happening by saying what you are doing to the child. Say, **I am going to pick you up.** Then when your child lifts his or her arms up, say, **I can see you're ready for me to pick you up. I'm going to take you to the store with me. So we'll go to the car. I will need to put you in the car seat.** Then talk to your child about what he or she might see as you drive along. **Look! I see a dog.** "Talking through" everyday situations such as these gives your baby a sense of what words apply to what he or she is seeing.

❖ Singing short songs or saying short poems to signal transition times (such as nap time, meal time, etc.) help a child to understand what is coming next by helping a child to associate the often-repeated words with certain activities. This is helpful because babies are not only learning words and their meanings at a very fast rate, but they are also learning to recognize the rhythms and sounds of language.

❖ Remember, your baby recognizes many more words than he or she can say. Don't expect verbal responses too early; rather, use simple signs (such as pantomiming drinking from a cup) to encourage your child to use signs you both understand. Also watch for other facial and verbal cues that indicate response.

❖ When your child makes sounds or tries out a new word, repeat the sound or word back to the child and watch for the child's response. He or she will probably be delighted! This may even lead to a simple language game: after you repeat the sound your child made (ba-ba), add another simple sound (ba-ba-da). Watch to see if the child repeats both sounds. Continue as long as the child is interested.

Planting

❖ Either outdoors or with a pot and soil, plant a seed with your child. Show your child a seed and a picture of what the seed will grow into when planted. You may want to choose a quickly-germinating seed such as rye grass, radishes or marigolds.

❖ Carefully supervise as your child feels the soil. Talk about the color and texture of the soil. Let your child help dig a hole for the seed or put soil in the pot. Then let your child plant the seed.

❖ Give your child a spray bottle for watering the seed. If your seed only requires a small amount of water, give your child a cup with some water in it and an eyedropper to water the plant with. You may need to put your hand over your child's hand to help him or her use an eyedropper at first.

❖ Help your child water the plant and watch it grow. Talk about the seed opening and the little shoot coming up. Talk about growing and do the finger play "I'm a Little Seed" with your child.

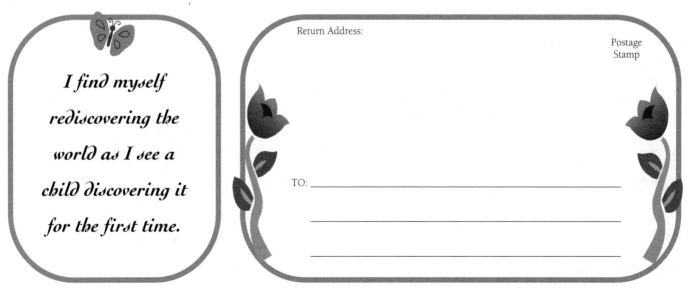

I find myself rediscovering the world as I see a child discovering it for the first time.

Return Address:

Postage Stamp

TO: _____

_____

_____

Parent's Home Page

TIPS AND ACTIVITIES FOR PARENTS OF CHILDREN UNDER TWO

Do these activities with your child to continue the learning your child has experienced at church.

May

People at Church Help Me

"God gives people to help me."
(See 1 Corinthians 12:28.)

This month we will help your child:

❖

develop an awareness of Jesus;

❖

and associate Jesus with being loved and helped.

Little Activities for Little People

Babies

❖ When looking at a book or magazine with pictures of familiar objects around the house, call your child's attention to the real object along with the picture. Say, **Here is a picture of a rattle. Here's one of your rattles. Listen to the rattle.** Such comparisons help develop your child's awareness.

❖ Talk about people and activities your child has enjoyed at church. Assure your child that the teachers at church love him or her. Say, **I like to go to church with you. Mrs. Stevens loves to take care of you and help you at church.**

Toddlers

❖ When your toddler shows affection in caring for a doll (and boys need dolls as much as girls), comment about the way he or she is loving the doll just as you love him or her. Say, **You put the doll to bed just like I put you to bed. Putting your tired baby to bed is a good way to help him or her.**

❖ Provide blocks of several different sizes for your child to use. While your child is stacking or piling blocks, look for indications of awareness of differing sizes. Point to and identify the big and little blocks. Ask your child to bring you a big block, then a little block. Praise these efforts. Emphasize that you enjoy being with your child and helping him or her to learn new words.

DO iT!

People Help Me

People at church help me.

They say "hello!"

and smile at me.

They hold me close

and play with me

and give me good things to eat!

Say and do this finger play as you play with your child. Use your child's name instead of "me." Talk about the people who care for your child at church. (If your church has a picture directory, show pictures of these people to your child.) Do this finger play many times, but especially immediately before and after your child has been to the church nursery. Your child's confidence and pleasure in the nursery will grow as he or she sees you affirming and enjoying your child's experiences in the nursery, too.

SiNG iT!

Showing God's Love

(Tune: "Twinkle, Twinkle, Little Star")

I will smile and play with you.

Jesus helped His good friends, too.

I can show I care for you

to help you know that God loves you.

Sing this song as you serve a meal to or play with your child. Talk about how you enjoy caring for your child. Smile at your child and tell him or her that you smile to show you love him or her. Talk about how people at church like to smile and take care of your child. If a child knows the name of a nursery worker, sing the song using the person's name in place of the word "I."

Children Won't Wait

There is a time to anticipate the
baby's coming, a time to consult
a doctor;

A time to plan a diet and exercise,
a time to gather a layette.

There is a time to wonder at the
ways of God,
knowing this is the destiny for
which I was created;

A time to dream of what this child
may become,

A time to pray that God will
teach me how to train this child
which I bear.

A time to prepare myself that
I might nurture my child's soul.

But soon there comes the time for
birth,

For babies won't wait.

There is a time for night feedings,
and colic and formulas.

There is a time for rocking and a
time for walking the floor,

A time for patience and self-
sacrifice,

A time to show that my child's new
world is a world of love and
goodness and dependability.

There is a time to ponder what my
child is—not a pet nor toy;
but a person, an individual—
a soul made in God's image.

There is a time to consider my
stewardship. I cannot possess
my child.

This child is not mine. I have been
chosen to care for, to love,
to enjoy

to nurture and to answer to God
for this child.

I resolve to do my best
for this child,

For babies don't wait.

There is a time to hold my child
close and tell the sweetest story
ever told;

A time to enjoy earth and sky and
flower, to teach my child of
wonder

and reverence for God and
all He has made.

There is a time to leave the dishes,
to swing my child in the park,

To run a race, to draw a picture,
to catch a butterfly, to give my
child happy comradeship.

There is a time to point the way,
to teach infant lips to pray,

To teach my child's heart to love
God's Word, to love God's day.

For children don't wait.

Originally published by *20th Century
Christian*. Used by permission.

Goop

❖ Here is a great sensory development experience. Pour 1/2 box of
cornstarch onto a shallow cookie
tray. Slowly add water (with
small amount of food coloring)
and stir. Consider putting your
child with cookie tray in the
bathtub or other easy-to-clean
area.

❖ Your child can play with goop by
squeezing, pulling and letting the
goop drip through his or her fingers. Though goop does not taste
good, and you will want to
encourage your child to touch—
not taste, goop will not harm a
child who manages to get a bit
into his or her mouth.

*Little children
know how to
make us laugh—
even when we
probably shouldn't!*

Return Address:

Postage
Stamp

TO: _____

_____

_____

Parent's Home Page

TIPS AND ACTIVITIES FOR PARENTS OF CHILDREN UNDER TWO

Do these activities with your child to continue the learning your child has experienced at church.

June

God Cares for Me

"God cares about you."
(See 1 Peter 5:7.)

This month we will help your child:

❖

associate God with the loving care experienced at church;

❖

show interest in conversation and songs about God's care.

Little Activities for Little People

Babies

❖ Respond to your baby's babbling. Imitate the sound he or she makes, or make new sounds for your child to mimic. It's not important that the sounds match, just that you both have fun making noises with each other.

❖ Provide your baby with a variety of viewing points to observe goings-on around the house. If your child is not yet crawling, a washable blanket in the middle of the floor is a fine place to play with a few toys. Periodically, move close to your baby for a few words, pats and a little play. Your child needs your frequent attention even when he or she is playing happily.

Toddlers

❖ Conversation about God's care for your child must be accompanied by loving demonstrations of care. As your child experiences having his or her needs met, the idea of God's loving concern will begin to make sense. As your child hears you talk lovingly about God, he or she will begin to associate God with good feelings and experiences.

❖ Take your child outside to play and discover things outdoors. You will have many opportunities to help your child see or touch something new. Connect what your child sees and touches with God's loving care. Say, **I see the birds. God made the birds and He cares for them. God made you and He cares for you, too.**

DO IT!

God Cares for Me

God cares for me
when I sleep.
God cares for me
when I play.
God cares for me
all the time,
every night and
every day.

Say and do this finger play with your child. Replace the words "me" and "I" with your child's name. Use the finger play when putting your child to sleep or when playing with him or her. On a bright sunny day, talk about the color of the sky and the sunshine and then say the finger play. In the evening, take your child out to look at the moon and the stars and talk about the nighttime. Repeat the finger play.

SING IT!

I'm So Glad

(Tune: "Skip to My Lou")

I'm so glad that God loves me,
God loves me, God loves me.
I'm so glad that God loves me,
He loves me all the time.
I'm so glad that God loves you,
God loves you, God loves you.
I'm so glad that God loves you,
He loves you all the time.

Sing this song to your child, replacing "you" with your child's name. Hold your child and sway or bounce while you sing. Clap your hands as you sing this song and encourage your child to clap with you. These first attempts at clapping are the beginning steps of learning rhythm. Say, **God cares for you when you play and when you sleep! I love you and care for you, too, when you are sleepy or playing!**

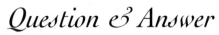

Question & Answer

Q: My child has begun crying when I leave her. I feel awful! What can I do?

A: When your child cries at separation time, first remember that it is a normal part of growth to know and to prefer one's parents! Recognize and accept both your own feelings of anxiety as well as those of your child. If you communicate comfort by your calm voice and relaxed body posture, your baby will likely "pick up" on these cues and calm down also. However, if your child still has a difficult time calming down, try:

Staying for awhile, then leaving for a few minutes and returning. Over a period of weeks, increase the length of your absences until both you and your child become more comfortable. Once you return, stay with your child for the remainder of the nursery program. More than one good-bye in a session is too hard on a baby or toddler.

Providing a "comfort object" (a familiar blanket, toy or pacifier) and creating a separation routine. Give the "comfort object" to your child and always say the same "good-bye" words. Try words such as, "I know you are sad. We will come back." or "It's hard to be away from you, but we will be back. Then we will give you a big hug!" By establishing a separation routine, your child will begin to understand what's coming next and will likely react with more calmness.

Pots and Pans

❖ Pots and pans are ready-made nesting toys. And they are interesting to the youngest children, because they have seen their parents use them.

❖ Set out several pots, pans and their lids on the floor near your child. If your child is enjoying playing with these, add wooden spoons and metal or plastic measuring cups to the array.

❖ In playing with the pots and pans, children will find out the different weights of these items, discover what fits in what, use a wooden spoon and pan as a ready-made drum or pretend to cook with them.

❖ Say, **We use pots and pans to cook with. I like to cook good food for you to eat. I like to care for you and give you good things to eat. God cares for you, too.**

Bonus Activity: Put pots and pans in a low cupboard. When you have a cooking project, set your child near this cupboard and open the doors. Let your child explore the contents of the cupboard as you cook. Make it possible for your child to see some of the stages of your cooking project.

"God sends children for another purpose than merely to keep up the race — to enlarge our hearts and to make us unselfish."
Mary Howitt

Return Address:

Postage
Stamp

TO: _____

_____

_____

Parent's Home Page

TIPS AND ACTIVITIES FOR PARENTS OF CHILDREN UNDER TWO

Do these activities with your child to continue the learning your child has experienced at church.

July

God Made Me

"God made me."
(See Job 33:4.)

This month we will help your child:

❖

enjoy success in using the body God made for him or her;

❖

begin to develop an awareness that God made his or her body.

Little Activities for Little People

Babies

❖ While feeding your baby, talk about the parts of the child's body. Say, **God made your mouth so you can eat.** Touch the child's mouth when you mention it. Repeat the word "mouth." Continue similarly, naming and touching fingers, toes, nose, ear, etc.

❖ During bath time, comment on the things that God made and the child's activities. Say, **It feels good to touch the warm water. God made water. Your hands and legs are in the water. God made your hands and legs. God made you!**

Toddlers

❖ Touch your nose and say, **This is my nose. Where is Jeremy's nose?** If your child is unable to touch his or her own nose, gently touch your child's nose. Say, **There's your nose!** Repeat the sequence several times, then move to another body part. As your child touches each part of his body, tell him or her that God made it. Continue as long as your child is responding with interest.

❖ Compare the facial and body features of a doll or stuffed animal with those of your child.

❖ Point to facial and body features of people pictured in magazines and books. Ask the child to touch his or her own nose, ears, chin, etc.

DO iT!

God Made

God made my ears.
God made my nose.
God made my fingers.
God made my toes.
God made my eyes.
They're both open wide.
God made my mouth
with a tongue inside!

Say and do this finger play with your child frequently. Connect the words of the finger play to your child's activity. For example, if your child is playing with a toy say, **God made your fingers to play with toys.** Then repeat the finger play, pointing to or gently touching the named body parts. Pray, **Thank You, God, for making my child.** Use your child's name when you pray for him or her.

SiNG iT!

I Have Two Eyes

(Tune: "Pop Goes the Weasel")

I have two eyes.
I have two ears.
I have two hands and feet.
I have one mouth
and one little nose,
but, oh, so many fingers and toes!

Sing this song to your child while he or she is playing. Hold a doll or stuffed animal and point to the body parts you are singing about. Ask your child to point to his or her body parts as you name them. Take off your shoes and your child's shoes and wiggle toes for the last line of the song. Sometimes a child will listen to the song, doing nothing but waiting to do the very last motion or sound, if it is particularly satisfying to him or her. If your child is interested, sing the song several times to allow time for him or her to respond.

Your Child Is Learning

Do you realize how intensely your young child hungers to learn? Watch as he or she explores the house from corner to corner. Your child probably delights in unwinding the toilet paper, pulling out the pots and pans, eating the dog food or feeling the texture of the screen door.

Children learn the way God designed them to learn—from their everyday experiences. And it's important for parents to know how to participate in the process.

Children learn a significant part of their fundamental life skills through play activities. Their physical development is strengthened, refined and improved through climbing, crawling, running, throwing, etc. Their mental development progresses through stacking, manipulating and experimenting with the everyday objects around them. Their social development is enhanced as they learn to play near others.

Recognize that each child is unique in the way he or she develops and learns. Don't fall into the worrisome trap of comparing one baby's development with another's, for every one of them will develop differently! Relax and enjoy your child's individual pace.

Exploring, manipulating, inquiring, creating, putting together, taking apart, stacking up, knocking down, tasting, smelling, feeling, looking, listening—what a potential rests in your child! That potential can be released, guided and encouraged by a loving parent. There is no thrill like being able to share with God in the growth and development of a child!

A Nature Experience

❖ Even the youngest child will be fascinated with living creatures. If you have ever wanted to have an aquarium, terrarium, or caged pet, get it now. If you don't want the expense or ongoing upkeep of one of the previous suggestions, do the following: Punch holes in the lid of a clear jar. Then simply collect a bug or two and some of the dirt and leaves where you found the bugs. Put the bugs, leaves and dirt in the jar and secure the lid.

❖ Hold your child in your lap and let him or her watch the bugs in the jar. Your child will be fascinated with the colors and the movement he or she observes. Be sure to place the jar where your child can get to it only when you are present. After your child has had sufficient time observing, let your child watch you return the bugs to the outdoors.

"Children have more need of models than of critics."

Joseph Joubert

Return Address:

Postage Stamp

TO: _____

_____

_____

Parent's Home Page

TIPS AND ACTIVITIES FOR PARENTS OF CHILDREN UNDER TWO

Do these activities with your child to continue the learning your child has experienced at church.

August

God Gives Me Friends

"Love each other."
(John 15:12.)

This month we will help your child:

❖

enjoy happy encounters with other children at church;

❖

associate God with happy experiences with others.

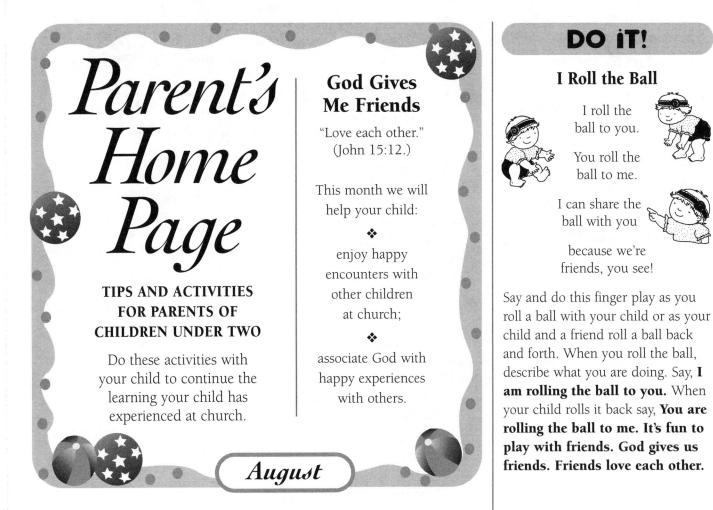

DO iT!

I Roll the Ball

I roll the ball to you.

You roll the ball to me.

I can share the ball with you

because we're friends, you see!

Say and do this finger play as you roll a ball with your child or as your child and a friend roll a ball back and forth. When you roll the ball, describe what you are doing. Say, **I am rolling the ball to you.** When your child rolls it back say, **You are rolling the ball to me. It's fun to play with friends. God gives us friends. Friends love each other.**

Little Activities for Little People

Babies

❖ One of the first words a baby learns to recognize is his or her own name. Toward the end of the first year, a baby will sometimes show signs of having heard his or her name in the middle of normal conversation. Babies also enjoy hearing their names in a song. Almost any simple children's song can be easily adapted to include your child's name.

❖ A cool breeze is always refreshing in August. Open a window or simply blow gently on your baby's arm, cheek or hair to give your child a refreshing treat.

Toddlers

❖ When holding your toddler in your lap, gently and briefly tickle his or her legs or feet. If your child shows enjoyment, join in the laughter. Talk about your enjoyment in playing with your child.

❖ Do you have any clean, old clothes your toddler can use for "dressing up"? A hat, loose-fitting shirts or blouses, purses and scarves are fun for starters. A lightweight pair of your shoes or castoffs from an older child may also be included. Dress-up is much more fun when two are involved, so try on the hat yourself before putting it on your child. Provide a mirror in which you can admire yourselves. If your child resists the strange garments, that is all right, too. Stay with a game only as long as it is fun for both of you.

SiNG iT!

Friends

(Tune: "The Farmer in the Dell")

We can smile and wave.
We can smile and wave.
Because it's fun to be with friends,
we can smile and wave.

Sing this song as you play with your child or as your child plays alongside another child. Smile at your child. Point to your smile. Say, **I am smiling at you. I like to see you smile. Friends smile at each other.** Wave to your child. Say, **I am waving to you. I like to see you wave, too.** Sing the song several times to give your child time to smile or wave or anticipate what you will do.

Question & Answer

Q: Is "time out" a good way to correct my child's misbehavior?

A: If you mean by "time out" forcing a child to sit alone, not allowing him or her to express strong feelings or talk with anyone, and using a timer to monitor the time instead of a caring person, then "time out" is not a good way to help a child learn how to behave. The child has simply been punished, not helped to learn how to behave in an acceptable way.

To help a child learn to behave acceptably, think about what you want the child to do. Then carefully and calmly explain to the child what is expected . Here are some examples of helpful conversation:

❖ **When I see you up on the table, I feel afraid because you could fall down and hurt yourself. I will not let you walk on the table because you could get hurt.** Then gently but firmly put the child on the floor.

❖ **I'm moving you away from baby Zachary. You need to remember to pat him gently.** Then move the child away from the baby. Some children will immediately repeat the previous misbehavior. When this happens say, **I can see that you still need to play away from the baby. I will move baby Zachary. You are still not patting him gently.**

If you are consistent and gentle, communicating and demonstrating what is expected, your child will learn what is acceptable.

Sprinkle Water Everywhere!

❖ Watering plants with you is a fun activity for a young child on a warm summer day.

❖ You will need a large plastic bottle. Use a scissors to poke nine holes in the bottom of the bottle (three rows of three holes each).

❖ Bring your toddler outside and fill the bottle with water.

❖ Ask your child to sprinkle the grass and flowers with water. Praise your child whenever he or she succeeds in following your directions.

❖ If it is a hot day, you and your child can take off your shoes and socks. Let your child sprinkle water on your feet. Sing the following song to the tune of "Skip, Skip, Skip to My Lou."

Sprinkle, sprinkle water here.

Sprinkle, sprinkle water there.

Sprinkle, sprinkle water here.

Sprinkle water everywhere!

Little children

are both

our reasons

and our excuses

to be playful.

Return Address:

Postage
Stamp

TO: _____

_____

_____

Parent's Home Page

TIPS AND ACTIVITIES FOR PARENTS OF CHILDREN UNDER TWO

Do these activities with your child to continue the learning your child has experienced at church.

September

I See God's Love at Church

"I like to come to church." (See Psalm 122:1.)

This month we will help your child:

❖

feel secure and comfortable at church as we demonstrate God's love to him or her;

❖

begin to associate God and Jesus with loving people and enjoyable activities.

Little Activities for Little People

Babies

❖ Getting out the door to church with baby, diaper bag and bottle can be hectic! Once you're in the car, however, help ease everyone's stressful feelings by saying the finger play poem, "I Come In," or singing "It's Fun to Go to Church." Even a few moments of quiet conversation and cuddling when you arrive at church will help your baby (and you!) to relax and feel secure, lessening the child's uneasiness at being separated from you.

❖ Hold your baby while looking at a sturdy book picturing families. Point to and name each family member, relating the people in the picture to your family. Say, **Samantha, here's a picture of a brother. You have a brother, too. His name is Andrew. God loves you, and God loves Andrew.**

Toddlers

❖ Expect your child to use dolls or stuffed animals in a variety of ways. Dolls are likely to be dragged, pulled, sat on or ignored. When a doll is being loved and cared for, comment, **Sarah, you are hugging that doll just like I hug you. I love you.** Sing a lullaby as your child hugs or rocks the doll. A cassette or CD of both quiet and active songs is a good resource to have.

❖ Keep your child's toys on a low shelf or on the floor. Toys that are being ignored should be stored. Toddlers need open space more than they need a vast array of toys. While your child is playing say, **You're having fun playing with your blocks. You have fun playing with toys at our church, too. I'm glad to go to church with you. God loves us.**

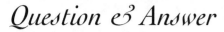
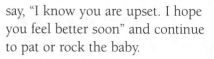

Question & Answer

Q: Why do babies cry and what can we do when they cry?

A: It's important to remember that crying is a baby's first language. Here are a few things to remember:

When a baby's cries are met with a loving response, it teaches the baby that language (in this case, crying) works. This is the foundation of all language development.

All healthy babies cry. (We would worry if they didn't!) The cries may say, "I'm hungry" or "I'm wet" or "I'm in pain." Crying can also be a way of releasing tension or a way of saying, "I'm overstimulated," expressing a need for a quiet place with softer light and no stimulating adult attention. Sometimes the cry means "I'm lonely." Some babies also learn to "call" before they cry! When you respond before the baby goes into a full-blown cry, he or she will call more often and cry less.

While it takes time to learn the meanings of your baby's crying language, you will soon know how to interpret his or her language.

There will be times when your baby cries for no apparent reason. Sometimes, the harder you try to stop a baby's crying, the more tension you communicate and the more anxious the child becomes! However, always do your best to listen to your baby's language and talk back to him or her, even if (after you've tried everything!) you simply say, "I know you are upset. I hope you feel better soon" and continue to pat or rock the baby.

It is not only what you do when the baby cries, but what you do when he or she is NOT crying that can help your infant learn to feel secure. When you respond quickly and consistently to your child's expressions (crying or other "language") and provide a predictable daily routine, he or she will feel more secure and thus be better able to handle minor upsets.

Box Wagon

❖ Cover a clean shoe box with colorful adhesive paper. Punch a hole in the end of box near the top. Slip a 2-foot (60-cm) length of sturdy cord through the hole. Knot cord inside the box and also at pulling end.

❖ Help your child fill the wagon with some favorite toys or a snack and go for a short walk, pulling the wagon. Play with your child or eat the snack together.

"Children have never been very good at listening to their elders, but they have never failed to imitate them."
James Baldwin

Return Address:

Postage
Stamp

TO: _____

_____

_____

Parent's Home Page

TIPS AND ACTIVITIES FOR PARENTS OF CHILDREN UNDER TWO

Do these activities with your child to continue the learning your child has experienced at church.

October

Jesus Loves Children

"Jesus loves the children."
(See Mark 10:16.)

This month we will help your child:

❖

develop an awareness of the name of Jesus and associate Him with being loved;

❖

enjoy the activities provided.

DO IT!

Jesus Loves Us All

Who are the children Jesus loves?

Jesus loves us all!

He loves us when we clap;

He loves us when we crawl.

He loves us when we walk;

He loves us when we fall.

Who are the children Jesus loves?

Jesus loves us all.

Jesus loves you!

Show your child a picture of Jesus from a child's Bible story book (available at most bookstores). Point to Jesus and say His name. Tell your child that Jesus loves every child. Say the finger play, making the motions with your fingers. If your child is interested, repeat the finger play slowly and encourage him or her to act out the actions with you by clapping, crawling, walking and plopping down on the floor. Say your child's name in the last line of the finger play.

SING IT!

Each Little Child

(Tune: "Mary Had a Little Lamb")

Jesus loves each little child,
little child, little child.
Jesus loves each little child.
He loves you, yes, He does.

Sing this song to your child, inserting your child's name in place of "each little child." Show your child a picture of Jesus. Say, **Jesus loves you!** Sing the song. Point to Jesus when you sing His name. Point to your child when you sing his or her name.

Little Activities for Little People

Babies

❖ Your baby will enjoy pushing his or her feet against your hands. Talk with and encourage your baby about his or her leg movement. Say, **Your feet are pushing my hands. You are getting very strong! Jesus loves you!** While your baby is having fun moving his or her legs, your baby will also be growing in understanding language.

❖ Babies enjoy looking at books with pictures of familiar items. Since babies like to not only study the pictures but also taste and handle the pages, it's important to have durable, washable books for your baby. As you enjoy a book with your baby, point to and describe what your child sees. For instance, **I see the yellow truck. Here's the blue bird.**

Toddlers

❖ When your toddler plays near another toddler, make sure you have several toys available. Children at this age play side by side in their own little worlds—unless one has a toy that another just has to have! Having several interesting toys helps solve this problem. Sharing is a concept yet to be learned by toddlers.

❖ Help your child safely explore a variety of seasonal items: pumpkin, Indian corn, squash, fall leaves. Talk with your child about the variety of colors and textures. Say, **Look at the colors of these leaves. I see an orange leaf. I see a yellow leaf. God made leaves. God loves you.**

Talking with Your Child Brings Results

One of the most amazing accomplishments of the entire human life span takes place by the age of three years: learning to understand almost all normal conversation. At birth, all words are meaningless. But within 36 months, the child has broken the code!

Long before a child can speak, he or she can grasp the general meaning of words spoken or sung. Usually by the eighth month, a child can understand his or her first word; by the child's first birthday, several dozen words have meaning for him or her. However, a child is not likely to say his or her first words until he or she is several months older. This gap between understanding and speaking often causes parents to talk very little to a child, thereby delaying speech development. Extensive research has shown that one of the most helpful things parents can do to stimulate intellectual and social growth is to talk with their baby. Dr. Burton White of Harvard University offers these suggestions for talking with children in their first two years of life:

❖ Whenever you care for your baby—feeding, changing, comforting or playing—talk to him or her. Add a smile to your voice. This interaction builds a strong connection in the baby's mind between your presence, your voice and the good feeling of being cared for.

❖ A baby can easily distinguish his or her mother's voice from other voices and often responds with smiles and focused attention.

❖ Talk frequently to your child, describing your actions and feelings, as well as the child's actions and responses. Talk about the here and now: the dishes you are putting on the table, the toy the baby is playing with.

❖ Read very simple stories to your baby just before he or she falls asleep. Story reading builds a close relationship between parent and child.

Flashlight Games

❖ Give your child a flashlight. Name the things your child shines the light on. Say, **You are shining the light on (the table).** With an older toddler, you may call out the name of a familiar object in the room. Ask your child to shine his or her light on the object.

❖ Play tag with flashlights. Use the beam of your own flashlight to catch your child's flashlight beam. Continue as long as your child shows interest.

"The first essential in a happy Christian home is that love must be practiced." **Billy Graham**

Return Address:

Postage Stamp

TO: _____

_____

_____

Parent's Home Page

TIPS AND ACTIVITIES FOR PARENTS OF CHILDREN UNDER TWO

Do these activities with your child to continue the learning your child has experienced at church.

November

God Gives Me Food

"God gives us food." (See Genesis 1:29.)

This month we will help your child:

❖

develop an awareness that God made food;

❖

enjoy eating food with teachers and other children. (Alert nursery staff of any food allergies your child has.)

DO iT!

My Food

This is my nose
to smell my cracker.
These are my eyes
to see my cracker.
These are my hands
to hold my cracker.
This is my tongue
to taste my cracker.
Thank You, God,
for my cracker.

Do this finger play with your child before giving him or her a snack. If your child is interested in what you are doing, ask, **Where is your nose? Where is my nose?** Watch your child point to the noses. Then do the whole finger play, encouraging your child to do it with you. While your child is eating his or her snack, do the finger play again. (If you are having a different snack than crackers, use the name of your snack in the finger play instead of crackers.)

Little Activities for Little People

Babies

❖ Move a toy slowly in front of a baby. As the baby tracks the movement with his or her eyes or reaches for the toy, stop the movement briefly, then begin again. As you play with the baby, talk about the toy and the baby's movements. Say, **I like to play with you and take care of you. God cares about you, too.**

❖ As your baby touches a soft doll or stuffed animal say, **The doll is soft. You feel soft, too.** Place the doll next to your baby or in his or her arms. **Daniel loves this soft lamb. I love Daniel.** Hug and cuddle your baby to provide an atmosphere of security and love.

Toddlers

❖ At your child's eye level, post magazine pictures of food and of people eating. (For safety, attach pictures with tape.) Talk about the pictured food. Say, **God gives us good food to eat.** Then pray, **Thank You, God, for bananas.**

❖ Observe how your child uses a toy. Toddlers are often more interest in the color, shape and texture of a toy than in its intended purpose. Your efforts to show how a toy is used are often met with indifference. That's OK. Your child's use of the toy fits his or her own need at the moment.

SiNG iT!

I Thank God

(Tune: "Mulberry Bush")

Apples taste so good to me,
so good to me, so good to me.
Apples taste so good to me.
I thank God for my food.

Show your toddler an apple. Say, **Is this an apple or a banana?** Wait for his or her answer. **Are apples red or blue?** Give your child a chance to respond, then say, **These apples are red!** Sing this song with your toddler. Do the motion of rubbing the tummy when saying the words "so good to me." Serve your child an apple. (When having a different snack than apples, sing this song about the snack you are having—bananas, pears, crackers, etc.)

Question & Answer

Q: What do I do when my toddler tries to take a toy from another child?

A: Parents need to understand that toddlers don't know how to share yet. This is not just a result of human nature; it's also that a toddler cannot reason beyond "If I want it, it's mine!"

Respond first by identifying the child's feelings. **It looks like you want Monica's truck.** Then suggest a solution by saying, **Monica wants to play with her truck right now. Look! Here is another truck to play with. Here is a yellow dump truck. Let's put some blocks in the truck.** Offering a substitute item often will distract a toddler, especially if you interest the child in playing with the item by playing with it yourself. Offering another choice often helps, too. **Would you like to play with the dump truck or with this boat? The boat has a horn. Listen!**

Your child may become interested in the new toy; however, he or she may want Monica's truck and only Monica's truck will do! In this case your child will probably scream, cry or try to take the truck again. Simply respond, **You cannot take Monica's truck away from her. It's Monica's turn with the truck.** Offer an alternative again. **We can play with this boat.** Be gentle, but do not allow your child to take the truck. If your child screams, identify his or her feelings again and give an option by saying, **Sounds like you are upset. Let me know when you're finished screaming. Then we'll find a new toy to play with.** As soon as the child is calm, quickly respond with a new toy or an activity. This helps reinforce to the child that his or her calming down has a positive benefit.

If the child continues screaming or grabbing, simply remove the child from the toy area. **I can see you need to come and rock with me. It will help you calm down.**

Jell-O Finger Painting

❖ Make two bowls of Jell-O in different colors. Place paper in front of your child and put a glob of each color of Jell-O on the paper. Spread and swirl the Jell-O like finger paint. Encourage your child to touch and play with the Jell-O, too. Say, **You're painting with the red Jell-O. The Jell-O feels smooth. It feels cold on your fingers.** Describe your child's actions as he or she plays with the Jell-O. **We can eat this Jell-O. It tastes good. God gives us food to eat.**

❖ Let your child continue painting with the Jell-O as long as he or she is interested, giving the child more Jell-O and sheets of paper as needed.

"That energy which makes a child hard to manage is the energy which afterward makes him a manager of life."
Henry Ward Beecher

Return Address:

Postage Stamp

TO: _____

_____

_____

Parent's Home Page

TIPS AND ACTIVITIES FOR PARENTS OF CHILDREN UNDER TWO

Do these activities with your child to continue the learning your child has experienced at church.

Jesus Was a Baby

"His name is Jesus." (See Luke 1:31.)

This month we will help your child:

❖

show interest in pictures, conversation and songs about baby Jesus;

❖

receive personal attention and love as teachers seek to show Jesus' love in ways a child understands.

December

Little Activities for Little People

Babies

❖ Securely fasten several large jingle bells to cradle gym strap. Each pull on the gym will reward your baby with an instant and cheerful ringing.

If your baby is too young to have the coordination to grab the cradle gym, he or she can still make it jiggle. With your hand, tap the mattress near your baby's feet. The objects hanging from the cradle gym will move. Gently take your baby's feet and tap them on the mattress to create the same motion.

❖ Collect several Christmas cards picturing baby Jesus. Hold your baby in your lap to look at the cards. Talk about the pictures. Say, **See the baby. The baby is sleeping. When Jesus was a baby, His mother and father took good care of Him. We're glad Jesus was born.**

Toddlers

❖ Provide items such as large cardboard cartons (with staples removed) for your child to crawl through. As your child starts through one end of the tunnel, look in the other end and call his or her name. Say, **Emmy, you are growing big. You can crawl through the tunnel. The Bible says that baby Jesus grew up, too.**

❖ Your child will undoubtedly be interested in your home's seasonal decorations. Place several pinecones and fresh evergreen boughs on a low table where your child can touch them. Avoid poisonous plants such as poinsettia and holly berries. As your child touches and smells the items, with your supervision, talk about baby Jesus. Say, **We want our house to look pretty to show how happy we are that baby Jesus was born. We love Jesus.**

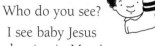

DO IT!

Look into the Stable

Look into the stable now.

Who do you see?
I see baby Jesus
sleeping in Mary's arms.

Look into the stable now.
What do you hear?
I hear baby Jesus
laughing in Joseph's arms.

Before doing this finger play, show your child a picture of baby Jesus in the manger from a story book or Christmas card. Or purchase a nativity scene (be certain it is unbreakable and has large pieces) for your child to look at and handle. Then do the finger play with your child. If your child is interested in what you are doing, ask, **How do you rock a baby?** Let your child show you how by pretending to rock a baby. **Show me how a baby laughs.** Enjoy and imitate your child's sounds. **It's fun to laugh together. We're happy because Jesus was born. We love Jesus.**

SING IT!

Happy Birthday, Jesus!

(Tune: "Jesus Loves Me")

It's Jesus' birthday, time to sing!
Shake the bells and make them ring.
Let's all sing a happy song.
Bring your drums and march along.

Happy birthday, Jesus,
Happy birthday, Jesus,
Happy birthday, Jesus.
We sing this happy song.

Sing this song and shake jingle bells. When your child shows interest, give him or her a child-safe rhythm instrument to play as you sing. Say, **It's fun to sing about Jesus! I'm glad Jesus was born.**

Looking Back

For little children, the days following Christmas are usually as much a part of Christmas as were the days preceding this joyous Christian festival.

As the year reaches its final days, take time to look back over these past months to sort out the special moments—those highlights of happy times and accomplishments for your little one. Set aside a time to look at the baby book or journal, noting the milestones of this past year. And take a few moments to thank God specifically for each of these milestones!

As the mother of Jesus watched the miraculous events surrounding the birth of her baby, she realized the importance of storing up memories that would often return to her throughout her lifetime. In one of the most appealing moments of motherhood in Scripture, Luke 2:19 relates, "But Mary kept all these things, and pondered them in her heart" (*KJV*).

As you move into a new year, remember often this is your child's most formative period of his or her entire life. By the time your little one is around the age of five, his or her basic life pattern of attitudes and responses will probably be established. What a very short time to instill the lifetime patterns that you wish him or her to develop! God has entrusted this tiny life to you to mold—a blessed responsibility.

As you guide and encourage your child's physical, mental and spiritual growth, you may understand anew and relate your experiences to those of Mary—"but his mother kept all these sayings in her heart. And Jesus increased in wisdom and stature, and in favour with God and man" (Luke 2:51,52, *KJV*).

Christmas Book

❖ Cut off the covers of six to eight similarly-sized Christmas cards. Staple them together, forming a book. Cover staples with electrical tape.

❖ Give the book to your child as his or her special Christmas book. Talk about the story of Jesus' birth as your child looks at the pictures. Continue as your child shows interest.

"We had from childhood not only the experience of love and truth common to all family life, but the idea of them embodied in the person of Jesus, a picture always present to our imagination as well as our feelings."
Joyce Cary

Return Address:

Postage Stamp

TO: _____

_____

_____

Parent's Home Page

TIPS AND ACTIVITIES FOR PARENTS OF CHILDREN UNDER TWO

Do these activities with your child to continue the learning your child has experienced at church.

January

God Helps Me to Grow

"God made us."
(See Malachi 2:10.)

This month we will help your child:

❖

associate new accomplishments with God and Jesus;

❖

enjoy the success of new accomplishments.

DO iT!

I'm Growing

When I was a baby,
I was very, very small.
Now I'm growing older.
I'm growing big and tall.

When I was a baby,
I could only crawl.
Now I can walk, and I can jump.
But, sometimes, down I fall!

Say and do this finger play with your child. Use your child's name instead of "I." Infants and toddlers will enjoy the sounds and actions, although they will not be able to do the finger play with you yet. Acting out the poem as you say it will also be enjoyable for your child. Encourage a toddler to crawl with you or to gently sit down.

SiNG iT!

I Am Growing

(Tune: "Are You Sleeping?")

I am growing.
I am growing.
Yes, I am.
Yes, I am.
One time I was smaller.
Now I am much taller.
Watch me grow.
Watch me grow.

Sing this song to your child as you rock, feed, dress or play with him or her. Show your child a picture of him- or herself when younger and smaller. Talk about how much bigger he or she has grown. **Lindsay, you're growing! You've learned to sit up, and now you're learning to crawl. God made you, and He helps you grow.** Children will begin to associate God's care with their growth and new accomplishments.

Little Activities for Little People

Babies

❖ Take advantage of nature's beautiful "mobiles"—the quiet floating of falling snow; leaves and branches dancing in the wind or rain trickling down a windowpane. Hold your baby near a window and comment on what you see. **Look at the branches blowing in the wind. God made the wind. God made the leaves. God made you! God is helping you grow!**

❖ Rocking your baby or preparing him or her for a nap can be a special "I love you" time. **You're growing, Zachary. Sometimes you like to rest. Sometimes you like to play. God loves you when you rest or play.** Having a favorite blanket or toy to hold helps most children relax. Play a quiet song from a children's cassette or CD.

Toddlers

❖ Touch your nose and say, **This is my nose. Where is your nose?** If your child is unable to touch his or her own nose, gently take your child's hand and touch it to his or her nose. Say, **There's your nose!** Repeat the sequence several times, then move on to another body part, saying, **God made your ears. God made your fingers. God made all of you—and you are growing!** Continue as long as your child is responding with interest.

❖ Rocking can be a delightful experience when a little one is alert and happy. Even the most active child will enjoy a few moments in your lap looking at a book or playing with a toy. Gentle and brief moments of tickling are also great fun and good introductions to singing "I Am Growing" or doing the finger play "I'm Growing."

Question & Answer

Q: My toddler is fascinated by television. He loves to watch it. Should I be concerned about any possible ill effects?

A: There is significant evidence that toddlers have a great need to explore their surroundings and manipulate objects in order to nurture their curiosity and stimulate their intelligence. If you are willing to allow your toddler to explore and manipulate each button on your TV and VCR, he or she will probably quickly learn how to operate the

machines. There's some real learning value in that—but the question is, do you want your child to be able to turn on the TV at will? On the other hand, children who spend time sitting and watching rather than moving and doing are likely to be slowed in their mental development. They also will be more likely to become sedentary (and often overweight) physically as they grow older. But most important, television simply offers a toddler very little in comparison with firsthand interactions with people and objects. Real life is a hands-on experience that teaches far more than TV, no matter how highly-touted the "educational" quality of a show.

If your child must watch, limit your child's exposure. Do your best to make viewing a special event done with an adult (complete with a time to talk about the show), rather than using it as an electronic baby-sitter.

The following comment from a parent, Jack Wiens, puts another light on the subject: "The thing that nags at me when I watch a lot of television is not so much what TV does to me and my family, but what it keeps us from doing. Things like...

- ❖ talking and listening to each other
- ❖ looking at each other
- ❖ hugging, holding, tickling, dancing
- ❖ reading, thinking
- ❖ painting, building, creating
- ❖ exercising, playing, singing."

Shakers

- ❖ Wash empty plastic soda bottles and caps thoroughly, inside and out. Pour a handful of macaroni, beans, hard candy, etc. into the bottle. Coat the inside of the cap with superglue and close tightly. When the cap is dry, cover cap seam completely with duct tape.

- ❖ Use the shakers as you listen to music with your child. Say, **What do you hear? I like to listen to music. It is fun to shake my shaker.** Continue playing with shakers as long as your child shows interest.

"Blessed be childhood, which brings down something of heaven into the midst of our rough earthliness."
Henri Amiel

Return Address:

Postage Stamp

TO: _____

_____

_____

Parent's Home Page

TIPS AND ACTIVITIES FOR PARENTS OF CHILDREN UNDER TWO

Do these activities with your child to continue the learning your child has experienced at church.

My Family Loves Me

"God gives us families." (See Psalm 68:6.)

This month we will help your child:

❖

to begin to associate God and Jesus with loving people at home and at church;

❖

respond to demonstrations of affection.

February

Little Activities for Little People

Babies

❖ Encourage your child's activity with smiles and words of approval. Stimulate your baby to reach or crawl by holding an attractive toy slightly beyond easy reach. Hold the toy steady so your child can succeed in reaching it. Next time, make the task slightly more challenging. Do not tease your child by continuing to move the toy when he or she moves toward it.

❖ When bathing your child say, **I like to give you a bath and take care of you. I love you. God loves you, too. God gives us families so we have people to take care of us.**

Toddlers

❖ If singing to your toddler makes you feel self-conscious, here is a cure: keep singing! The more you sing, the more natural it will seem, even if musical talent is not one of your strengths. Just keep your attention on your child and you will soon be enjoying the music as much as your child is. And you will probably never have a more appreciative audience!

❖ Put a small amount of water in a plastic dish pan or baby tub. With your child, wash a baby doll in the water, then dry it with a towel. Say, **Luis, you are taking good care of this baby. Your grandma takes good care of you, too. God made your grandma to care for you. Grandma loves you, and I love you, too.** Your child may also enjoy wrapping the doll in a blanket and rocking the doll.

DO iT!

Families

We all live in families,

you and me.

What kinds of families?

Let me see!

Tall ones and short ones;

big ones and small ones.

We all live in families,

you and me.

Say and do this finger play with your child. Use your child's name instead of "you." Draw your child's attention to a photo of your family and other pictures of families as you say and do this finger play.

SiNG iT!

My Family

(Tune: "Row, Row, Row Your Boat")

Thank, thank, thank You, God, for my family!

God made families to love and care for you and me!

Sing this song to your child as he or she plays with a doll, toy dishes or household items. Talk about ways you show love to your child. Say, **I give you good things to eat because I love you. I play with you because I love you. I'm glad we're a family together. God gives us families.** Your child will begin to develop an awareness of God being associated with the love he or she experiences with you at home.

Teaching by Example

Scripture makes it clear that it is God's plan for parents to be responsible for the spiritual training and nurture of their children. There are two basic ways to "bring children up in the training and instruction of the Lord"—by example, and by direct instruction and teaching. For children under two, teaching by example is the more effective method.

❖ We can never teach our children to walk in God's ways by merely telling them that they should. We must demonstrate with our lives the reality of Christianity.

❖ Even secular psychologists recognize the power of human behavior to communicate values. J.A. Hadfield, a British psychologist who observed the growth patterns of thousands of children, made the following observation: "We see that it is by a perfectly natural process that the child develops standards of behavior and a moral sense. If you never taught a child one single moral maxim, he would nevertheless develop moral—or immoral—standards of right and wrong by the process of identification."

❖ The most powerful way to teach young children is by parental example. If we show that we enjoy being with our children, if our children feel comfortable with us, they naturally—particularly as they enter the third year of life—want to be like us. They will talk like us and even their tone of voice will sound like ours. If we're loud and boisterous and yell a lot, our children will do the same. If we are sensitive, honest and understanding, they will learn to live by those values. Putting it simply, if we want our children to reflect Jesus Christ in their lifestyle, we must be good examples of Jesus Christ.

Gene Getz, Pastor and Author

Scribbling

❖ Young children first write by swinging their arms up and down, back and forth, and by jabbing and poking at the paper. This scribbling helps develop the hand-eye coordination that will be needed for drawing and writing.

❖ Provide plenty of paper when your child is interested in scribbling. Let your child use one material at a time. He or she will enjoy contrasting materials such as a red marker on white paper or a black crayon on yellow paper. Talk to your child about the colors he or she is using. Say, **I see you are coloring with the blue crayon. You're making a lot of blue marks.**

"There is no vocabulary
For love within a family,
*   love that's lived in*
But not looked at, love
*   within the light of which*
All else is seen, the love
*   within which*
All other love finds speech.
This love is silent."
*   T.S. Eliot*

Return Address:

Postage
Stamp

TO: _____

_____

_____

Parent's Home Page

TIPS AND ACTIVITIES FOR PARENTS OF CHILDREN UNDER TWO

Do these activities with your child to continue the learning your child has experienced at church.

Jesus Loves Me

"Jesus loves us."
(See Revelation 1:5.)

This month we will help your child:

❖

enjoy activities in which teachers talk lovingly of Jesus;

❖

frequently hear the words "Jesus loves us."

March

Little Activities for Little People

Babies

❖ When adults play with a baby, they may overwhelm the child. Adults can do so many things that the baby cannot, it's easy for the adult to become a performer while the baby merely watches. Your child's development will be better served if you remember to let your child set the pace for awhile, with you imitating your child's actions.

❖ Provide interesting textures for your baby to feel: a furry stuffed animal, a cardboard book, a soft blanket, your hand or arm. comment, **You can feel the soft blanket, Anna. Jesus loves you, Anna. I'm glad Jesus loves us.**

Toddlers

❖ Give your child a scarf or tie to wave in the air as you play a lively song on a cassette or CD. Wave a scarf or tie, too. Comment, **We're having fun playing. Jesus loves you when you play. Jesus loves you all the time!**

❖ When your child has difficulty fitting a shape into a shape-sorter, give some assistance without robbing your child of the accomplishment of putting the piece in by him- or herself. You may point to the place where the piece goes, asking, **Do you think it goes here?** You may also substitute an easier piece for your child to try. When your child puts a piece in the correct place, praise his or her effort. **Jessie, you put the fire engine piece into the puzzle. Good for you!**

YEAR B   ©1997 by Gospel Light. • Permission to photocopy granted. • Nursery Smart Pages • 177

DO iT!

Day and Night

When the sun is in the sky,

Jesus loves me.

When the stars are way up high,

Jesus loves me.

In the day and in the night,

while I play and then sleep tight,

Jesus loves me.

Say and do this finger play with your child. Use the child's name instead of "I" and "me." Take your child outside on a sunny day and again on a starry evening and do this finger play each time. Do this finger play with your child at nap time or bedtime or when he or she is having fun playing.

SiNG iT!

Yes, Jesus Loves You

(Tune: Refrain to "Jesus Loves Me")

Yes, Jesus loves you.

Yes, Jesus loves you.

Yes, Jesus loves you!

The Bible tells us so.

Show your child a Bible. Say, **This book is called the Bible. The Bible tells us that Jesus loves us. Jesus loves you.** Then sing the song with your child. Use your child's name instead of "you." This song can be sung while you rock or bounce your child or hold hands. Finish each song by reminding your child of your love for him or her.

Question & Answer

Q: How can I best prepare my baby-sitter to care for my child?

A: Be sure to provide your baby-sitter with some basic guidelines.

❖ Start with what you plan to pay. Talk to other parents to see what is normally paid. Be sure the baby-sitter knows what you will pay before he or she agrees to work for you.

❖ Demonstrate and explain basic care routines which are familiar for your child such as feeding, changing, preparing for bed. If your sitter is new, schedule an hour or two when he or she can practice while you are there. Pay the sitter for the time, as well!

❖ Provide materials your sitter can use in playing with your baby. Describe some of your baby's favorite activities.

❖ Provide written guidelines, including the schedule you want followed, rules of importance to you and information of what to do in case of a problem. Provide phone numbers where you can be reached; also numbers of a responsible adult as well as police and fire departments.

❖ Indicate the time you will return. Then return on time.

Q: How can I best prepare my child for the baby-sitter?

A: If your child has never been cared for by this sitter, inviting the sitter over for some paid "practice time" will not only benefit the sitter and satisfy your mind but will also help your baby build familiarity with the sitter. When the sitter is a familiar person, your child will likely adjust better when the care time comes.

Before a sitter arrives, talk with your child about the sitter's arrival. Tell your child where you will be going and that you will be coming back. Even if your child is too young to respond to your words, he or she will be comforted by the attention and the tone of your voice.

A child will also benefit by your establishing a "good-bye" routine for every parting, even before you have selected a sitter. Using the same words, songs or poems along with hugs and kisses every time you part from your child will help him or her make sense of what's coming next, helping the child remain calm.

Sand Play

❖ Sandboxes aren't just for the summer. Children love to pour and manipulate all kinds of materials. Make a small indoor sandbox using a small plastic tub or baby bath. Supply strainers, funnels, plastic containers and shovels. Instead of sand you may want to use puffed rice or other cereal so your child can safely eat the "sand."

❖ Say, **You are playing with the sand. We can pour the sand together. I like to play in the sand with you!** Continue playing with sand as long as your child shows interest.

"Give a little love to a child, and you get a great deal back."
John Ruskin

Return Address:

Postage Stamp

TO: _____

_____

_____

Parent's Home Page

TIPS AND ACTIVITIES FOR PARENTS OF CHILDREN UNDER TWO

Do these activities with your child to continue the learning your child has experienced at church.

April

God Makes Growing Things

"God made everything."
(See Genesis 1:1.)

This month we will help your child:

❖

associate God with items of His creation;

❖

enjoy exploring items God has made.

Little Activities for Little People

Babies

❖ Help your baby touch the leaves of growing plants. Say, **God made the leaves. God made everything.**

❖ When feeding your baby, talk to the baby about growing. Say, **You're drinking good milk. God made milk. God made you.**

❖ Observe your baby's actions when lying in a crib or on the floor. Comment on what the baby is doing. **Rebekah, you are kicking your legs. God made your legs. God made you.** Repeat similar short sentences as your baby moves his or her arms and legs. Emphasize the idea that God made us. Show pleasure as the baby succeeds at any challenge. **You can roll over now. God mad you, Collin. God made everything that grows.**

Toddlers

❖ Show your child pictures of growing things such as a dog with puppies, a cat with kittens and other animals with their young. Use the words "little" and "big" as you talk about each animal and its young. Say, **This is a big duck; these are little ducks. This is a big horse, this is a little horse.** Ask your child to point to a big animal and then a little animal. **God made all the animals.**

❖ As your child plays, talk about his or her actions. Say, **You are stacking the blocks. You are using your strong arms to lift the big blocks. God made your arms. Thank You, God, for Derek's arms.**

I'm a Little Seed

I'm a little, tiny seed in the earth so low.
God sends sun and rain, then I start to grow.
Up, up, up, slowly I grow, then my leaves and flowers show!

Say and do this finger play with your child. Use the child's name instead of "I" and "I'm." To act out the poem in another way, sit on your knees with your head down to be the seed. As you say "Then I start to grow," begin to stretch your head up, then your arms, and then stand up. As you say the words "Then my leaves and flowers show!" stretch your arms out and wiggle your fingers or cup your hands to represent leaves or flowers.

SiNG iT!

Animal Friends

(Tune: "Jingle Bells" chorus)

Oh, God made ducks and rabbits and squirrels and little birds to sing.
God made you and God made me.
Yes, God made everything!
(Repeat.)

Show your child books picturing ducks, rabbits, squirrels and birds. Ask your child, **What does the duck say? Show me how a squirrel runs. I can wiggle my nose like a rabbit. Can you? Can you flap your arms like a bird flaps its wings?** Then sing the song with your child. Your child may enjoy pretending to be a bird by flapping his or her arms, chirping and moving around while you sing and pretend to be a bird, too.

Discipline: The Child's Legacy

Parents have always worried about discipline. Articles and books on the subject have been in demand since ancient times. While "experts" sometimes disagree with each other on how to deal with certain problems, there is much common ground that has proven solid for generations of parents.

❖ First, discipline means teaching. And young children are very quick learners. Unfortunately, parents sometimes teach just the opposite of what they intend. For example, angry words and harsh punishment confuse a child, resulting in resentment rather than repentance.

❖ Children learn best in pleasant surroundings. Therefore, discipline is most effective when the child knows he or she is loved and understood. The natural response when a child has displeased a parent is for the parent to punish the child. However, the parent's action should help the child learn what to do instead of the wrong action. Discipline is for the child's benefit, not simply to release adult frustration.

❖ Another factor in helping children learn acceptable behavior is the parents' pattern of meeting the child's needs. The child whose needs have been frustrated will find it hard to respond positively to parental guidance.

❖ Since young children have limited understanding of words, their unacceptable behavior is most effectively guided through actions, not talk. Usually the best approach is to distract the child with an acceptable activity. In some cases it is necessary to remove some item from the child, or the child from the item. In either case, a simple statement of why you are taking action is helpful. Avoid dwelling on the problem. Focus your attention and the child's attention on the desired new activity.

❖ If the child continues to misbehave, look behind the action to discover the reason. Your child may be trying to get your attention. Or the child may be intensely curious about a particular item. Whatever the cause, seek to meet your child's need in a healthy manner. Remember, when it comes to the human heart, love wins more battles than force.

Bird Watching

❖ Take a walk with your child. Say, **We are going to look for some birds.** As you walk, point out and talk about birds you see. Say, **I see a bird flying. There is a bird looking for food to eat.** Listen to the sounds the birds make. Talk about other things you see that your child shows interest in.

❖ Place a simple bird feeder outside a window your child can see out of. When you see birds at the bird feeder, talk with your child about what you see.

"There are one hundred and fifty-two distinctly different ways of holding a baby—and all are right."
Heywood Broun

Return Address:

Postage Stamp

TO: _____

_____

_____

Parent's Home Page

TIPS AND ACTIVITIES FOR PARENTS OF CHILDREN UNDER TWO

Do these activities with your child to continue the learning your child has experienced at church.

May

People at Church Help Me

"God gives people to help me."
(See 1 Corinthians 12:28.)

This month we will help your child:

❖

develop an awareness of Jesus;

❖

and associate Jesus with being loved and helped.

People Help Me

People at church help me.
They say "hello!" and smile at me.
They hold me close and play with me
and give me good things to eat!

Say and do this finger play as you play with your child. Use your child's name instead of "me." Talk about the people who care for your child at church. (If your church has a picture directory, show pictures of these people to your child.) Do this finger play many times, but especially immediately before and after your child has participated in the church nursery program. Your child's confidence and pleasure in the nursery will grow as he or she sees you affirming and enjoying your child's experiences in the nursery program, too.

Little Activities for Little People

Babies

❖ Make up or sing to your child songs that you know about church to help your child develop happy and safe feelings about church. Sing often to your child to calm him or her or to accompany your child's play. Your baby enjoys your voice more than any other sound. So don't be shy—sing silly or sweet or any way you like!

❖ Even a young baby will enjoy watching soap bubbles as you blow them. Point to the bubbles and talk about how they are floating around the room. Gently blow a bubble toward your baby. Say, **I'm blowing bubbles for you to see, Alysha. I'm glad to be with you. Jesus loves you.**

Toddlers

❖ Most nesting toys frustrate a toddler at first. Make the task simpler by removing every other piece. Avoid correcting your child if some pieces are left out. At this age your child needs the freedom to experiment without having adults impose standards beyond his or her capabilities.

❖ Participate with your child when he or she is eating a snack. Sit with your child and eat your snack at a relaxed pace. Smile at your child. say, **I'm eating a cracker, and Michael is eating a cracker. Crackers are good. God gives us good food to eat.** Pray, **Thank You, God, for crackers.**

❖ If you have toys or furniture similar to those in your church nursery, comment on them to your child. **This toy is just like the one at our church. The people at our church love you.**

Showing God's Love

(Tune: "Twinkle, Twinkle, Little Star")

I will smile and play with you.
Jesus helped His good friends, too.
I can show I care for you
to help you know
that God loves you.

Sing this song as you serve a meal to or play with your child. Talk about how you enjoy caring for your child. Smile at your child and tell him or her that you smile to show you love him or her. Talk about how people at church like to smile and take care of your child. If a child knows the name of a nursery worker, sing the song using the person's name in place of the word "I."

Question & Answer

Q: How can I tell what my baby wants when he or she can't talk yet?

A: You can learn most about your baby by slowing down and being observant. A great deal of communication goes on with even the youngest child. The first and most basic part of this process is simply to *watch* your child. One well-known psychologist has said, "If you want to know how a baby feels, watch his feet." That's good advice! Notice your baby's facial expressions, sounds, body posture and gestures. These provide the foundation for understanding what your baby is trying to communicate.

Always place yourself at your child's eye level. Smile and talk quietly with him or her. As you make eye contact, especially when doing something routine like changing diapers, watch and talk to your child to indicate your interest and care. This encourages the child to respond.

Rather than going into action only when your child fusses, work towards paying attention and responding to your child even when he or she is not fussing. You may find that as you become better at this, your child fusses less and communicates more!

Because everything is new to your baby, it is very easy for him or her to become overstimulated. If your baby looks flushed, try reducing the stimulation—lower the lights, turn down the noise, remove some of the toys and gently stroke your child. Children's reactions don't instantly change, but by paying attention to your child's reactions, you will discover what

helps to soothe him or her.

If you observe your child trying hard to grab a rattle, but unable to do so, or trying hard to do something else but failing, he or she will fuss to express frustration. Instead of saying, "Don't cry!" move the rattle closer or help your child hold the rattle and bring it to his or her mouth, talking to your child as you do so. In this way babies and toddlers learn that communication works.

Bottle Bowling

❖ Wash and dry several empty plastic liter pop bottles. Stand the bottles upright on the floor. Help your child roll a ball toward the bottles to knock them down. Clap and cheer when the bottles fall down. Say, **You knocked the bottles down!**

❖ Let your child set up the bottles however he or she wants to. Your child may also want to knock down other toys as well. Continue to play as your child shows interest.

"Children are God's apostles, day by day Sent forth to preach of love, and hope, and peace."
James Russell Lowell

Return Address:

Postage Stamp

TO: _____

_____

_____

Parent's Home Page

TIPS AND ACTIVITIES FOR PARENTS OF CHILDREN UNDER TWO

Do these activities with your child to continue the learning your child has experienced at church.

June

God Cares for Me

"God cares about you." (See 1 Peter 5:7.)

This month we will help your child:

❖ associate God with the loving care experienced at church;

❖ show interest in conversation and songs about God's care.

DO IT!

God Cares for Me

God cares for me
when I sleep.
God cares for me
when I play.
God cares for me
all the time,
every night and
every day.

Say and do this finger play with your child. Replace the words "me" and "I" with your child's name. Use the finger play when putting your child to sleep or when playing with him or her. On a bright sunny day, talk about the color of the sky and the sunshine and then say the finger play. In the evening, take your child out to look at the moon and the stars and talk about the nighttime. Repeat the finger play.

Little Activities for Little People

Babies

❖ Hold your baby on your lap and sit facing a mirror. Wave your hand. Watch to see if your baby imitates your motion. Say, **I see your face in the mirror. I see your eyes and your mouth. God made you, Jessie. God cares for you!**

❖ Let your baby look at and carefully touch a flowering plant. Say, **Look at this pretty flower. God cares for flowers and helps them to grow. God cares for you, too. God gives you food to eat and people to care for you. I love you.**

❖ While changing your baby's diapers, lean over him or her, making sounds to draw your baby's attention to you. When your baby is looking at you, slowly move your face back and forth, continuing to make the sounds. Move slowly and quietly to help assure the baby of your complete attention.

Toddlers

❖ When your child brings a book to you, let him or her turn the pages. Talk about the pictures in the book, connecting the items in the pictures with the ways in which God cares for your child. Say, **Here is a bunny. God cares for bunnies. He gives grass to eat. God cares for you. God gives you food to eat, too. God loves you!** Your child may want to turn the pages in the same book several times, usually not in any particular order. And they may point to the same items each time. Children cannot learn without repetition.

❖ Provide a simple rhythm instrument (shaker, rattle or bell) for your child to play with. Briefly demonstrate use of the instrument. Then give it to the child. Play lively music from a children's cassette or CD.

SING IT!

I'm So Glad

(Tune: "Skip to My Lou")

I'm so glad that God loves me,
God loves me, God loves me.
I'm so glad that God loves me,
He loves me all the time.
I'm so glad that God loves you,
God loves you, God loves you.
I'm so glad that God loves you,
He loves you all the time.

Sing this song to your child, replacing "you" with your child's name. Hold your child and sway or bounce while you sing. Clap your hands as you sing this song and encourage your child to clap with you. These first attempts at clapping are the beginning steps of learning rhythm. Say, **God cares for you when you play and when you sleep! I love you and care for you, too, when you are sleepy or playing!**

Laying the Foundation

There is no more appropriate place for a child to learn trust than in your family! Such security becomes the basis for learning to trust God and beginning to feel His love. Make sure your child understands that your home is safe and that the people there are caring ones.

Here are some specific ways to lay a foundation of secure feelings in babies and toddlers:

❖ Respond. Don't ignore your baby or toddler or dismiss his or her crying or other behavior as "just crankiness." Make the effort to understand and help.

❖ Provide interesting things to do, to look at, to listen to.

❖ Talk in a quiet, respectful and soothing way. Never respond in anger. Singing to your child may calm both of you. Or try talking to your child about how you want to respond gently and helpfully to his or her fussiness—it will help you do that. Pray, asking God to give you gentleness in place of anger.

❖ Be observant. When you see trouble coming, distract your child with another activity or toy.

❖ Remove your child from danger or potential problems, talking to him or her as you do so to help your child understand what you are doing.

❖ Take time to watch your child, to ask and to respond in appropriate ways to him or her. This tells your little one he or she is important to you—and to God.

Bubble Games

❖ Buy some bubble solution or make your own (1/4 cup clear dishwashing liquid, 1/4 cup glycerin [purchase at the drugstore], 3/4 cup water and 1 tablespoon sugar). Make big bubbles by dipping the large end of a plastic kitchen funnel into the bubble solution and blowing through the small end. Play with the bubbles along with your child.

❖ Get your hands wet. Blow bubbles through your hands.

❖ Have your child try to stomp on the bubbles as they land on the floor or grass.

❖ Break bubbles by clapping your hands together. Play some music and clap to the beat with your child as you both try to break the bubbles.

❖ Blow bubbles to your child in the bathtub.

"A baby is God's opinion that the world should go on."
Carl Sandburg

Return Address:

Postage Stamp

TO: _____

_____

_____

Parent's Home Page

TIPS AND ACTIVITIES FOR PARENTS OF CHILDREN UNDER TWO

Do these activities with your child to continue the learning your child has experienced at church.

July

God Made Me

"God made me."
(See Job 33:4.)

This month we will help your child:

❖

enjoy success in using the body God made for him or her;

❖

begin to develop an awareness that God made his or her body.

DO IT!

God Made

God made my ears.
God made my nose.
God made my fingers.
God made my toes.
God made my eyes.
They're both open wide.
God made my mouth with a tongue inside!

Say and do this finger play with your child frequently. Connect the words of the finger play to your child's activity. For example, if your child is playing with a toy, say, **God made your fingers to play with toys.** Then repeat the finger play, pointing to or gently touching the named body parts. Pray, **Thank You, God, for making my child.** Use your child's name when you pray for him or her.

SING IT!

I Have Two Eyes

(Tune: "Pop Goes the Weasel")

I have two eyes.
I have two ears.
I have two hands and feet.
I have one mouth and one little nose,
but, oh, so many fingers and toes!

Sing this song to your child while he or she is playing. Hold a doll or stuffed animal and point to the body parts you are singing about. Ask your child to point to his or her body parts as you name them. Take off your shoes and your child's shoes and wiggle toes for the last line of the song. Sometimes a child will listen to the song, doing nothing but waiting to do the very last motion or sound, if it is particularly satisfying to him or her. If your child is interested, sing the song several times to allow time for him or her to respond.

Little Activities for Little People

Babies

❖ While your baby is learning to walk, he or she needs lots of practice in balancing. Let your baby push a stroller outdoors or a lightweight chair indoors. Say, **Max, you're learning how to walk! You're using your arms to push the stroller. You're using your legs to walk. God made you, Max.**

❖ Look at a book picturing babies. Connect what your child sees to this month's theme: God Made Me. For example, point to a child's ears in a picture. Say, **Here are the baby's ears.** Then place your hands on the child's ears as you say, **Here are your ears. God made your ears. God made you!**

❖ Comment on the body parts your baby uses in playing with a toy. Say, **Morgan, you picked up the rattle with your hand. God made your hand.**

Toddlers

❖ As your child plays with toys, comment on the parts of the body he or she is using in play. Show pleasure in your child's developing skills. Talk about God's love in giving us healthy bodies.

❖ Avoid pressuring a child to always play with a toy "the right way"—experimentation is necessary and satisfying. Simply affirm your child's efforts as you talk about the skills he or she has developed. Your acceptance and encourage helps your child develop confidence for further learning and exploration.

❖ Compare your features with those of your child. Say, **God made my nose. God made your nose.** Point to your nose, then your child's nose. Continue with other facial features: eyes, ears, mouth. Your child will enjoy this activity while looking into a mirror.

Question & Answer

Q: What type of books should I buy for my child and what can I do to help my child enjoy books?

A: Young children "read" the pictures in the book. So it is important to buy books with clear, bright pictures. Also select books with pictures of familiar settings and things—dogs, cats, toys, families, homes, parks.

Buy sturdy books, sometimes known as board books, that have cardboard-backed or coated pictures. This stiffness will enable a very young child to be able to turn the pages of the book. Often a child will look at a book for a very brief period of time. The child will want to turn the pages, as much for the pleasure of turning the page as to see what's on another page. This page turning will go backwards and forwards, pages will be skipped, and some pages returned to again and again. Help the child turn the page only if he or she has difficulty doing so.

Sometimes just seeing one object in a book and hearing its name will satisfy a young child. As the child gets older, he or she will enjoy saying the names of objects pictured on the page. Point to and name the objects in the pictures ("Look! I see a dog!"). Ask questions to which a child can point to give the answers ("Where is the dog? Can you point to the dog?"). Talk about the action in the pictures ("The dog is carrying a bone. Where is the tree?").

Describe the pictures, adding comments and asking simple questions that help children think of God's love ("That big green tree looks cool. God made big trees. Devon, do you have a tree in your yard?"). Remember that baby and toddler attention spans are very short! A toddler may only be interested in one picture before sliding off your lap.

An older toddler may enjoy hearing a short story, one that can be told in a minute and retold several times in one sitting. Books with repetitive rhymes are especially fun to read with children. Above all, be sure your child sees you reading books, magazines, newspapers—and the Bible. Your example will powerfully influence your child's attitude toward books. Providing a comfortable, loving time for busy babies and toddlers to settle in with a book teaches them a great deal about God's love and yours!

Mirror Fun

❖ Set up a variety of mirrors for your child to see. Young children enjoy looking at themselves in mirrors. They are learning to differentiate themselves from others. Point to his or her reflection whenever you see mirrors.

❖ Sit with your child on your lap in front of a mirror. Say, **I see your happy face. Do you see me?** Wave and make other motions. Imitate your child's facial expressions and motions. If your child is interested, continue to imitate his or her expressions and make others for your child to imitate.

❖ Point to your nose, ears, mouth, etc. Say, **Where is your nose? I like looking at you in the mirror. I like to see your happy face.**

"Bringing up a family should be an adventure, not an anxious discipline in which everybody is constantly graded for performance."
Milton R. Sapirstein

Return Address:

Postage Stamp

TO: _____

_____

_____

Parent's Home Page

TIPS AND ACTIVITIES FOR PARENTS OF CHILDREN UNDER TWO

Do these activities with your child to continue the learning your child has experienced at church.

God Gives Me Friends

"Love each other."
(John 15:12.)

This month we will help your child:

❖

enjoy happy encounters with other children at church;

❖

associate God with happy experiences with others.

August

Little Activities for Little People

Babies

❖ Cover a doll or toy with a small blanket, towel or diaper. Slowly remove the cover. Repeat. Show surprise and joy at each discovery of the "lost" toy.

❖ When your baby is learning to sit up or crawl, talk about how he or she is using the strong legs God made. Give assistance only when needed so the child can succeed.

❖ While holding your baby in your lap, look at pictures of friends and family members. Hold the pictures steady to help your baby focus his or her eyes on the picture. Talk about each picture, saying the person's name. **I see your friend, Dana, in this picture. She is with her mommy. God gives us friends. Friends love each other.** Continue as long as your baby shows interest.

Toddlers

❖ Take turns with your child in adding blocks to a structure. Since the child's concern is usually to make the stack taller, your participation can help make the stack longer or wider. A good rule-of-thumb for safety is to build towers only as high as a child's shoulder before knocking it down.

❖ Changing your child's diapers is a good time to play with your child's arms, hands, feet and legs and talk about how the child is growing. **You're getting bigger, Joseph, and you are learning to do new things. God loves you. And I love you, too.**

❖ If your toddler no longer takes morning naps, he or she may need some quiet moments to regain emotional and physical energy. Rock your child or snuggle on your bed together while listening to a quiet song on a children's tape or CD.

DO IT!

I Roll the Ball

I roll the ball to you.

You roll the ball to me.

I can share the ball with you

because we're friends, you see!

Say and do this finger play as you roll a ball with your child or as your child and a friend roll a ball back and forth. When you roll the ball, describe what you are doing. Say, **I am rolling the ball to you.** When your child rolls it back say, **You are rolling the ball to me. It's fun to play with friends. God gives us friends. Friends love each other.**

SING IT!

Friends

(Tune: "The Farmer in the Dell")

We can smile and wave.

We can smile and wave.

Because it's fun to be with friends,

we can smile and wave.

Sing this song as you play with your child or as your child plays alongside another child. Smile at your child. Point to your smile. Say, **I am smiling at you. I like to see you smile. Friends smile at each other.** Wave to your child. Say, **I am waving to you. I like to see you wave, too.** Sing the song several times to give your child time to smile or wave or anticipate what you will do.

Discipline and Little Children

Discipline means "teaching"—the very kind of teaching Jesus did with His disciples! It is an opportunity to teach a child appropriate ways to meet his or her needs. Teaching these ways is twofold: first, to immediately stop behavior that might hurt your child; second, to help your child find another way to behave.

Young children have a very small understanding of how the world works. They have no idea what the consequences of their acts will be! Good discipline helps your child make sense of things, even as you show him or her appropriate ways to act. Here are some discipline tips for very young children:

❖ Prevent Problems. Set up your home to be as safe and "trouble-free" as possible. If young children are able to explore freely, they can develop their own internal controls, reducing stress on babies and adults alike.

❖ Set Clear Limits. Use the word "no" as little as possible. It does not teach the child what TO do. Instead, give clear information. For example, "The food in the dish is for the dog. We leave the food in the dish." The word "no" is most effective when used for clearly dangerous situations.

❖ Redirect Behavior. "Let's get some food that's good for you to eat."

❖ Offer a Choice. Whenever possible, give your child a choice between two acceptable alternatives. "Do you want a round cracker or a fish cracker?"

❖ Acknowledge Feelings: Use the words, "I see..." often. "Dana, I see you really want to hold the dog's food." This shows the child you understand and helps him or her make sense of his or her feelings.

The most important part of this teaching is found in the way you behave! As you model caring and respectful behavior and follow the above guidelines, you will find not only that the relationship between you and your child is more peaceful but also that you are naturally helping your child make sense of the world. Your love and care is the essence of showing God's love to your little one!

Water Painting

❖ Take your child outside. Give him or her a large, soft paintbrush and a small pail of water. Show your child how to "paint" the house (or sidewalk) using water. Say, **The place you painted looks different. It is fun to paint.**

❖ Paint along with your child as long as he or she is interested. Your child will enjoy playing with the water and the paintbrush especially while you are painting also.

> *"This is what a father ought to be about: helping his son to form the habit of doing right on his own initiative, rather than because he's afraid of some serious consequence."*
> **Terence**

Return Address:

Postage Stamp

TO: _____

_____

_____

Teacher's Home Page

The Teacher's Home Pages provide teaching plans based on biblical concepts for each month of the year. Each caregiver who will be in the nursery needs to read the appropriate Teacher's Home Page as a way of preparing for the nursery session. These pages feature:

✓ an overview of the monthly theme, listing the song, finger play and Bible story for the month;

✓ a thoughtful devotional based on the Bible story;

✓ suggestions for theme-related activities for both babies and toddlers (activities are also suggested on the Parent's Home Page so that parents can reinforce their child's learning at home);

✓ a variety of bite-sized tips for interacting with babies and toddlers and their parents.

Photocopy the monthly Teacher's Home Page (on pages 189-238), mailing it to each caregiver during the week before he or she will serve in the nursery. (It's a quick and easy way to remind staff of their nursery commitment!) The nursery coordinator, a member of the nursery committee or the parent of a child in the nursery photocopies and distributes the Teacher's Home Pages.

If nursery workers care for both babies and toddlers in the same room, send the entire Teacher's Home Page to each worker. If babies and toddlers are cared for in separate rooms, send the first page and either the Activities with Babies or the Activities with Toddlers page to each worker.

Store the Teacher's Home Pages in a binder or folder for reuse each year.

Teacher's Home Page

I See God's Love at Church

"I like to come to church." (See Psalm 122:1.)

This month you will help each child:

❖ feel secure and comfortable at church as you demonstrate God's love to the child;

❖ begin to associate God and Jesus with loving people and enjoyable activities.

September

SING iT!

It's Fun to Go to Church

(Tune: "Farmer in the Dell")

It's fun to go to church!

It's fun to go to church!

With all the other boys and girls,

it's fun to go to church!

Sing this song to infants and toddlers as you rock, feed or play with them. Babies like to hear the same song over and over. They look forward to the familiar and happy sounds of a song sung many times. Children will experience God's love at church when they are having enjoyable experiences with loving caregivers.

DO iT!

I Come In

I come in,

there's a smile on my face.

I come in,

my friends are in this place.

I come in,

my friends say "hi" to me.

I'm in church,

what a happy place to be!

Say and do this finger play as a child comes into the nursery or at any time during the session. Use the child's name instead of "I" and "my." Infants and toddlers will enjoy the sounds and actions, although they will not yet be able to do actions with you.

TELL iT!

When Jesus was a baby,

His parents brought Him to church.

People at church were glad to see baby Jesus.

They talked to Him.

They smiled at Him.

They held Him close.

Jesus was happy to be at church.

You can be happy at church because people show God's love to you here.

(See Luke 2:22-38.)

Tell this brief story about Jesus' first visit to the Temple as you show a child the September Toddler Picture from *I Love to Look!* If child remains interested, use the Picture Talk suggestions on the back of the picture. The story can also be told while a child is playing with toys. Connect the child's action with the story by saying, **Daniel, you're playing with blocks. I can see you're happy at our church today. When Jesus was a baby, His parents brought Him to church, too.**

Choose one or two of these learning activities to provide for babies during a session. Continue the activity as long as one or more children are interested. Additional learning activities may be found in the *I Love to Wiggle and Giggle!* easel book.

Pictures and Books

❖ Display the September Teaching Poster and photo from the *Nursery Posters*, making sure the photo is at child's eye level. Refer to the poster if you need help remembering the words to the story, song or finger play. Talk about the photo with children. **These children are playing with toys just like you play with the toys at our church. I'm glad you're here. God loves you and I do, too.**

❖ Hold a baby while looking at a sturdy, washable book picturing families. Point to and name each family member. Relate the baby and his family to the people in the picture. **Megan, here's a picture of a big brother. You have a brother, too. You and your brother come to church.** Talk about families coming to church. (Babies will also want to explore the book with hands and mouths!)

Movement

❖ While a baby is lying in the crib or sitting in your lap, offer a finger for him or her to grasp. Older babies may pull themselves to a sitting or standing position. Younger babies will simply enjoy pulling on your finger. Say, **Your hands are so strong! I'm glad you're here today at our church.**

Music

❖ Sing "It's Fun to Go to Church" while a child is busy playing or during a quiet moment when you are the focus of the child's attention.

❖ Frequently use the finger play "I Come In," repeating it as often as babies show interest. Play songs from the *I Love to Sing!* cassette/CD at various times throughout the session.

God's Wonders

❖ Hold a hand mirror so the child can see his or her face, then hands. Talk about and gently touch each part of the child's face while child looks in the mirror. Say, **God loves you, Becca.**

"To bring up a child in the way he should go, travel that way yourself once in a while."
Josh Billings

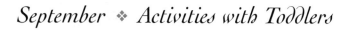

Choose one or two of these learning activities to provide for toddlers during a session. Beginning an activity yourself will usually attract the interest of several children. Continue the activity as long as one or more children are interested. Additional learning activities may be found in the *I Love to Wiggle and Giggle!* easel book.

Pictures and Books

❖ Display the September Teaching Poster and photo from the *Nursery Posters*, making sure the photo is at child's eye level. Refer to the teaching poster if you need help remembering the words to the story, song or finger play. Talk about the photo with children. **These children are playing with toys just like you play with the toys at our church. I'm glad you're here. God loves you and I do, too.**

❖ Provide two or three books picturing children, families and toys. Stand the books against the wall where children can see them easily. Sit beside the books and begin looking at one. Invite a nearby child to join you. Talk about the pictures, pointing to the things you name.

❖ Use books with children who are involved in various areas of the room. For example, take a book to where children are playing with toys. Compare the toys they have with the pictures in the book. Talk about the good times children have at church.

Music and Rhythm

❖ Move close to one or more children and begin to sing "It's Fun to Go to Church," substituting words describing what the child is doing. For example, if the child is playing dolls, sing "It's fun to play with dolls." A child may continue playing, may pause momentarily, or may stop playing to listen. **I'm glad Nate is having a good time at church today. I like being with Nate at church.**

❖ When children show interest in your songs and conversation, repeat them several times.

❖ Play "Together" on the *I Love to Sing!* cassette/CD. Sing along with the song, following along with the actions suggested in the song.

God's Wonders

(Use only with teacher supervision. Store items out of children's reach.)

❖ Let each toddler have a chance to hold and look into an unbreakable mirror. Ask, **Can you see your brown eyes in the mirror? God made your eyes. God loves you.** Continue talking about other parts of the child's face: nose, mouth, eyebrows, ears, hair. Comment, **I'm glad you're here today at our church.**

Toys and Blocks

❖ Before children arrive, place several favorite toys on a low shelf or on the floor. The first children need only a few toy options as they begin play. Add one or two new toys periodically as more children arrive. Toys that are being ignored should be removed from sight to avoid clutter. Toddlers need open space more than they need a vast array of toys.

❖ As children play, look for signs of enjoyment and pleasure. Comment on each child's expressions of positive feelings. **Laura, I like your happy smile. You seem happy when you play with the balls at church.** Sing "It's Fun to Go to Church" using the words "It's fun to play with balls."

❖ When two children struggle over the same toy, provide an identical toy or an attractive substitute for one child. Distraction is the most practical way to resolve a toddler conflict. Although a substitute toy may suffice, recognize that toddlers do not yet understand the idea of sharing. However, a toddler can begin to learn to take turns if guided gently, but firmly by an understanding adult.

Devotional

As you watch and learn from the babies and toddlers you teach, notice how anxious each one is for food to satisfy the pangs of hunger. No substitute will do! You may try bouncing and tickling, rocking and caressing, but a little one's crying will not stop until physical hunger is satisfied. This is one time when the child knows exactly what he or she needs.

Read 1 Peter 2:1-3. The apostle Peter urges us to have the same single-minded drive in satisfying our spiritual needs. Unfortunately, we often allow ourselves to be sidetracked. We try a wide variety of ways to find fulfillment or to eliminate problems. But our spiritual hunger continues, often making us as cranky as a hungry baby! Peter tells us that only the "pure milk of the word" (verse 2) can nourish the deepest needs of the human soul. Take time to be fed. Recognize the symptoms of your need and satisfy that hunger!

As a teacher of very young children, the gentle care you provide introduces them to the nurture and love of the people who love God and His Son, the Lord Jesus. Your tasks may seem to involve only the physical care of changing, feeding, playing, cuddling and singing. However, those actions must be bathed in the warmth of Jesus' love. Such love will radiate from you as you take time each day to "taste" the goodness of the Lord (see Psalm 34:8). Just as babies single-mindedly demand to be fed, demand "time out" from your busy schedule to feed your soul from God's abundant resources.

Getting to Know Parents

If it's your job to check in children as they arrive at the nursery, make it easy for parents to remember your name by wearing a child-safe name tag. Greet each parent and make a positive, specific comment about some new development or characteristic you have noticed about the child. Parents appreciate teachers who are aware of their child as an individual. Encourage parents in what you observe them doing well rather than criticizing them for mistakes. Parents need the confidence of success to help them deal with the challenges of family living.

Your service reminder: _____

Return Address:

Postage Stamp

TO: _____

_____

_____

Teacher's Home Page

Jesus Loves Children

"Jesus loves the children." (See Mark 10:16.)

This month you will help each child:

❖ develop an awareness of the name of Jesus and associate Him with being loved;

❖ enjoy the activities provided.

October

TELL iT!

Jesus loved the little children.
Mommies and Daddies brought
their children to Jesus.
Jesus held the little babies close.
Big boys and girls walked to
Him all by themselves!
Jesus smiled at all the children,
and the children smiled at Him.
Some children came
and sat near Jesus.
Some children climbed
right up in His lap!
Jesus loved each one.

(See Mark 10:13-16.)

Tell this brief story as you show a child the October Toddler Picture from *I Love to Look!* If the child remains interested, use the Picture Talk suggestions on the back of the picture. The story can also be told while you are holding or rocking a child. Connect your action with the story by saying, **I like to hold you and rock you. Jesus liked to be with children, too.**

DO iT!

Jesus Loves Us All

Who are the children Jesus loves?

Jesus loves us all!

He loves us
when we clap;

He loves us
when we crawl.

He loves us
when we walk;

He loves us when we fall.

Who are the children Jesus loves?

Jesus loves us all.

Jesus loves you!

Show a child the October Toddler Picture from *I Love to Look!* Point to Jesus and say His name. Say, **Jesus loves the children. Jesus loves you.** Then say and do this finger play. If the child is interested, say the finger play slowly and encourage the child to act out the actions with you by clapping, crawling, walking and gently plopping down on the floor. Say the child's name in the last line of the finger play. Repeat the finger play several times during the session.

SiNG iT!

Each Little Child

(Tune: "Mary Had a Little Lamb")

Jesus loves each little child,

little child, little child.

Jesus loves each little child.

He loves you, yes, He does.

Sing this song to a child while rocking in a chair, while playing with a toy, or while gently bouncing the child in your lap. Every time you sing the words "little child," look into the child's eyes and pat his or her head. Sing the child's name in place of the word "you." At another time when you sing this song, clap your hands. Invite a child to clap his or her hands along with you.

Choose one or two of these learning activities to provide for babies during a session. Continue the activity as long as one or more children are interested. Additional learning activities may be found in the *I Love to Wiggle and Giggle!* easel book.

Toys

❖ While a baby plays with a toy, describe the toy and the baby's actions. Occasionally play with the toy yourself. For example, move the cradle gym, shake a rattle, turn a dial. Respond to the baby with a smile and a nod when he or she attempts to imitate your actions.

❖ While a child is playing with a toy, talk about Jesus' love for you and the children. Say, **I'm glad Jesus loves me. Jesus loves you, too, Nathan.**

Movement

❖ A young baby enjoys pushing his or her feet against your hands and soon learns to put his or her own effort into the game. Talk about what the baby is doing and encourage his or her abilities. Talk about the parts of his or her body he or she is using. This activity will provide valuable stimulation for the baby's growing understanding of language. **I'm glad to play with you. Jesus loves you!**

God's Wonders

(Use only with teacher supervision. Store items out of children's reach.)

❖ Bring in a pumpkin or two. Place pumpkin on the floor or in the crib where a child can pat it. **Michelle, you're touching the pumpkin. It's orange! I'm glad you're here at our church today. I love you, Michelle. Jesus loves Michelle, too.**

Music and Rhythm

❖ Even the youngest infant usually responds positively to soft, quiet singing. Hearing simple, yet rhythmic melodies again and again gives babies great pleasure.

❖ Frequently sing "Each Little Child." Also, sing along with and/or gently bounce the baby to "We're Special" on the *I Love to Sing!* cassette/CD.

Little children remind us not to take ourselves so seriously.

Pictures and Books

❖ Display the October Teaching Poster and photo from the *Nursery Posters*, making sure the photo is at child's eye level. Refer to the poster if you need help remembering the words to the story, song or finger play. Talk about the photo with children. **Look at this boy sitting next to the pumpkin. This boy looks happy! Jesus loves children. Jesus loves you!** The baby is showing interest in the photo when simply looking at it. Point to items in the photo and talk about them. If the baby responds with sounds, smile at the baby and repeat the sounds to let the baby know you enjoy his or her responses.

❖ A baby enjoys looking at books with pictures of familiar items. The child's pleasure comes from studying the pictures, tasting and handling the pages. Therefore the books used with babies should be durable and washable. As you look at a book with a baby, point to a picture and describe what the baby is seeing. For instance say, **See the yellow truck. Look at the blue bird.**

Choose one or two of these learning activities to provide for toddlers during a session. Beginning an activity yourself will usually attract the interest of several children. Continue the activity as long as one or more children are interested. Additional learning activities may be found in the *I Love to Wiggle and Giggle!* easel book.

Toys and Blocks

❖ A large number of toys displayed at once tends to confuse and frustrate toddlers. Choosing what to play with first is an overwhelming decision! One or two toys at a time is usually sufficient to involve a child. When the child drops one toy for something else, another child usually comes along and investigates the dropped one. If you notice that certain toys are not being used, put them away to help reduce clutter and confusion, and to provide open spaces for beginning walkers.

❖ As children play, look for smiles or intense concentration that show when a child is enjoying him- or herself. Comment on the child's expressions of enjoyment. Sing "Each Little Child." Share a child's delight and excitement when the child's block tower goes tumbling down. **Just look at how Katy can build the blocks and knock them down! Jesus loves you, Katy!**

❖ Toddlers do not usually play together or interact with each other extensively: rather, they play side by side in their own little world—unless one has a toy that another just has to have! Having duplicates of the most popular toys helps solve this problem. Sharing is a concept yet to be learned by toddlers.

God's Wonders

(Use only with teacher supervision. Store items out of children's reach.)

❖ Bring in several seasonal items for children to explore: pumpkin, Indian corn, squash, fall leaves. Talk with children about the variety of colors and textures. Say, **I'm glad you're here today, Terri. Jesus loves you. Jesus loves all the children.** Sing "Each Little Child."

Music and Rhythm

❖ Be prepared during any activity to sing "Each Little Child." Singing may attract several other children.

❖ Songs with simple actions encourage a child to participate. Just the action of clapping helps children to be involved. Play "Watch Me!" on the *I Love to Sing!* cassette/CD.

❖ A tired toddler will enjoy being held and hearing a song from the Quiet Time Songs of the *I Love to Sing!* cassette/CD. Play the music or sing along with it. Gently patting the child to the rhythm of the song can be soothing, too.

Pictures and Books

❖ Display the October Teaching Poster and photo from the *Nursery Posters*, making sure the photo is at child's eye level. Refer to the teaching poster if you need help remembering the words to the story, song or finger play. Talk about the photo with children. **Look at this boy. He looks happy! He's having fun playing in the leaves. Jesus loves children. Jesus loves you, Ashlee.**

❖ When you and a child look through a book in the nursery, talk about the pictures. Ask the child to point to the things you name. Toddlers will need help taking care of books. When children have finished looking at books, show them where to put the books and help children put books away.

❖ Keep one copy of the October Toddler Picture from *I Love to Look!* where you can easily use it to tell a child about Jesus' love for children. Display your copy of the October Toddler Picture for the children to look at and talk about throughout the month.

Devotional

What does it mean to become like a child? How can an adult humble him- or herself to be childlike?

These questions must have gone through the minds of some of Jesus' disciples when He set a child in their midst in answer to their question about who is greatest. Read Matthew 18:1-4. This formula for greatness with the emphasis on little children sounded quite contrary to all the commonly accepted ideas about status. Perhaps as the disciples looked at the child Jesus had recruited for His object lesson, they began to see some of the qualities of the child that Jesus valued.

As you observe the babies and toddlers in your church, one of the first characteristics you may notice is their total dependence on others. Surely Jesus was calling attention to our dependence on God. How often do we impair our effectiveness by thinking we can get by with just our own ability! What new horizons of growth might become visible to us if we could see beyond the limits of our own resources to what God has made available to us?

What other valuable childlike qualities can you nurture in your own life? Perhaps the openness of an infant should be cultivated? Might not the child's demonstrations of affection be good examples to imitate? What if adults showed a toddler's desire to learn? Carefully watch a child during the next session. Look for attributes in that child for you to imitate spiritually. It's the path to greatness!

Getting to Know Parents

With an instant camera, take a photo of each child with his or her parents. Put the picture up on a bulletin board (preferably near the entrance to the nursery), writing parents' and child's names under the photo. You and other nursery caregivers will learn the parents' names easier this way and an usher or helper will be helped to find the parents, should the child need them.

Your service reminder: _____

Return Address:

Postage Stamp

TO: _____

_____

_____

Teacher's Home Page

God Gives Me Food

"God gives us food." (See Genesis 1:29.)

This month you will help each child:

❖ develop an awareness that God made food;

❖ enjoy eating food with teachers and other children.

November

TELL iT!

Jesus' friends were hungry.
So Jesus cooked some
fish and bread.
"Come and eat!" Jesus said.
The fish and bread tasted good.
Jesus' friends were glad
He gave them food.
We are glad for our food, too.

(See John 21:9-13.)

Tell this brief story as you show a child the November Toddler Picture from *I Love to Look!* If child remains interested, use the Picture Talk suggestions on the back of the picture. The story can also be told while a child is looking at a picture of food in a book. Connect the picture with the story by saying, **Benjamin, this is a picture of a banana. I like to eat bananas. Jesus' friends enjoyed eating together, too. They ate some bread and fish.** Optional: Bring fish-shaped crackers for toddlers to eat.

DO iT!

My Food

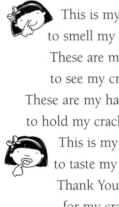

This is my nose
to smell my cracker.
These are my eyes
to see my cracker.
These are my hands
to hold my cracker.
This is my tongue
to taste my cracker.
Thank You, God,
for my cracker.

Say and do this finger play with children at the snack table before passing out the snack, or at any time during the session. Help a child or children who are interested in what you are doing by asking, **Where is your nose?** Let children point to their noses. Then do the whole finger play, encouraging the children to do the motions with you. While the children are eating their crackers, say the finger play and do the motions again. (If children are having a different snack than crackers, use the name of your snack in the finger play instead of crackers.)

SiNG iT!

I Thank God

(Tune: "Mulberry Bush")

Apples taste so good to me,

so good to me, so good to me.

Apples taste so good to me.

I thank God for my food.

Show children an apple. Say, **Is this an apple or a banana?** Wait for children to answer. **Are apples red or blue?** Give children a chance to respond. Then say, **These apples are red!** Sing this song with children. Rub your tummy when singing the words "so good to me." Sing the song when looking at pictures of food in a children's book, using the names of the pictured foods.

Choose one or two of these learning activities to provide for babies during a session. Continue the activity as long as one or more children are interested. Additional learning activities may be found in the *I Love to Wiggle and Giggle!* easel book.

Toys

❖ Move a toy slowly in front of a baby. As the baby tracks the movement with his or her eyes or reaches for the toy, stop the movement briefly, then begin again. Let the child grasp the toy. When the child lets go, begin the movements again. As you play with the baby, talk about the toy and the baby's movements. Say, **I like to play with you and take care of you. God cares about you, too.**

❖ As the baby touches a soft doll say, **The doll is soft. Daniel is soft, too.** Hug and cuddle the baby to provide an atmosphere of security and love. Place the doll in the baby's arms. **Daniel loves the dolly. I love Daniel.** Sing "A Happy Place" from the *I Love to Sing!* cassette/CD.

God's Wonders

(Use only with teacher supervision. Store items out of children's reach.)

❖ Have some fresh fruit (pear, orange) available for baby to touch. Name foods for the baby. Use finger play poem "My Food." Talk about God giving us food. Sing "I Thank God."

Books and Pictures

❖ Display the November Teaching Poster and photo from the *Nursery Posters,* making sure the photo is at child's eye level. Refer to the poster if you need help remembering the words to the story, song or finger play. Talk about the photo with children. Say, **This baby is learning to feed herself. She's eating good food. God gives us good food to eat. Thank You, God, for our food.** Talk about other items in photo as long as the baby shows interest by looking at it, touching it or making sounds.

❖ Show books and pictures of babies being fed. Mount food pictures on wall or bulletin board where babies can see them. Hold a baby and talk about food. Say, **See the baby. The baby has a bottle. Thank You, God, for milk.** Name other foods shown. Thank God for them.

> *"Before I got married I had six theories about bringing up children; now I have six children and no theories."*
> **John Wilmot (1647-1680)**

Movement

❖ Hold the baby in your lap on the floor and have an older toddler or another adult roll the ball to you. Show the baby how to push the ball back to the toddler. Sing "My Friends" from the *I Love to Sing!* cassette/CD. A baby masters skills by repeating an action again and again. The first time you roll a ball to the baby, the baby will hardly be able to hold it in his or her arms, let alone be able to return it to you. A baby cannot be forced to learn. However, if the activity is within the baby's capabilities and the baby enjoys repeating it, skills and self-satisfaction will soar.

Music and Rhythm

❖ Sing "I Thank God" as you care for a child. Play times and quiet times are more pleasant with singing.

❖ Use the finger play "My Food" whenever your hands are free and you have a child's attention. A baby enjoys watching the motions and hearing the rhythm of the poem. The child enjoys him- or herself even more when you help the child participate by moving the child's hands or touching the child's body.

Choose one or two of these learning activities to provide for toddlers during a session. Beginning an activity yourself will usually attract the interest of several children. Continue the activity as long as one or more children are interested. Additional learning activities may be found in the *I Love to Wiggle and Giggle!* easel book.

Toys and Blocks

❖ Provide food puzzles with large, colorful pieces. Talk about each food picture. Sing "I Thank God." **I'm glad God gives us such good food to eat.** Help when needed by moving a puzzle piece close to where it fits, by turning a piece so it is almost in place, or by putting a piece in and letting the child take it out and replace it.

❖ Toddlers are explorers. They are often more interested in the color, shape and texture of a toy than in its intended purpose. Thus, they frequently seem to be playing aimlessly, merely looking at, holding or waving a toy. Adult efforts to show how a toy is used are often met with indifference. Observe how children use a toy. Is there another toy which could be more effective for that purpose? Could an adult example stimulate the child to a new discovery with the toy? Or is the child's use of the toy fitting his or her own need at the moment?

❖ Optional: One at a time, peel and/or slice a banana, pear and orange into small portions. Talk about the peeling, the fruit, the seeds. Let the toddlers see, smell, and touch the food. Say, **Eating fruit helps Jeffrey grow big.** Offer each child a small bite of each fruit. (Check to be sure no child is allergic to foods you are offering.) Say, **Thank You, God, for such good food to eat.**

Music and Rhythm

❖ Be ready to sing "I Thank God" at appropriate moments during the session. Even if singing is not your talent, toddlers enjoy hearing the rhythm and melody. Play "Thank You" or "Food for Me" from the *I Love to Sing!* cassette/CD as children are playing. Sing along with the songs. If a child shows interest in the music by clapping or moving, respond to his or her interest. Clap your hands, too, or hold the child's hands and gently rock to the music.

❖ Use the finger play "My Food" whenever you talk with children about food. Point to the toddler's eyes, nose, hands, mouth. Just for fun, clap your hands each time you say the words "to (see) my cracker." Thank God that we can enjoy our food.

Pictures and Books

❖ Display the November Teaching Poster and photo from the *Nursey Posters*, making sure the photo is at child's eye level. Refer to the teaching poster if you need help remembering the words to the story, song or finger play. Talk about the photo with children. Say, **What is the child doing? What is the child eating? I like to eat good food, too. God gives us good food to eat.**

❖ At child's eye level, post magazine pictures of food and of people eating. (For safety, attach pictures with tape, not tacks or pins.) Talk about the pictured food. Older toddlers can help you name foods as you point to the appropriate picture. Others can point as you name the foods. Compare real fruits with the pictures.

God's Wonders

(Use only with teacher supervision. Store items out of children's reach.)

❖ Play "What Is This?" by holding up a fruit or vegetable and asking an older toddler to name what he or she sees. Or, hold two items in your hand. Say, **Mara, point to the (banana). Good! Now point to the apple. God gave us good apples and bananas to eat.**

Devotional

After fishing all night, Jesus' disciples should have needed no coaxing to begin eating. Yet, there they stood on the beach, dumbfounded that their Lord who had recently risen from the dead, made two miraculous appearances in locked rooms, and produced an abundant catch of fish from previously sterile water was now standing beside a fire, cooking their breakfast. Read John 21:9-13.

As the disciples stood there, Jesus served their food. He knew that His earthly ministry was quickly drawing to a close. He knew He must give great attention to preparing the disciples for their coming responsibility. Nevertheless, Jesus took time for a simple act of kindness to meet a basic physical need. When we meet the basic needs of babies and toddlers, we are a reflection of Jesus' kindness.

Have you recently recounted the needs in your life that Jesus has helped you meet? What problems has He helped you cope with successfully? What challenge has He helped you to meet? What burdens has He helped make lighter? And then, have you thanked Him for the many ways in which He has helped you? Scripture reminds us, "Do not be anxious about anything, but in everything, by prayer and petition, with thanksgiving, present your requests to God. And the peace of God, which transcends all understanding, will guard your hearts and your minds in Christ Jesus" (Philippians 4:6,7).

Getting to Know Parents

Remember when you are working with infants and toddlers, you are serving the parents as well. Many parents are very busy and already feel inadequate. Be sure to acknowledge the great job they have done in getting themselves and their children to church, even if they have forgotten the expected extra diaper. Pray for the parents during the week. Though parenting is a wonderful job that offers many rewards, it is perhaps the hardest to do well. Be ready to offer any resources your church provides for families (parenting classes, a list of recommended baby-sitters, a hot meal or two, etc.).

Your service reminder: _____

Return Address:

Postage Stamp

TO: _____

_____

Teacher's Home Page

Jesus Was a Baby

"His name is Jesus." (See Luke 1:31.)

This month you will help each child:

❖ show interest in pictures, conversation and songs about baby Jesus;

❖ receive personal attention and love as teachers seek
to show Jesus' love in ways a child understands.

December

SING IT!

Happy Birthday, Jesus!

(Tune: "Jesus Loves Me")

It's Jesus' birthday, time to sing!

Shake the bells and make them ring.

Let's all sing a happy song.

Bring your drums and march along.

Happy birthday, Jesus,

Happy birthday Jesus,

Happy birthday, Jesus.

We sing this happy song.

Sing this song and shake a bell or other rhythm instrument. When a child shows interest give him or her a bell, drum or other child-safe instrument to play as you sing. Often when one child is exploring an instrument, other children will want to participate. Have several instruments ready to hand out. Sing the song several times while walking around the room. Encourage interested children to follow you. Say, **It's fun to sing about Jesus! We're happy Jesus was born!**

DO IT!

Look into the Stable

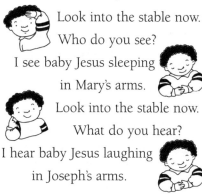

Look into the stable now. Who do you see?

I see baby Jesus sleeping in Mary's arms.

Look into the stable now. What do you hear?

I hear baby Jesus laughing in Joseph's arms.

Show the child the December Toddler Picture from *I Love to Look!* (Optional: Provide a child-safe nativity scene for child to handle.) Then do this finger play with a child. Ask a child who is interested in what you are doing, **How do you rock a baby?** Let child pretend to rock a baby. **Show me how a baby laughs.** Imitate the sounds the child makes. Then do the whole finger play, encouraging the child to do it with you.

When a child is playing with a doll, hold a doll, too, and act out the motions to the finger play with the doll. Encourage the child to do the motion with a doll, too.

TELL IT!

Mary held her baby.

Her baby's name was Jesus.

She rocked Him gently in her arms and sang a quiet song to Him.

Joseph held baby Jesus and watched Him wiggle and laugh.

All through every day, and all through every night,

Mary and Joseph loved and cared for baby Jesus.

We are glad baby Jesus was born.

(See Luke 2:4-7.)

Tell this brief story as you show a child the December Toddler Picture from *I Love to Look!* If child remains interested, use the Picture Talk suggestions on the back of the picture. The story can also be told while a child is playing with a doll. Connect the child's action with the story by saying, say, **Adrienne, you are rocking and caring for the doll just like your mommy cares for you. When Jesus was a baby, His mommy and daddy cared for Him, too.**

Choose one or two of these learning activities to provide for babies during a session. Continue the activity as long as one or more children are interested. Additional learning activities may be found in the *I Love to Wiggle and Giggle!* easel book.

Movement

❖ Securely fasten several large jingle bells to cradle gym strap, high enough so the baby can't grasp them. Each pull on the gym will reward him or her with an instant and cheerful ringing. (Remove any straps from crib long before child is able to reach them.)

❖ If a baby is too young to have the coordination to grab the cradle gym, he or she can still make it jiggle. With your hand, tap the mattress near the baby's feet. The objects hanging from the cradle gym will move. Gently take the baby's feet and tap them on the mattress to create the same motion. If the baby shows interest in the movement, repeat the foot tapping. The baby may gradually begin to move his or her own feet to make the bells jingle.

❖ Limit the time a baby spends in a crib or playpen. Extend times when the baby is being fed or changed to give some extra attention. Carry the baby with you as you check on others. Sit down and play with the baby for a few minutes, or put the baby on a protected area of the floor. When a baby is in a crib, play, sing or talk with the baby frequently. Use any of these moments with a baby to lovingly introduce pictures, songs and conversation about Jesus.

Books and Pictures

❖ Display the December Teaching Poster and photo from the *Nursey Posters*, making sure the photo is at child's eye level. Refer to the poster if you need help remembering the words to the story, song or finger play. Talk about the photo with children. Say, **See the baby. The baby is sleeping. The blanket looks soft.** Point to items in the picture and tell the baby what they are called. **When Jesus was a baby, His mother and father took good care of Him. We're glad Jesus was born.**

❖ Hold a baby in your lap to look at books picturing babies and families. Or, hold the book about 6 to 8 inches (15 to 20 cm) from a baby lying or sitting in a crib. Hold the book steady. Point to the dominant items in a picture. Describe what you see in the picture. When the baby's interest wanes, provide another activity.

God's Wonders

(Use only with teacher supervision. Store items out of children's reach.)

❖ Babies enjoy looking at displays of Christmas greens. However, use caution to keep a baby from grabbing a handful of pine needles or putting them in his or her mouth. Also, avoid poinsettias and holly with berries, which are poisonous. Pitch-free pinecones without sharp points offer interesting textures to touch.

Music and Rhythm

❖ Play "Christmas Party" from the *I Love to Sing!* cassette/CD or recorded Christmas carols at low volume to help create a cheerful atmosphere. Sing along with the songs. Babies will enjoy and respond to the sound of your voice. Use the name of the baby to whom you are singing, where appropriate. **I'm glad Jesus was born. I like to sing about Jesus.**

"Childhood is not a disease to be cured or endured. It is a God-ordained part of human life with value and significance that continually enriches the experiences of those who may have forgotten what it is like to see the world from a fresh, unspoiled point of view."
Wes Haystead

Choose one or two of these learning activities to provide for toddlers during a session. Beginning an activity yourself will usually attract the interest of several children. Continue the activity as long as one or more children are interested. Additional learning activities may be found in the *I Love to Wiggle and Giggle!* easel book.

Caring Times

❖ December's holiday excitement may produce a group of very tired, irritable toddlers. Rocking, therefore, can be an effective way to lessen a child's anxiety. Play a song from the Quiet Time Songs on the *I Love to Sing!* cassette/CD or sing a favorite Christmas song as you rock a child.

Toys and Blocks

❖ With a child watching, place a toy under one of two containers. Move the containers around, then ask the child to find the toy. When the child succeeds, repeat the game using three containers. Each time praise the child's efforts. Say, **I like to play with you. Mary and Joseph played with baby Jesus, too.** Allow child to hide toy and help you find it, too.

❖ When a child holds a doll, talk about Mary holding baby Jesus. Show the December Toddler Picture from *I Love to Look!* and tell the story of Jesus' birth. Say, **Mary loved baby Jesus and took care of Him. How can we take care of this baby doll?**

❖ Provide items such as large cardboard cartons (with staples removed) for toddlers to crawl through. Say, **Madeleine, you are growing big. You can crawl through the tunnel. The Bible says that baby Jesus grew up, too.**

God's Wonders

(Use only with teacher supervision. Store items out of children's reach.)

❖ Place several pinecones and fresh evergreen boughs on a low table or shelf where toddlers can touch. Avoid poisonous plants such as poinsettia and holly berries. Invite children to smell evergreen boughs. Say, **We put greens and pinecones in our church. We want our church to look pretty to show how happy we are that baby Jesus was born. We love Jesus.**

Music and Rhythm

❖ Let toddlers participate in making some happy sounds to accompany recorded music. While playing "Christmas Party" from the *I Love to Sing!* cassette/CD or other song from a children's Christmas cassette tape, provide toddlers with jingle bell bracelets for shaking. Children will also enjoy making animal sounds to go along with this song.

❖ Children at this age will explore an activity and change to a new one very quickly. As one child joins your music-making, another will likely see if his or her instrument fits into a stacking toy. When the environment is child safe and there are enough adult helpers, it is important to let the children explore and learn about what interests them.

Pictures and Books

❖ Display the December Teaching Poster and photo from the *Nursery Posters*, making sure the photo is at child's eye level. Refer to the teaching poster if you need help remembering the words to the story, song or finger play. Talk about the photo with children. Say, **What is the baby doing? The baby's blanket looks soft. When Jesus was a baby, He slept just like this baby, too. We love Jesus.**

❖ In addition to putting the December Poster and Christmas Photo up in the room, cover both sides of several Christmas cards (showing Jesus' birth, and families celebrating Christmas) with clear Con-Tact paper. Lean cards up against a wall or shelf. When a child shows interest in a picture, talk about it with him or her. **Jesus was born as a baby, just like you. We're glad Jesus was born. We love Jesus.** (Cards can also be cut into two- or three-piece puzzles for toddlers to put together.)

Devotional

There was never a birth announcement to equal it! On a nearby hillside angels were proclaiming joy, salvation and peace. In a faraway land, a group of wise men were stunned by the appearance of a star.

Immediately after hearing the news, the shepherds rushed into Bethlehem; the wise men began to plan for their trek westward. The accounts in Luke and Matthew reflect great excitement and joy. Read the accounts of their journeys in Matthew 2:1-12 and Luke 2:4-20. But what followed the first flush of emotion, the awe and wonder of the event?

The shepherds returned to their hillside, continuing their daily rounds of herding the flocks. The wise men faced an arduous journey through strange and possibly dangerous lands. And Mary and Joseph faced the daily routines of caring for an infant. The excitement lasted only a short time, then the familiar patterns of normal life were resumed. But even though the angel choir was gone, "Mary treasured...all these things...in her heart" (Luke 2:19).

December may be filled with much excitement for your family and church. However, in the midst of the celebrations, take time to treasure the presence of Christ in daily living. Set aside moments to ponder the ways He touches your life with joy, salvation and peace.

Getting to Know Parents

Be consistently supportive of each child. Your relationship with parents will be greatly influenced by the ways they see you caring for their child. Signs of impatience with a child's behavior can drive a wedge between a teacher and parents. Your open acceptance of the child makes parents feel you also accept them.

Whenever possible, take advantage of relaxed times to talk with parents (a brief phone call during the week, a few moments at an adult event at church). Openly share ways you have enjoyed caring for the child, seeking to learn from parents insights about their child. Avoid discussing the child in his or her presence. Even young children know when they are the topic of conversation.

Your service reminder: _____

Return Address:

Postage
Stamp

TO: _____

_____

_____

Teacher's Home Page

God Helps Me to Grow

"God made us." (See Malachi 2:10.)

This month you will help each child:

❖ associate new accomplishments with God and Jesus;

❖ enjoy the success of new accomplishments.

January

SING iT!

I Am Growing

(Tune: "Are You Sleeping?")

I am growing.

I am growing.

Yes, I am.

Yes, I am.

One time I was smaller.

Now I am much taller.

Watch me grow.

Watch me grow.

Sing this song to infants and toddlers as you rock, feed or play with them. Use the child's name instead of "I." Babies like to hear the same song over and over. Talk about when the child was smaller and couldn't do some of the things he or she can do now. Say, **Now you can walk and climb and reach up so high. We can thank God for helping you to grow and do new things.** Children will be encouraged to do new things when they experience affirmation and help from loving caregivers.

DO iT!

I'm Growing

When I was a baby,

I was very, very small.

Now I'm growing older.

I'm growing big and tall.

When I was a baby,

I could only crawl.

Now I can walk, and

I can jump.

But, sometimes,

down I fall!

Say and do this finger play at any time during the session when a child is crawling, walking or playing with toys. Say the child's name instead of "I" and "I'm." Encourage an interested child to do the actions with you, or to do even one action with you. Infants and younger toddlers will participate by enjoying the sounds and actions. Optional: Crawl, walk, jump and gently sit down as you say this finger play, encouraging children to do even one of the actions with you.

TELL iT!

Once Jesus was a baby.

Jesus learned to crawl.

Then He learned to walk.

Jesus grew to be a bigger boy.

He learned to do many things.

You are growing, too.

You are learning to talk and sing and run and climb.

God made you.

God will help you grow.

(See Luke 2:52.)

Tell this brief story as you show a child the January Toddler Picture from *I Love to Look!* If child remains interested, use the Picture Talk suggestions on the back of the picture. The story can also be told while a child is playing with toys. Connect the child's action with the story by saying, **Olivia, you're stacking the blocks. You have grown and you can do so many things now! Jesus grew and learned to walk and play just like you.**

Choose one or two of these learning activities to provide for babies during a session. Continue the activity as long as one or more children are interested. Additional learning activities may be found in the *I Love to Wiggle and Giggle!* easel book.

Pictures and Books

❖ Display the January Teaching Poster and photo from the *Nursery Posters* making sure the photo is at child's eye level. Refer to the poster if you need help remembering the words to the story, song or finger play. Talk about the photo with children. **I see a baby and a big sister in this picture. You're a baby now, but you're growing. God helps you to grow.**

❖ Show a baby a sturdy book picturing people of various ages. Talk about evidences of his or her growth. Sing "I Am Growing." Pray, **Thank You, God, for loving Micah and helping him grow.** Allow the baby time to hold and even put the book in his or her mouth. (Wipe off the book with a disinfectant before allowing another child to handle it.)

God's Wonders

(Use only with teacher supervision. Store items out of children's reach.)

❖ Position an unbreakable mirror so the baby can look at different parts of his or her growing body. Touch the parts of the body as you discuss them; also talk about what the child can do with that part of his or her body. For example, **Here is Tanya's hand. Tanya can touch my hand. God made Tanya's hand. God loves Tanya.** Use the finger play poem "I'm Growing."

Movement

❖ Use smiles and conversation to encourage a baby who is learning to sit up, crawl or walk. Talk about how the baby is using the strong legs God made. Give assistance only when needed so the child can succeed, then acknowledge and encourage the successes.

❖ Saying, **God helps Caleb grow** and similar short sentences helps to emphasize the idea of growing as the baby moves his or her body. Show pleasure as the child succeeds at any challenge. **Michael, you are growing. Now you can roll over.** Sing "I Am Growing," replacing "I" and "me" with the child's name.

Toys

❖ Babies enjoy toys they can easily hold in their hands and chew. (A baby cannot fully experience a toy without mouthing it!) Toys too large to be manipulated by small hands are frustrating. Also, make sure the toys for babies are safe and are washed after each use.

❖ As the child grows, he or she likes toys that respond to his or her actions. A transparent ball with objects inside, a pull toy that makes a special sound when moved, or a toy that bounces back when hit are favorites. To increase a child's interest and response, respond enthusiastically when a child accomplishes a new task.

Caring Times

❖ Spend at least a few minutes talking to even the tiniest baby, frequently using the baby's name. Hold each baby while feeding. Make sure you are comfortable so your complete attention can be focused on the baby you are holding. This relaxed setting gives you the opportunity to cuddle and talk, giving the baby a sense of security and love.

❖ When changing a baby, be gentle and loving in your attitude. Smile and talk to the baby as you make him or her dry and comfortable. Talk about how his or her legs are getting longer as the baby grows bigger. Sing, "I Am Growing."

❖ Rocking a baby or preparing him or her for a nap can be a special "I love you" time. **You're growing, Shana. Some times you like to rest. Some times you like to play. God loves you when you rest or play.** Having a favorite blanket or toy to hold helps most children relax. Play Quiet Time Songs from *I Love to Sing!* cassette/CD.

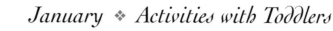
Choose one or two of these learning activities to provide for toddlers during a session. Beginning an activity yourself will usually attract the interest of several children. Continue the activity as long as one or more children are interested. Additional learning activities may be found in the *I Love to Wiggle and Giggle!* easel book.

Pictures and Books

❖ Display the January Teaching Poster and photo from the *Nursery Posters*, making sure the photo is at child's eye level. Refer to the poster if you need help remembering the words to the story, song or finger play. Talk about the photo with children. **Look at this little baby and her big sister. Micah, you are growing and learning to do so many new things. God made you and He helps you to grow.**

❖ Show books picturing children at different stages of growth: a baby sleeping, then crawling, and walking. Talk about how God helps children to grow and do new things. **God helps you to grow. God made you!**

God's Wonders

(Use only with teacher supervision. Store items out of children's reach.)

❖ Toddlers enjoy looking at themselves in a mirror. Talk about Keith's big smile that shows his teeth. **Keith uses his teeth to chew his food. Good food helps him grow. Keith, you are growing bigger just like God plans for you to grow. God loves you, Keith.** Repeat the finger play, "I'm Growing."

Music and Rhythm

❖ Songs that can be accompanied by lots of action are fun. Sing "I Am Growing" or use the finger play "I'm Growing."

❖ Sing-song rhymes about what a child is doing are especially enjoyable; a personalized rhyme often increases a child's interest in the activity. Sing or play "Grow Song" on the *I Love to Sing!* cassette/CD as toddlers roll a ball back and forth or play another game.

❖ Sing or play Quiet Time Songs from the *I Love to Sing!* cassette/CD during snack or rest time and Active Time Songs as children are playing. From time to time, sing or hum along with the music.

❖ When children show interest in your songs and conversation, repeat them several times.

Toys and Blocks

❖ Pull toys that have some kind of action delight toddlers. However, these toys require enough open space for a toddler to walk safely while he or she is looking over his or her shoulder at the toy. Assist the child by clearing an open space in the room.

❖ Older toddlers use blocks to build pretend houses, towers, etc. Their structure may not look recognizable. But that's the purpose of imagination! Comment on a child's abilities. **God planned for your arms to grow strong so you can build a tower, Jaleel. God made you!**

❖ Use a doll to demonstrate the different parts of a child's body; then ask the toddler to find his or her own eye, arm, leg, feet, etc. Talk about the fact that God made our (eyes, arms, etc.) so we can see, talk, walk, etc. Sing "I Am Growing."

❖ Puzzles are fascinating to toddlers. If these puzzles also have a little knob on the top of each piece, all the better. Toddlers enjoy the feelings of accomplishment in completing puzzles. Puzzles also help a child relate sizes and shapes, as well as improving eye-hand coordination.

❖ As a child completes a puzzle comment, **Nathan, you are growing so big! Once you needed my help with that puzzle. Today you can do it all by yourself. God loves you. God is helping you to grow.**

> *"You can talk to God about your children. You can tell Him everything, ask Him anything. You can even laugh with Him about the funnier things. I believe He understands laughter, for He is the One who made your child so funny in the first place."*
> *Ethel Barrett*

Devotional

Read Luke 2:21-40. Mary and Joseph must have closely observed their infant son in the days and weeks following their visit to the Temple. The prophecies of Anna and Simeon, added to the previous announcements by angels, undoubtedly stirred expectations of unusual qualities in their child. Would this child with such a special destiny show special abilities at an early age?

If Mary and Joseph had anticipated some dramatic evidence of Jesus' divine nature, they must have been disappointed. After the excitement of the prophecies, life settled back into normal routines. Jesus gradually began to mature. The Gospels do not record any amazing intelligence, precocious abilities, or supernatural authority. Like all babies and toddlers, He simply continued to grow. Gradually, daily, He kept increasing in wisdom and stature, and in favor with God and men (see Luke 2:52).

When we discover significant insights or have dramatic spiritual experiences, we often expect that life will suddenly become different. We are frequently disappointed that the impact of Sunday seems so weak on Monday. We would like to reach maturity in large, bold moves. We become impatient with the slow, small steps that seem to make so little difference.

Yet, as Jesus grew normally through all the stages of infancy, child-hood and adolescence, Scripture assures us the grace of God was upon Him (see Luke 2:40). That same grace works today in each Christian's heart and mind, guiding the gradual but powerful process of growth, as we seek to become more like Jesus.

Getting to Know Parents

Keep a camera handy. Throughout the year as you see a child having a particularly good time, take a picture. Talk about the picture with the child. Post the pictures on the nursery bulletin board. When you remove a picture from the board, be sure to send it home with the parent. Parents love to have a glimpse of their child's behavior away from home and they will appreciate your thought-fulness in displaying and sharing the picture.

Your service reminder: _____

Return Address:

Postage Stamp

TO: _____

_____

_____

Teacher's Home Page

My Family Loves Me

"God gives us families." (See Psalm 68:6.)

This month you will help each child:

❖ begin to associate God and Jesus with loving people at home and at church;

❖ respond to demonstrations of affection.

February

SING IT!

My Family

(Tune: "Row, Row, Row Your Boat")

Thank, thank, thank You, God,

for my family!

God made families to love

and care for you and me!

Sing this song to a child as he or she plays with a doll or toy, or looks at books with pictures of families. Talk about how moms and dads show love to children. Say, **Moms and dads help take care of you. They wash your clothes and give you food to eat. God gives us families.** Pretend to be a mom or dad talking to the child on a play telephone, then sing the song. As you do this activity, children will begin to develop an awareness of God being associated with the love they experience at home and at church.

DO IT!

Families

We all live in families, you and me.

What kinds of families?

Let me see!

Tall ones and short ones;

big ones and small ones.

We all live in families,

you and me.

Say and do this finger play at any time during the session while you are playing with or rocking a child. Say the child's name instead of "you." Draw a child's attention to the February photo from the *Nursery Posters* or to books with pictures of families as you say and do this finger play.

TELL IT!

Timothy was a little child, just like you.

Timothy liked good things to eat, and he liked to play, just like you.

Timothy's mommy and grandma loved God.

They taught him about God.

Timothy learned that God loves boys and girls and grown-ups, too.

Timothy learned to love God, just like you.

(See 2 Timothy 1:5; 3:15.)

Tell this brief story as you show a child the February Toddler Picture from *I Love to Look!* If child remains interested, use the Picture Talk suggestions on the back of the picture. The story can also be told while a child is looking at a Bible story book. Connect the child's action with the activity by saying, **Jessica, you're looking at a book with pictures of Jesus. When Timothy was a little boy, he learned about Jesus, too.**

Choose one or two of these learning activities to provide for babies during a session. Continue the activity as long as one or more children are interested. Additional learning activities may be found in the *I Love to Wiggle and Giggle!* easel book.

Pictures and Books

❖ Display the February Teaching Poster and photo from the *Nursery Posters*, making sure the photo is at child's eye level. Refer to the poster if you need help remembering the words to the story, song or finger play. Talk about the photo with children. **Look at this family. Here's a mommy and here's a little child. Mommies and daddies love their children and take care of them. God gives us families to take care of us.**

❖ Hold a baby while looking at a sturdy book picturing families. While the baby touches and pats the book, point to and name each family member. Relate the baby and his or her family to the people in the picture. **Megan, here's a picture of a big brother. You have a brother, too. God gives us brothers. God gives us families who love us.**

Movement

❖ Be sure babies are free to move as much as they can, whether in cribs, playpens or on the floor. Remove any unnecessary clothing or blankets; avoid cluttering the area with toys that inhibit movement. Encourage a child's activity with smiles and words of approval. Stimulate a child to reach or crawl by holding an attractive toy just beyond easy reach. Hold the toy steady so the child can succeed in reaching it. Next time, make the task slightly more challenging. Do not tease a child; hold the toy in one place until he or she reaches it.

> *"We are apt to forget that children watch examples better than they listen to preaching."*
> **Roy L. Smith**

Music

❖ Sing "My Family" while a child is busy playing or at a quiet moment when you are the focus of the child's attention.

❖ Frequently use the finger play "Families," repeating it as often as babies show interest. Play Quiet Time Songs from the *I Love to Sing!* cassette/CD at various times throughout the session.

God's Wonders

❖ Babies enjoy the feel of warm water on their hands. Provide a small amount of lukewarm water in a plastic bowl. Hold a baby so he or she can touch the water. (Or hold a baby near a sink to feel running water from a faucet.) Have a soft towel ready to dry the baby's hands. Say, **Your mommy and daddy use water to give you a bath. God made mommies and daddies to take care of their children. I'm glad God gives us families.** Play "Happy Family" and "My Family Cares" from the *I Love to Sing!* cassette/CD while a baby is playing with the water.

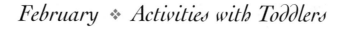

February ❖ *Activities with Toddlers*

Choose one or two of these learning activities to provide for toddlers during a session. Beginning an activity yourself will usually attract the interest of several children. Continue the activity as long as one or more children are interested. Additional learning activities may be found in the *I Love to Wiggle and Giggle!* easel book.

Pictures and Books

❖ Display the February Teaching Poster and photo from the *Nursery Posters*, making sure the photo is at child's eye level. Refer to the poster if you need help remembering the words to the story, song or finger play. Talk about the photo with children. **Look at this mom holding her baby. And here is a grandpa playing with a baby. Moms and dads, grandmas and grandpas love their children. I'm glad God gives us families.**

❖ Provide two or three books picturing children, families and toys. Stand the books against the wall where children can see them easily. Sit beside the books and begin looking at one. Invite a nearby child to join you. Talk about the pictures, pointing to the things you name.

❖ Use books with children who are involved in various areas of the room. For example, take a book to where children are playing with toys. Compare the toys they have with the pictures in the book. **Look at the toys in this picture. We have toys at church. And you have toys at home. Your dad gives you toys, Emilee, because he loves you. God gives us families.**

Music and Rhythm

❖ Move close to one or more children and begin to sing "My Family." Children may move to the music or clap their hands. Say, **God made our families to love us. It's fun to sing about our families. I'm glad God gives us families.**

❖ If singing to a toddler makes you feel self-conscious, here is a cure: keep singing! The more often you sing, the more natural it will seem, even if musical talent is not one of your gifts. Keep your attention focused on the child and you will soon be enjoying the music as much as he or she does. You will probably never find a more appreciative audience! Sing the songs for this month on the *I Love to Sing!* cassette/CD to reinforce the conversation about a child's loving family.

God's Wonders

(Use only with teacher supervision. Store items out of children's reach.)

❖ Bring a plastic dishpan (or baby tub) with a small amount of water in it. Let children wash a baby doll in the water, then dry it with a towel. Say, **Your grandma gives you a bath and takes care of you. God made your grandma to care for you. God gives us families because He loves us.**

Toys and Blocks

❖ Arrange (or remove) some of the furnishings in the room to provide open space where children can freely manipulate toys. Comment on a child's actions, noting the way he or she can make the toy do what he or she wants.

❖ Provide a few pieces of safe, familiar furniture for toddlers to climb on as they do at home. A footstool or large pillow provides interesting challenges. Help children only as they need it. Talk about ways their parents help them at home. (The more you know about each child's home situation, the more effective you can be in teaching.) Sing "My Family."

❖ Provide familiar home materials such as plastic dishes, pots and pans. A child will enjoy setting the table and cooking pretend food. Compare the child's use of these items with what families do at home. Say, **Brian, you are setting the table just like your daddy. Now I see you cooking dinner for your daddy. God gives us families. Our families love us.** As a child plays house, play "Happy Family" and "My Family Cares" from the *I Love to Sing!* cassette/CD.

Devotional

Three short verses about Timothy's early years tantalize us. Read Acts 16:1; 2 Timothy 1:5; 3:15. There is so much more we would like to know. How did his mother and grandmother go about teaching him the Scriptures? At what age did they begin their instruction? In what ways did Lois and Eunice share their faith with Timothy? How did they overcome the difficulty of Timothy's father probably being an unbeliever?

All we see are the results. Perhaps it is best that Paul did not share Eunice's child-raising "secrets." Every parent since would have felt compelled to follow the same exact procedures, possibly losing sight of the one crucial fact that the apostle Paul shares in this letter to Timothy, now an adult. Paul tells us that both Lois and Eunice possessed a sincere faith. Their task was to help make this faith meaningful to young Timothy. Because Christ dwelt within them, it was natural for His love to flow through them to Timothy. There must have been times of struggle and disappointment for Lois and Eunice, but sincere faith in Christ gave them a steady foundation.

As you seek to minister to young children, first make sure that Jesus is your Savior and Lord. Then your ministry to little ones will be based in the sincerity of personal experience.

Getting to Know Parents

Make sure that someone in your nursery program keeps track of children's attendance in the nursery. When parents have missed church because of a sick child, deliver a cassette tape of the worship service and/or mail a church bulletin to them. Offer to help if needed: provide a meal, pick up a prescription, baby-sit a child while the sick child is taken to the doctor, etc. Consider maintaining a list of people in the church who wish to minister to young families in these ways.

Your service reminder: _____

Return Address:

Postage
Stamp

TO: _____

_____

_____

Teacher's Home Page

Jesus Loves Me

"Jesus loves us." (See Revelation 1:5.)

This month you will help each child:

❖ enjoy activities in which teachers talk lovingly of Jesus.

❖ frequently hear the words "Jesus loves us."

March

SING iT!

Yes, Jesus Loves You

(Tune: Refrain to "Jesus Loves Me")

Yes, Jesus loves you.

Yes, Jesus loves you.

Yes, Jesus loves you!

The Bible tells us so.

Sing this song to infants and toddlers as you rock, feed or play with them. Babies like to hear the same song over and over. Encourage a child to clap or tap two blocks together with you as you sing. Children will experience Jesus' love at church when they are having enjoyable experiences with loving caregivers, who talk and sing about Jesus.

DO iT!

Day and Night

When the sun is in the sky,

Jesus loves me.

When the stars are way up high,

Jesus loves me.

In the day and in the night,

while I play and then sleep tight,

Jesus loves me.

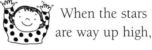

Say and do this finger play at any time during the session while looking at a book picturing Jesus, a child's daily activities, or different times of the day. Say the child's name instead of "me" and "I." Repeat this finger play to help a child prepare for a rest time or to enrich a play activity a child is enjoying.

TELL iT!

Zacchaeus wanted to see Jesus.

But Zacchaeus was little.

Zacchaeus couldn't see over the taller people.

So he climbed up into a tree!

Now he could see Jesus.

Jesus saw Zacchaeus, too.

Jesus loved Zacchaeus.

And Jesus loves you!

(See Luke 19:1-6.)

Tell this brief story as you show a child the March Toddler Picture from *I Love to Look!* If child remains interested, use the Picture Talk suggestions on the back of the picture. The story can also be told while a child is climbing on a climbing toy or stretching high to reach something. **Josh, you're climbing up the stairs. Zacchaeus climbed a tree one day, too. He wanted to see Jesus and learn about Him. You are learning about Jesus, too.**

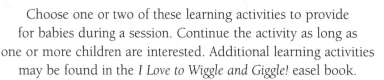

Choose one or two of these learning activities to provide for babies during a session. Continue the activity as long as one or more children are interested. Additional learning activities may be found in the *I Love to Wiggle and Giggle!* easel book.

Pictures and Books

❖ Display the March Teaching Poster and photo from the *Nursery Posters*, making sure the photo is at child's eye level. Refer to the poster if you need help remembering the words to the story, song or finger play. Talk about the photo with children. **See the daddy. The daddy loves his child. Jesus loves you, too!**

❖ Hold a baby while looking at a book with pictures of Jesus and children. Point to Jesus and say, **Jesus loves children. Jesus loves you, Monique.** Babies will explore the book using hands and mouths.

Movement

❖ Give a baby a colorful scarf (a bandanna or piece of lightweight fabric can also be used). Hold a scarf yourself. Wave your scarf, smiling and nodding your head as the baby imitates your actions. Say, **You're playing with the scarf, Jessica. Jesus loves you when you play. Jesus loves you all the time!** Also use the scarf to play a gentle tugging game with a baby. (Have enough scarves available so each child may have his or her own. Wash scarves after use.)

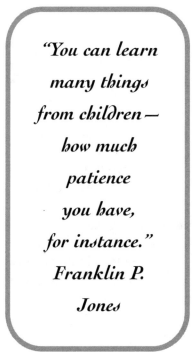

"You can learn many things from children — how much patience you have, for instance."
Franklin P. Jones

God's Wonders

❖ Provide interesting textures for a baby to feel: a furry stuffed animal (washable), a cardboard book, a soft blanket, your hand or arm. Comment, **You can feel the soft blanket, Kara. Jesus loves you, Kara. I'm glad Jesus loves us.**

Music

❖ Sing "Yes, Jesus Loves You" while a child is busy playing or at a quiet moment when you are the focus of the child's attention. Play "Jesus Loves Us All" and "Jesus Loves Me" from the *I Love to Sing!* cassette/CD and sing along, using the child's name instead of "you." Play Quiet Time Songs from the *I Love to Sing!* cassette/CD for a baby who is resting.

Choose one or two of these learning activities to provide for toddlers during a session. Beginning an activity yourself will usually attract the interest of several children. Continue the activity as long as one or more children are interested. Additional learning activities may be found in the *I Love to Wiggle and Giggle!* easel book.

Pictures and Books

❖ Display the March Teaching Poster and photo from the *Nursery Posters*, making sure the photo is at child's eye level. Refer to the poster if you need help remembering the words to the story, song or finger play. Talk about the photo with children. Say, **Where's the daddy?** If the child doesn't point to the dad, point to him and say, **There's the daddy. The daddy's holding the child. The daddy loves his child. Jesus loves you, too.**

❖ Provide one or more Bible storybooks with pictures of Jesus and children in them. Stand the books against the wall where children can see them easily. Sit beside the books and begin looking at one. Invite a nearby child to join you. Talk about the pictures saying, **Jesus loves and helps people. Jesus loves you and I do, too**. Use books with children who are involved in various areas of the room. For example, take a book to where children are playing with toys. Say, **Jesus loves children when they play. Jesus loves children all the time. Jesus loves you.**

Toys and Blocks

❖ The following episode shows some ways to connect a toddler's play to this month's theme, "Jesus Loves Me."

Jason deposits a doll in front of Mrs. Douglas and proudly announces: "Beebee."

"Right, Jason," replies Mrs. Douglas. "It's a baby. Babies are for hugging and loving. And so is Jason. I love Jason. Jesus loves Jason, too." While Mrs. Douglas talks gently and slowly, Jason picks up the doll, turns it upside down, replaces it on the floor, then on Mrs. Douglas's lap. "Beebee," Jason repeats, then toddles off in search of new fascinations.

Jason's next discovery is a large, soft, fabric block. He snatches it up and carts it across the room, then with a flourish, flings it to the floor at Mrs. Douglas's feet. "Block," Mrs. Douglas says. "Block, Jason, block." She then drops the block at Jason's feet.

Jason silently picks up the block, then drops it again.

"Block, Jason. Block," says Mrs. Douglas as she picks up the block and duplicates Jason's drop. Now Jason knows he is into a new game. The child and the teacher alternate picking up the block and then dropping it. Each time Mrs. Douglas repeats the word, "Block." But Jason is having too much fun with his newly invented sport to give attention to using words. Following lots of hearty laughter, Mrs. Douglas reaches out and gives Jason a hug. "I love you, Jason. Jesus loves you, too. Jesus loves Jason very much."

God's Wonders

(Use only with teacher supervision. Store items out of children's reach.)

❖ Collect a variety of textured fabrics or materials for children to feel: silk, towel, plastic mat, wool, corduroy, etc. If possible, remove children's shoes and socks so they can walk barefoot on the fabrics. Encourage children to feel the differences in the fabrics. Comment, **I'm glad to feel this shiny cloth. And I'm glad that Jesus loves you, Julie. Jesus loves you, too, Mark.** Play "Jesus Loves Me" and "Jesus Loves Us All" from the *I Love to Sing!* cassette/CD.

Music and Rhythm

❖ Move close to one or more children and begin to sing "Yes, Jesus Loves You," substituting the child's name for "you." Encourage child to clap with you while you sing.

❖ Play "Jesus Loves Us All" and "Jesus Loves Me" on the *I Love to Sing!* cassette/CD. Sing along with the songs, using the child's name where appropriate.

Devotional

Zacchaeus was a hated man. He boldly enriched himself at the expense of others, hiding behind the authority of the Roman government, hurting people right and left. His behavior was a lot like what we might see in a cranky toddler—grabby, aggressive, unable to focus on anyone but himself.

While Zacchaeus's focus on "ME" and "MINE!" was a normal response when he was only a toddler, he seems to have never grown beyond it to treat other people with compassion. Instead, he became an adult who was just plain selfish and cruel. Do you suppose he was treated cruelly as a little one, teaching him that cruelty was acceptable when one got big enough or powerful enough to bully other people? Did he live with selfishness that taught him it was the way to live? Although it's true that children learn what they live with, it may have been none of those factors. But whatever the cause may have been, the only cure for his toddler attitude was Jesus' love!

You may feel like there's a child or two in your nursery with real "Zacchaeus potential"! But remember that it is Jesus' love that changes people—no matter what their age or height or problem. And Jesus' love can flow through you as you sing, play, feed and change these little ones who learn what they live. Take time before you enter the nursery to ask Him to give you His love to share. He loves to answer such prayers! And recognize that as you treat these little ones with love—the kind of love God has shown you in Jesus—you are teaching powerful lessons, lessons that may help your toddlers outgrow the "Zacchaeus Syndrome"!

Getting to Know Parents

Part of getting to know the parents of children in the nursery is listening to their comments—positive and negative. It's important to let parents know you value their opinions. If a parent comments about a concern related to the nursery, acknowledge the concern and let him or her know you will see what can be done to improve the situation. If you don't know how to respond to a suggestion made by a parent, talk with other nursery staff or the nursery director about the best way to solve the problem. Let the parent know how the concern was resolved. And, of course, acknowledge with grateful thanks any positive comments about the nursery program and pass them on to other nursery workers!

Your service reminder: _____

Return Address:

Postage Stamp

TO: _____

_____

_____

Teacher's Home Page

God Makes Growing Things

"God made everything." (See Genesis 1:1.)

This month you will help each child:

❖ associate God with items of His creation;

❖ enjoy exploring items that God has made.

April

SING iT!

Animal Friends

(Tune: "Jingle Bells" chorus)

Oh, God made ducks

and rabbits and squirrels

and little birds to sing.

God made you and God made me.

Yes, God made everything!

(Repeat.)

Sing this song to infants and toddlers often during the session, especially while looking at a book picturing animals. Ask toddlers, **What does a duck say?** Wait for a response or make the sound and encourage children to join you. Then sing the song. If a child is interested in trying to say "quack, quack," sing the song replacing all the words with "quack, quack" and encourage the child to join you. **God made animals. I'm glad He made animals. God made everything that grows.** Repeat song using names of other animals.

DO iT!

I'm a Little Seed

I'm a little, tiny seed

in the earth so low.

God sends

sun and rain,

then I start to grow.

Up, up, up,

slowly I grow,

then my leaves

and flowers show!

Show a child a plant or look out the window, pointing out a tree, bush or flowers. Then say and do this finger play with the child. Repeat the finger play if the child is interested. Say, **God made the trees and plants. God made everything that grows! Thank You, God, for trees and plants.** Optional: Bring several seeds to show children.

TELL iT!

God made everything that grows.

He made green grass

and pretty flowers grow

on the ground.

He made trees grow way up high.

God made puppies grow into dogs

and kittens grow into cats.

Little pigs grow into big pigs and

little cows grow into big cows

that say "moo!"

God made little babies grow bigger

and bigger—just like you.

(See Genesis 1:11-31.)

Tell this brief story as you show a child the April Toddler Picture from *I Love to Look!* If child remains interested, use the Picture Talk suggestions on the back of the picture. The story can also be told while a child is playing with toy animals. Say, **Michael, you're playing with cows and pigs. What does a cow say? What does a pig say? God made all the animals.**

 Choose one or two of these learning activities to provide for babies during a session. Continue the activity as long as one or more children are interested. Additional learning activities may be found in the *I Love to Wiggle and Giggle!* easel book.

Pictures and Books

❖ Show magazine pictures of animals and plants on which you have glued pieces of fabric in a variety of textures for babies to touch. As you talk about a picture, rub the baby's hand gently on the fabric. Feeling textures helps the baby develop his or her sense of touch.

❖ Display the April Teaching Poster and photo from the *Nursery Posters*, making sure the photo is at child's eye level. Refer to the poster if you need help remembering the words to the story, song or finger play. Talk about the photo with children. **Look at this little girl. She's playing with the kittens. God made girls and boys. God made kittens, too. God made everything!**

Caring Times

❖ While feeding a bottle to a baby, talk to the baby about growing. Say, **You're drinking good milk. God made milk. God made you.**

❖ Cuddle a small soft toy animal while rocking a baby or getting ready for nap time. Sing "Animal Friends." Then say, **God made all these animals. God made you, Tasha.** Continue humming the song to the child.

God's Wonders

(Use only with teacher supervision. Store items out of children's reach.)

❖ Show a plant or branch with leaves to a baby. Help the child gently touch the leaves. Say, **God made the plants, Monique. God made everything that grows.** Play and sing "Growing Things" from the *I Love to Sing!* cassette/CD. Wash child's hands after he or she touches plant.

Dolls

❖ Show a doll to a baby. Compare the size of a doll with that of the baby. Say, **The doll has a little hand. Tasha's hand is big. Tasha is growing, just as God planned. God made you, Tasha.**

Music

❖ Sing "Animal Friends" at any time during the session. When babies are awake and moving, sing or play Quiet Time Songs from the *I Love to Sing!* cassette/CD during feeding and nap time.

❖ Say, **Rebekah, you are kicking your legs. God made your legs. God made you.** Repeat similar short sentences as a baby moves his or her arms and legs to emphasize the idea that God made us. Show pleasure as the baby succeeds at any challenge. Play "God Made Grins" from the *I Love to Sing!* cassette/CD. Say, **Seth can roll over now! God made you, Seth. God made everything that grows.**

> *I find myself rediscovering the world as I see a child discovering it for the first time.*

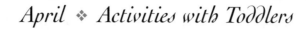

Choose one or two of these learning activities to provide for toddlers during a session. Beginning an activity yourself will usually attract the interest of several children. Continue the activity as long as one or more children are interested. Additional learning activities may be found in the *I Love to Wiggle and Giggle!* easel book.

Pictures and Books

❖ Display the April Teaching Poster and photo from the *Nursery Posters*, making sure the photo is at child's eye level. Refer to the poster if you need help remembering the words to the story, song or finger play. Talk about the photo with children. **I see a girl and some kittens in this picture. God made kittens. God made the little girl. What does a kitten say?** Wait for the child to respond, but if he or she doesn't, simply make the sound yourself.

❖ Use books with children who are involved in various areas of the room. For example, take a book to where children are playing with toy animals. Compare the toy animals they have with the pictures in the book. Say, **God made the horse and the dog.** Sing "Animal Friends."

❖ While looking at a book with a child, point to a flower and say, **There is a flower.** Then cover it with your hand and ask, **Where is the flower?** Uncover the item and announce, **Here is the flower! God made flowers! Thank You, God, for flowers.** Repeat the game to help the child enjoy anticipating discovery of each item.

Music and Rhythm

❖ Move close to one or more children and begin to sing "Animal Friends." Involve children by ask-ing, **What does a duck say?** and **Can you wiggle your nose like a rabbit?** A child may continue playing, may pause momentarily, or may stop playing to listen. **Marci and Zack, you're having fun making animal sounds. God made all the animals!**

❖ Play "Growing Things" and "God Made Grins" on the *I Love to Sing!* cassette/CD. Sing along with the song and invite the children to sing with you or play simple rhythm instruments or tap blocks together to the music.

God's Wonders

(Use only with teacher supervision. Store items out of children's reach.)

❖ Bring a flowering plant and a small plastic watering can. Help each child have a turn to water the plant. Place the plant by a sunny window. Say, **God made the flowers. God gives them water and sunshine to help they grow.** Do the finger play "I'm a Little Seed" with children.

❖ If possible, arrange for small caged animals such as birds, baby ducks or chicks to be brought to church each Sunday of this month. Provide constant adult supervision so children can look with safety. Say, **God made birds. God made all the animals.** Sing "Animal Friends" with children. Remove cage after curiosity has been satisfied. Wash child's hands if child has touched cage or animal.

Toys and Blocks

❖ As children play, focus conversation on the skill a child demonstrates as he or she uses a particular toy. To help the child relate your words to the actions, describe what the child is doing with the toy. Say, **Jamie is stacking blocks. Jamie is using his strong arms to lift the big blocks. God made your arms. Thank You, God, for Jamie's arms.**

❖ When a conflict arises between children, distraction is a simple and effective way to resolve it. Quickly provide an alternative activity or toy. Then remain near the children to offer understanding and support until both are purposefully occupied again.

❖ Cut four or five fabric or flannel shapes of birds, animals, fish, flowers, fruit, etc., providing duplicates of each. **God made all these animals that grow.** The child may place shapes on a flannel board (or on the floor) in any arrangement desired.

Once a child has recognized a shape, show the duplicate shape and one that is different. Say, **Which one is like your fish?** If the child cannot match the pieces, place the pair together and explain, **Here are two fish. They are just the same.** If the child shows interest, repeat the game until he or she can match the duplicates. **Good for you, Michael! God made fish like these. God made you, too!**

Devotional

And...it was good. These familiar words echo through the first chapter of Genesis. In springtime they seem to take on fresh luster as plants awaken from their long winter dormancy. There is something very good about new beginnings. Read Genesis 1:1-31.

Perhaps your spiritual life needs a new beginning, a reawakening from a period of seeming barrenness. Just as God's Spirit moved to bring beauty and order in the world's beginning, God Himself can bring light and life to the soul of anyone who is open to this love. God designed people in His own image to possess qualities that respond to His presence.

The good beginning for all creation came as God spoke. His Word still speaks today. Make time in your daily routines to read the Scriptures, asking God to help you respond.

Keep in mind that even the universe was not built in a day; six were needed to do the job! Expect God's work in your life to take place over a period of time as you gain spiritual insight according to His plan for you.

Getting to Know Parents

Every time you listen to a parent's specific comments on his or her child, you are creating a comfortable atmosphere for the parent. However, nurseries can be busy places. Sometimes a parent will try to tell you something just when you need to respond to a child. While going to the child say, **I need to help Benjamin get settled right now, but I want to hear what you are saying. Let's talk more after the service, or I'll phone you later today. Thanks!**

Your service reminder: _____

Return Address:

Postage
Stamp

TO: _____

_____

_____

Teacher's Home Page

People at Church Help Me

"God gives people to help me." (See 1 Corinthians 12:28.)

This month you will help each child:

❖ develop an awareness of Jesus;

❖ and associate Jesus with being loved and helped.

May

SING iT!

Showing God's Love

(Tune: "Twinkle, Twinkle, Little Star")

I will smile and play with you.

Jesus helped His good friends, too.

I can show I care for you

to help you know that

God loves you.

Sing this song to infants and toddlers as you rock, feed or play with them. Insert the child's name in place of "you." Even though it is often very busy in the nursery, look for times to sing this song to one child at a time and talk about ways you specifically enjoy him or her. Say, **Robin, I'm so glad you came to church today. I like to hold you and play with you**.

DO iT!

People Help Me

People at church help me.

They say "hello!" and smile at me.

They hold me close and play with me

and give me good things to eat!

Say and do this finger play while having a snack, while playing with a child or at any time during the session. Use the child's name instead of "me." Talk to a child about how happy you are when you see him or her come to the nursery and how much you like to play with, feed and hold the child. Then say the finger play to the child.

TELL iT!

One day Jesus and His friends walked and walked.

Their feet were very dirty!

So Jesus helped His friends.

He poured water into a big bowl.

Jesus washed His friends' feet and dried them with a towel.

Jesus loved to help His friends.

People at church love to help you, too.

(See John 13:2-5.)

Tell this brief story as you show a child the May Toddler Picture from *I Love to Look!* If child remains interested, use the Picture Talk suggestions on the back of the picture. The story may also be told after changing a child's diaper or clothing or after helping a child wash hands. Say, **It feels good to have clean hands. I'm glad to take care of you, Nate, and help you feel nice and clean.**

Choose one or two of these learning activities to provide for babies during a session. Continue the activity as long as one or more children are interested. Additional learning activities may be found in the *I Love to Wiggle and Giggle!* easel book.

Pictures and Books

❖ Display the May Teaching Poster and photo from the *Nursery Posters*, making sure the photo is at child's eye level. Refer to the poster if you need help remembering the words to the story, song or finger play. Talk about the photo with children. **I see a little child in this picture. The woman is reading a book to the child. I like to read books to you, Charlotte.**

❖ Show a baby a book with pictures of nursery items. Say, **Here is a picture of a rattle.** Show the child a rattle in the nursery and compare it to the one in the picture. Say, **Here is a rattle in our nursery. You play with rattles at church. Jesus loves you, Ryan.**

God's Wonders

(Use only with teacher supervision. Store items out of children's reach.)

❖ Even a young baby will enjoy watching soap bubbles as you blow them in the nursery. Point to the bubbles and talk about how they are floating around the room. Gently blow a bubble toward a baby. Say, **I'm blowing bubbles for you to see, Lorri. I'm glad to be with you today. Jesus loves you!**

Music

❖ Play "Helping" and "Helpers" from the *I Love to Sing!* cassette/CD at various times throughout the session. Sing along with the songs to heighten children's interest and to increase your own familiarity with the words and melodies. When you sing "Helpers," use the name of the child you are singing to. Maintain eye contact with a baby while you say, **Joseph, I like to come to church and sing happy songs to you. Jesus loves you!**

Caring Times

❖ Give a baby your undivided attention during feeding times. This one-to-one interaction gives you and the baby the opportunity to get to know each other. Say, **I'm glad to feed you, Dylan. I love you! Jesus loves you, too!**

❖ While changing a diaper, play a game of peekaboo with the baby using the clean diaper.

❖ Sing "Showing God's Love" while gently rocking a baby. If the baby responds by making sounds, imitate the baby's noises.

❖ Be alert to signs that a baby is tired or sleepy. Some babies resist taking a nap in strange surroundings. After being placed in the crib, a baby will often relax as you quietly stroke or pat his or her back. Be sure the child has something interesting to touch or look at before you move away from the crib.

Little children know how to make us laugh — even when we probably shouldn't!

Choose one or two of these learning activities to provide for toddlers during a session. Beginning an activity yourself will usually attract the interest of several children. Continue the activity as long as one or more children are interested. Additional learning activities may be found in the *I Love to Wiggle and Giggle!* easel book.

Pictures and Books

❖ Display the May Teaching Poster and photo from the *Nursery Posters*, making sure the photo is at child's eye level. Refer to the poster if you need help remembering the words to the story, song or finger play. Talk about the photo with children. **There's a lady reading a book to this child. I like to read books to you, too. I'm glad to help you at church.**

❖ Provide a book that shows pictures of adults lovingly caring for children and of familiar nursery items. Look at a book with a child. Say, **Here is a crib. We have a crib like that in our nursery.** Point out the crib to the child. Say, **Here is a climbing toy. Where is our climbing toy in the nursery?** Pause to allow child to point to the climbing toy. Continue your conversation about other items in the nursery. Say, **Here is a grown-up playing with a child. I like to play with you at church.** **Jesus loves you, Alisha.**

Music and Rhythm

❖ While singing a song to one child, you may find several others pausing in their play to listen. Include each listener's name in a song such as "Helping" or "Helpers" from the *I Love to Sing!* cassette/CD. Sing along with the Quiet Time Songs on the *I Love to Sing!* cassette/CD as you rock a child.

Caring Times

❖ Participate with children at snack time. Sit with them and eat your snack at a relaxed pace. Say, **I have a cracker. Jonathan has a cracker. Crackers are good.** Pray, **Thank You, God, for crackers.** Sing "Showing God's Love."

❖ As you change a child's diapers, talk about what you are doing to help the child. Say, **I'm taking off Claire's wet diaper. Now I'm going to put on a dry diaper. I like to help Claire. Jesus loves you, Claire.**

❖ When a toddler is upset, a few minutes of gentle rocking is often the best therapy. **Michael, I know you miss your daddy. It makes you sad that your daddy isn't here. I'll rock you for awhile to help you feel better.**

❖ A book or toy can often attract a child's interest to help overcome sad moments. However the child responds, it is important to accept the child's unhappy feelings. If a child senses that you dislike his or her crying, it will likely be more difficult for the child to stop.

❖ An overly tired child may need a nap, but he or she may strongly resist lying down. To help the child relax, rock him or her as you softly sing a quiet song. After a few minutes, the child may be willing to lie down. Or, the brief time of comforting may have renewed the child's energy enough to happily return to play.

Toys and Blocks

❖ Different-sized blocks create a variety of building options for a child. As you observe a child using blocks, look for indications that the child is aware of the differing sizes. Ask the child to bring you a big block, then a little block. Say, **This is a big block! And this one is little. Good for you, Cara. You know about blocks! I like to be with you at church, Cara. Jesus loves you!**

❖ Nesting toys may frustrate a toddler at the first attempt. To simplify the task, remove every other piece. Avoid correcting the child when some pieces are left out. At this age the child needs to be free to experiment without having adults impose advanced standards. As children work, comment about the ways you assist them to show you enjoy helping.

God's Wonders

(Use only with teacher supervision. Store items out of children's reach.)

❖ In an open area where children can move freely, blow soap bubbles for them to try to catch. Join in their spontaneous expressions of joy and wonder. Comment on their smiles and laughter. Say, **I like to blow the bubbles for you to catch. I like you, Kelsey. Jesus loves you!**

Devotional

Time in the nursery often seems a bit like a tornado: whoosh, babies suddenly arrive; fully absorbed, you whirl and turn and move through a series of caregiving tasks—then suddenly, they are gone! You sit breathlessly, assessing the needed cleanup and asking, "What on earth happened here?"

On such days, it may seem that one menial task after another took up all your time and energy. Was anything accomplished beyond basic physical care? In some nurseries, no more is expected. But Jesus shows us that in even the most menial act of care, there is potential for ministry. When Jesus washed His friends' feet, He taught them not only about being washed physically, but by the way in which He washed their feet, He also taught them the depth of His servanthood and the value He placed on each one of them—even the one who would betray Him. The disciples learned about servanthood and how Jesus valued each of them not by simply having their feet washed, but from the way in which it was done.

You are not merely a provider of menial services to babies. You are a teacher of very young children. On the surface, those menial tasks may seem to involve only the physical care of changing, feeding, playing, cuddling and singing. However, your actions go far beyond mere physical care and become ministry when you use them to express the warmth of Jesus' love. The gentle way in which you talk to, play with and love each child for whom you care teaches each of them something about Jesus' love and about the people at church who love God. That's a powerful lesson!

Such love will radiate from you only as you take time each day to "taste" God's goodness. As you consider His love for you and as you pray for each little one for whom you care, menial can become ministry!

Getting to Know Parents

The time when parents and children arrive at the nursery can be hectic. However, if it's your job to check in children as they are brought to the nursery, it's helpful for you to briefly greet and talk with each parent. Parents will always feel more comfortable leaving their child with someone who has demonstrated friendship to them. And a child who is reluctant to leave his or her parent will be reassured by the sound of your friendly conversation. *Daddy thinks this person is a friend. So maybe she's my friend, too.*

Here are some questions you can ask which will not only help you build a relationship with the parent, but will give you insight into caring for the child: What does Tyler like to play with? What have you noticed Tyler likes to do in our nursery? When did Tyler wake up this morning? Does he usually wake up cheerful or sad? How does Tyler show that he's interested in other babies?

Your service reminder: _____

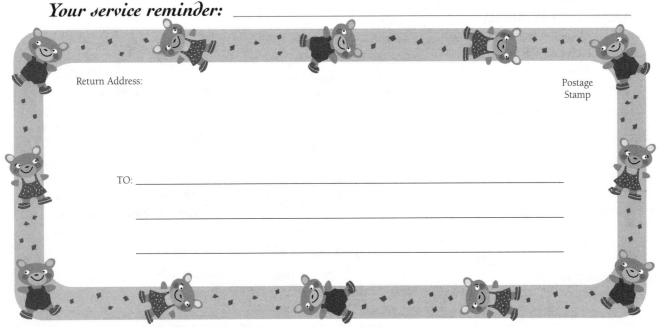

Return Address:

Postage
Stamp

TO: _____

_____

Teacher's Home Page

God Cares for Me

"God cares about you." (See 1 Peter 5:7.)

This month you will help each child:

❖ associate God with the loving care experienced at church;

❖ show interest in conversation and songs about God's care.

June

SING iT!

I'm So Glad

(Tune: "Skip to My Lou")

I'm so glad that God loves me,
God loves me, God loves me.
I'm so glad that God loves me,
He loves me all the time.

I'm so glad that God loves you,
God loves you, God loves you.
I'm so glad that God loves you,
He loves you all the time.

Sing this song to a child, replacing "you" with the child's name. Hold the child's hands and walk in a circle as you sing this song. Or hold the child and sway or bounce as you sing. Occasionally clap your hands as you sing this song to a child, encouraging the child to clap, too. Young children usually do not have the skill yet to clap in time to the music, but their efforts are the beginning steps in recognizing rhythm. Talk about the things your child does. Say, **God loves and cares for you when you eat and when you cry and when you play and when you sleep! God loves and cares for you all the time. I love you and care for you, too.**

DO iT!

God Cares for Me

God cares for me when I sleep.
God cares for me when I play.
God cares for me all the time, every night and every day.

Say and do this finger play with a child. Replace "me" and "I" with the child's name. Say the finger play while playing or putting a child down for a rest. Take the child outside or to look out a window to see the blue sky and the sunshine. Talk about the daytime and how God cares for him or her during all the activities of the day. Say, **God cares for you. He gives you food to eat and time to play and people to love you and help you.** Talk about the nighttime and show the child a picture of the night sky. Say, **God cares for you all night, too. He helps you rest and sleep.** If the child is interested, say the finger play several times during this conversation.

TELL iT!

"Look at the pretty flowers," Jesus said.
"God makes them grow. He makes red, yellow and white flowers.
God made these flowers, and He cares for them.
God made you.
God loves you and cares for you, too.
God loves you even more than flowers."

(See Matthew 6:28-32.)

Tell this brief story as you show a child the June Toddler Picture from *I Love to Look!* If child remains interested, use the Picture Talk suggestions on the back of the picture. Tell this story to a child as he or she looks at real flowers or pictures of flowers. Say, **God cares for the flowers. He gave them the rain and sunshine they need to grow. God cares for you, too. He gave you food and people to care for you.**

Choose one or two of these learning activities to provide for babies during a session. Continue the activity as long as one or more children are interested in it. Additional learning activities may be found in the *I Love to Wiggle and Giggle!* easel book.

Caring Times

❖ Maintain a relaxed, unhurried manner while feeding a baby; continue to hold the baby for a few minutes after the feeding is finished. Quiet conversation and singing can make feeding a satisfying time. Younger babies occasionally spit up some milk shortly after their feeding. Have a clean cloth or soft paper towel handy to protect your clothing. Consider these hints to minimize spitting up:

Stop midway through the feeding to burp the baby. Repeat at the end of the feeding and a few minutes after.

❖ Provide a mobile of attractive objects over the changing area. Brightly-colored shapes attract the babies' interest.

❖ Singing gentle lullabies or singing along with the Quiet Time Songs on the *I Love to Sing!* cassette/CD is effective while rocking a child in preparation for a nap. You demonstrate God's care for a baby when you do these things.

Pictures and Books

❖ Display the June Teaching Poster and photo from the *Nursery Posters*, making sure the photo is at child's eye level. Refer to the poster if you need help remembering the words to the story, song or finger play. Bring a baby to see the photo. Point to the flowers and say, **Here are some flowers. God made the flowers and cares for them. God cares for you and so do I!**

Movement

❖ While baby is lying in a crib or sitting in your lap, offer a finger for him or her to grasp. Older babies may pull themselves to a sitting or standing position. Younger babies will simply enjoy pulling on your finger. Talk to the baby about what he or she is doing, commenting on the baby's strong hands. **God made your hands. God cares for you!**

God's Wonders

(Use only with teacher supervision. Store items out of children's reach.)

❖ Bring a small flowering plant that can be taken to each baby for a brief time of viewing (and careful touching). Say, **Look at this pretty flower. God cares for flowers and helps them grow. God cares for you, too. God gives you food to eat and people to care for you.**

> *"God sends children for another purpose than merely to keep up the race—to enlarge our hearts and to make us unselfish."*
> *Mary Howitt*

Music

❖ Play Quiet Time Songs and Active Time Songs on the *I Love to Sing!* cassette/CD throughout the session, paying attention to a child's need for quiet or lively music (or even for no musical stimulation!).

❖ Frequently say the finger play "God Cares for Me," repeating it as often as babies show interest.

Toys

❖ Here is an example of how a teething baby uses toys: Amy is cutting a few new teeth, so every object in reach is fair game for gnawing. Her teacher checks her diaper bag and finds two teething toys her parents have brought. Amy immediately prefers the familiar toys and gums away happily for an extended period. When her teacher moves Amy from the crib to a playpen, the toys go with her. When it is time for a bottle, the toys go back into the diaper bag. After finishing the bottle, and being changed, Amy is placed on a blanket and given several of the nursery's clean toys. The teacher periodically stops next to her for a few moments of playing and talking. As Amy finishes with the toys, they are placed in the "to be washed" container.

Choose one or two of these learning activities to provide for toddlers during a session. Beginning an activity yourself will usually attract the interest of several children. Continue the activity as long as one or more children are interested. Additional learning activities may be found in the *I Love to Wiggle and Giggle!* easel book.

Pictures and Books

❖ Display the June Teaching Poster and photo from the *Nursery Posters*, making sure the photo is at child's eye level. Refer to the poster if you need help remembering the words to the story, song or finger play. Talk about the photo with children. **I see lots of flowers and I see a little girl. What is the girl doing? Show me the flowers. God cares for flowers by giving them sunshine and rain to help them grow. God cares for you, too. God gave you people to love you. God wants you to have the things that you need to grow.**

❖ When a few books are placed within children's reach, a child can choose a book to look at. When a child brings a book to you, let the child turn the pages. Talk about the pictures in the book, connecting the items in the pictures with the ways in which God cares for the child. Say, **There is a picture of a daddy holding his child. God gives you people to care for you. God cares for you.** Or say, **Here is a picture of a bunny. God cares for bunnies. He gives grass to eat. God cares for you. God gives you food to eat, too.**

God's Wonders

(Use only with teacher supervision. Store items out of children's reach.)

❖ Bring fresh flowers or leaves. Place them in one or more unbreakable containers without water. Invite children to touch and smell the flowers. Say, **God made the flowers. God cares for the flowers. God cares for you, too.** Talk with children about the colors and feel of the flowers.

Caring Times

❖ While changing a child, talk about how you are caring for him or her. Say, **I like to take care of you, Dawna. I love Dawna. God loves and cares for you, too.**

❖ While rocking a child, play and sing Quiet Time Songs from the *I Love to Sing!* cassette/CD. Talk softly about God's love saying, **Gabe, God loves us. God cares for us very much. And I'm glad!**

❖ When you place a child in a crib for a nap, stay next to the crib for a few minutes. Rub the child's back, gently rock the crib and sing softly. Provide a cuddle toy for the child to hold. Your loving actions demonstrate God's care for the child.

Music and Rhythm

❖ Provide simple rhythm instruments (tambourine, shakers, drums) children can play to accompany the Active Time Songs of the *I Love to Sing!* cassette/CD. Briefly demonstrate the use of each instrument. Then give it to the child. Accept each child's own method of making music. A child's enjoyment in experimenting with the instrument will insure that he or she will want to use it again. A child will naturally watch how you use the instrument and imitate you. A child learns rhythm and how to use instruments by being given many enjoyable experiences with music and instruments.

Toys and Blocks

❖ Observe how children use the toys in your department. Are the toys the kind that can be used in a variety of ways? Or do children merely pick them up, look at them and drop them? Remove those toys that children seem to ignore. In a month or so, bring them out again to see if children will use them more purposefully.

❖ Always remove all broken or damaged toys. Avoid cluttering the room or shelves with a vast array of toys. A few well-selected toys are preferable to an unorganized pile, which tends to confuse and frustrate children.

Devotional

It's easy to see how God could care for babies: sweet and snugly, they delight us with their coos and giggles. It's a joy to tell them of His love as we play with them and rock them. No doubt God cares for them even more than we do! But what kind of care does God have for us grown-ups? Let's look at Peter's statement in 1 Peter 5:7: "Cast all your anxiety on him because he cares for you."

How much worrying do you think babies do? Do you suppose they wake in the morning, stressed over where their milk will come from? Does their blood pressure rise as they fret over the possible problems of the day? Here they are, helpless, completely dependent on the caregivers—and instead of being stressed about their dependency, they respond in a blessed confidence, nestling in the arms of one who loves them and falling asleep in a relaxed lump of total trust. That's not just a sweet picture; it's the reality of God's care!

Now take a moment to think about the anxieties you faced this week: from the plumbing to the trouble your child had at school to worries about whether or not the groceries will stretch until payday. Adult lives seem to swell with anxiety-producing situations! Our blood pressure rises, our stomachs churn—and all the while, God invites us with open arms to give our anxieties to Him, relax in that baby-like blessed confidence and stop losing sleep over our troubles! Perhaps we don't coo and snuggle as well as we once did, but God wants us to remember that no matter how big and responsible we are, we're still His little ones. He is willing—and waiting—to care for our anxiety. So give your anxieties to Him. Rest in Him. He cares for you!

Getting to Know Parents

One of the best gifts you can give to parents is to pray for them and with them about their children. Individual caregivers or the nursery director can send a letter to parents stating their own prayers for the nursery program and inviting parents to pray along with them. Or write prayers on a sheet of paper and display it at the nursery entrance. This effort to encourage parents to pray with you will help nursery workers and parents unite in their common desire to depend on and express God's love for the children. Remember that God cares for the children in your nursery more than anyone.

Your service reminder: _____

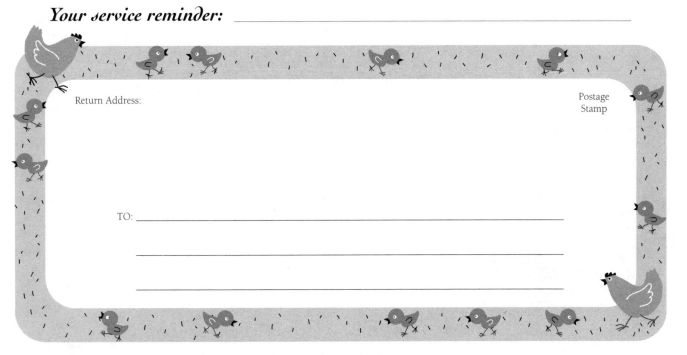

Return Address:

Postage Stamp

TO: _____

_____

_____

Teacher's Home Page

God Made Me

"God made me." (See Job 33:4.)

This month you will help each child:

❖ enjoy success in using the body God made for him or her;

❖ begin to develop an awareness that God made his or her body.

July

SING iT!

I Have Two Eyes

(Tune: "Pop Goes the Weasel")

I have two eyes.

I have two ears.

I have two hands and feet.

I have one mouth

and one little nose,

but, oh, so many fingers and toes!

Sing this song to infants and toddlers while playing with a doll or stuffed animal. Point to the body parts of the doll and name them. Ask the child to point to eyes, ears, hands, feet, mouth, nose, fingers and toes. If possible, take off your own shoes and the child's shoes, wiggling toes on the last line.

> "Children have
> more need
> of models than
> of critics."
> Joseph Joubert

DO iT!

God Made

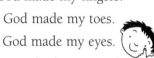

God made my ears.

God made my nose.

God made my fingers.

God made my toes.

God made my eyes.

They're both open wide.

God made my mouth

with a tongue inside!

Say and do this finger play frequently during the session. Insert child's name in place of "my." Connect the words of the finger play to the child's activity. For example, if the child is playing with a toy say, **God made your fingers to play with toys.** Then repeat the finger play, pointing to or gently touching the appropriate body parts. Each time you repeat the finger play children will be more likely to enjoy it as they begin to anticipate the next movement. Say the following prayer: **Thank You, God, for making Pieta, David and Rachel. Thank You for making our ears and noses and toes.**

TELL iT!

God made everything!

God made the cold water we drink.

God made the big waves in the sea.

God made the land
that's all around us.

God made all the people, too—

big ones and little ones,

people like me, and people like you.

God made us, and we are glad!

(See Psalm 95:3-7.)

Tell this brief story as you show a child the July Toddler Picture from *I Love to Look!* If child remains interested, use the Picture Talk suggestions on the back of the picture. The story can also be told while you and a child are outside or looking out a window. Point out several things God made such as a tree, grass, birds or other people. Say, **God made you and God made me. God made so many wonderful things!** Connect what the child sees with the story by saying, **We can see so many things that God made.**

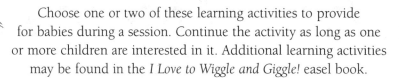

Choose one or two of these learning activities to provide for babies during a session. Continue the activity as long as one or more children are interested in it. Additional learning activities may be found in the *I Love to Wiggle and Giggle!* easel book.

Pictures and Books

❖ Display the July Teaching Poster and photo from the *Nursery Posters*, making sure the photo is at child's eye level. Refer to the poster if you need help remembering the words to the story, song or finger play. Talk about the photo with children. Say, **Here is a little girl. This girl is learning to walk. You'll be learning to walk, too. God made your legs so you'll be able to walk, Andrea.**

❖ Look at books picturing babies. Connect what the child is seeing to this month's theme: God Made Me. For example, point to a child's ears in a picture. Say, **Here are the baby's ears.** Then place your hands on the child's ears as you say, **Here are your ears. God made your ears. God made you!**

Music and Rhythm

❖ Sing, "I Have Two Eyes," inserting the child's name into the song. Repeat the song several times as the child is interested. Add a smile to your singing! Play the Active Time Songs and Quiet Time Songs of the *I Love to Sing!* cassette/CD.

Caring Times

❖ While feeding a baby, talk about parts of the child's body. Say, **God made Greg's mouth so Greg could eat.** Touch the child's mouth when you mention it. Repeat the word "mouth."

❖ While changing a diaper, sing "Here I Am!" from the Active Time Songs of the *I Love to Sing!* cassette/CD. Touch each body part as you sing about it. Usually by the fourth month a child will respond to gentle and brief tickling. A few tickles as you sing will often stimulate giggles from both child and teacher.

❖ Sing a favorite hymn or lullaby from the Quiet Time Songs of the *I Love to Sing!* cassette/CD while rocking a baby. If the baby shows signs of drowsiness, switch to soft humming. Continue humming as you carry the baby to a crib. Softly playing Quiet Time Songs from the *I Love to Sing!* cassette/CD can help maintain an even sound level in the nursery, making napping easier for babies.

Toys

❖ Comment on the body parts a baby uses in playing with a toy. Say, **Lauren, you picked up the rattle with your hand. Now you're shaking the rattle with your arm. You like to chew on the rattle with your mouth.** Sing "Here I Am!" and mention those parts of the body the child is using.

❖ When a baby is showing interest in a doll, point out the doll's body parts, comparing them with the child's. Say, **This is Mike's hand. This is the doll's hand. Mike's hand. Doll's hand.** Repeat this conversation several times slowly, touching as you talk. Sing "I Have Two Eyes," gently touching or pointing to each body part as you sing about it.

God's Wonders

❖ Fasten an unbreakable mirror inside a crib, about 12 inches (30 cm) from baby's head. Touch the baby's face and head so he or she can see your hand in the mirror.

❖ Talk about specific skills each child has mastered. Touch the body parts involved as you mention them. Your attention and demonstration of pleasure will help the child feel increased satisfaction with each achievement. Say, **Monique, you can roll over. What fun! You used your arms to roll over. God made your arms. God made you.** Sing "God Made Me" and "Here I Am!" from the *I Love to Sing!* cassette/CD.

Choose one or two of these learning activities to provide for toddlers during a session. Beginning an activity yourself will usually attract the interest of several children. Continue the activity as long as one or more children are interested. Additional learning activities may be found in the *I Love to Wiggle and Giggle!* easel book.

Pictures and Books

❖ Display the July Teaching Poster and photo from the *Nursery Posters*, making sure the photo is at child's eye level. Refer to the poster if you need help remembering the words to the story, song or finger play. Talk about the photo with children. Say, **Here is a little girl. God made girls and boys. God made you! This girl is learning to walk. You've learned to walk, too. God made your legs so you could walk.**

God's Wonders

(Use only with teacher supervision. Store items out of children's reach.)

❖ Involve children in looking into a mirror as you point to their eyes, ears, nose, mouth and chin. Repeat "God Made" finger play while touching each part of a child's face.

Music and Rhythm

❖ As you sing "Here I Am!" from the *I Love to Sing!* cassette/CD, encourage the child to touch each body part named in the song. An older toddler will do this without help. If he or she cannot keep up with the words, slow the tempo. Ask, **Where are Lydia's ears?** If Lydia finds them, respond with, **You found your ears! And where is Lydia's nose?** If Lydia

needs help, point to your own nose. Also sing "God Made Me" from the Active Time Songs on the *I Love to Sing!* cassette/CD.

Caring Times

❖ As children enjoy their snack, talk about the body parts they use in eating. Say, **Shannon, God made your hands to hold your cracker. And God made your eyes to see your cracker. And God made your mouth to eat your cracker. God made you!** Sing "I Have Two Eyes."

❖ Be sure to check each child's diaper at least once each hour. A busy toddler may not appreciate the interruption of play, so provide a toy for the child to hold while being changed. Talk with and help the child avoid becoming bored while the task is being completed.

❖ Rocking a crying child is a time-proven method for soothing upset feelings. Rocking can also be a delightful experience when a little one is alert and happy.

❖ All toddlers need a few quiet moments during an active play session. A nap may be unnecessary; however, all toddlers can benefit from resting briefly. You may hold or sit next to a child, gently stroking his or her arm, leg, back or head. Softly sing a lullaby or hymn you enjoy. Or sing along with the Quiet Time Songs on the *I Love to Sing!* cassette/CD.

Toys and Blocks

❖ Observe how children respond to the puzzle toys you provide. (Puzzles with three or four pieces are best for toddlers.) Often a child will find an interesting use for a toy that was not intended by the manufacturer. For example, even when the rings on a toy are designed to be assembled in a particular way, a toddler may enjoy putting the smallest ring instead of the largest ring on first—just to see what happens. Or a child may prefer playing with shape blocks rather than putting them through the holes in the shape sorter box.

❖ Avoid pressuring a child to always play with a toy "the right way"—experimentation is necessary and satisfying. Simply affirm the child's efforts as you talk about the skills he or she has developed. Your acceptance and encouragement helps a child develop confidence for further learning and exploration.

❖ Compare a doll's features with those of a child. Say, **God made your nose. God made you, Eric!** Point to the doll's nose, Eric's nose, then your nose. Identify your actions with words. Then ask Eric to play the pointing game with you.

Devotional

Perhaps Adam felt like a child with a new toy when the Lord brought the animals for him to name. What an array of creatures! All shapes, sizes, colors—each one was uniquely fascinating, deserving of extended scrutiny. Imagine Adam's delight as he first stroked the lion's mane, admired a peacock's tail fan out, observed a monkey's antics. Yet even as Adam delighted in each new form of life, God was aware that none of these creatures could ever be a suitable companion for Adam. Only another human could meet Adam's wide range of needs and interests.

Every descendant of Adam and Eve carries the same need for human companionship. While the child's intense curiosity can be satisfied with toys, pictures, books and animals, contact with people remains his or her overpowering interest. Just as God recognized Adam's need, adults who care for young children must recognize that each child needs the companionship of a caring person. Meeting that need calls for giving more than bottles or crackers. It requires patient and understanding adults who give themselves willingly to the task of showing God's love to each of His little ones.

Getting to Know Parents

Several times a year, send out a short questionnaire or a request for feedback from parents. Ask parents to tell you what they found most helpful in the nursery program and their ideas for improving it. Enclose a stamped, addressed envelope with the request. (If your church already receives parental feedback in written form, ask to read the comments.)

While realizing the difficulty of pleasing everyone, parental feedback can help you improve the care you give. You will learn which parts of the nursery procedures parents don't understand, and what parts of your program they especially value. When parents think about and communicate what they feel is best for their children, they are simultaneously encouraging themselves to continue in the hard task of doing the very best for their children.

Your service reminder: _____

Return Address:

Postage
Stamp

TO: _____

_____

Teacher's Home Page

God Gives Me Friends

"Love each other." (John 15:12.)

This month you will help each child:

❖ enjoy happy encounters with other children at church;

❖ associate God with happy experiences with others.

August

SING iT!

Friends

(Tune: "The Farmer in the Dell")

We can smile and wave.

We can smile and wave.

Because it's fun to be with friends,

we can smile and wave.

Sing this song as you play with a child or as two children play together. Smile and point to your smile. Say, **I am smiling at you. I like to see you smile. Friends smile at each other.** Wave to the child and say, **I am waving to you. I like to see you wave, too.** Sing the song several times to give a child time to smile, wave or anticipate what you will do. Talk about the children in the nursery. **Nathan and Abbey are friends.** Pray, **Thank You, God, for our friends.**

DO iT!

I Roll the Ball

I roll the ball to you.

You roll the ball to me.

I can share the ball with you because we're friends, you see!

Say and do this finger play as you roll a ball to a child. When you roll the ball say, **I am rolling the ball to you.** When the child rolls it back say, **You are rolling the ball to me.** Then roll the ball to another child. Say, **We're playing with our friends. I'm glad for our friends at church. God gives us friends. The Bible tells us to love each other.**

TELL iT!

David and Jonathan were friends.

They played like good friends do.

They helped each other, too.

Jonathan gave David his coat.

Jonathan said, "I love you."

"Thank you, Jonathan," David said, "I love you, too."

God gives us friends, and we are glad.

(See 1 Samuel 18:1-4.)

Tell this brief story as you show a child the August Toddler Picture from *I Love to Look!* If child remains interested, use the Picture Talk suggestions on the back of the picture. The story can also be told while children are playing with toys next to each other. Say, **I like to play with you, Brian and Kimiko. I'm glad God gives us friends. Friends love each other.**

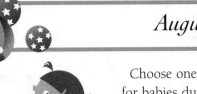

Choose one or two of these learning activities to provide for babies during a session. Continue the activity as long as one or more children are interested. Additional learning activities may be found in the *I Love to Wiggle and Giggle!* easel book.

Pictures and Books

❖ Display the August Teaching Poster and photo from the *Nursery Posters*, making sure the photo is at child's eye level. Refer to the poster if you need help remembering the words to the story, song or finger play. Talk about the photo with children. **Look at the friends in this picture! The girl is handing a book to her friend. God gives us friends. I see lots of friends in this room, too.** Name children in the room.

Toys

❖ Place a doll in front of a baby. Then cover the doll with a small blanket or diaper. Slowly remove the cover. Repeat the game, joining in the baby's enjoyment of rediscovering the "lost" doll.

❖ Place two babies near each other. Give each one a doll. If they show any interest in each other say, **Samantha sees Mark. I'm glad Mark and Samantha came to church today. They have lots of friends in this room. Friends love each other.**

❖ Hold a baby in your lap and roll a ball toward another child. Repeat the finger play, "I Roll the Ball."

Movement

❖ An adult's lap is one of baby's most versatile play spaces. It can provide a safe base while exploring buttons and buckles. A lap is fine for standing on. It can provide a jiggly ride. It can rock or sway or hold completely still. A baby can lie on his or her back or tummy on a lap and wave arms and legs with wild abandon. A lap can be a great perch from which to view the rest of the room, and it can also be a safe haven on the floor—perfect for crawling in and out. Some laps are a good place for meeting other babies. What are some other ways you can let babies use your lap?

Little children

are both

our reasons

and our excuses

to be playful.

God's Wonders

(Use only with teacher supervision. Store items out of children's reach.)

❖ A cool breeze is always refreshing in August. If possible, open a window and hold a baby where the breeze can be felt. Or use a hand fan (make a fan by accordion-folding a sheet of paper) to blow a breeze gently on a baby's arm, cheek or hair. While holding the baby, sing or play Quiet Time Songs from the *I Love to Sing!* cassette/CD.

Music

❖ Many babies learn to recognize their names in normal conversation. They also enjoy hearing their names in a song. Insert a child's name into songs wherever possible. "Friends" and "My Friends" from the Active Time Songs of the *I Love to Sing!* cassette/CD are good songs in which to use a baby's name. Occasionally touch the child as you sing, to help the child associate the name with him- or herself.

Choose one or two of these learning activities to provide for toddlers during a session. Beginning an activity yourself will usually attract the interest of several children. Continue the activity as long as one or more children are interested. Additional learning activities may be found in the *I Love to Wiggle and Giggle!* easel book.

Pictures and Books

❖ Display the August Teaching Poster and photo from the *Nursery Posters*, making sure the photo is at child's eye level. Talk about the photo. Say, **I see two girls taking turns looking at a book. They are sharing. These girls are friends. God gives you friends, too.** Refer to the poster if you need help remembering the words to the story, song or finger play.

❖ Here is an example of how to use books with toddlers: Denise, a nursery worker, picks up a book showing toddlers at play. She sits down in the middle of the room next to a toddler, opens the book and begins to look at the pictures, occasionally commenting on a pictured item. In a few moments, Elliot comes over to investigate. Tuan and Kyle quickly follow. As Denise continues talking about the pictures, she comments on things she has seen each child do during the morning. **Elliot, I see a picture of a toy car in this book. You played with a car today.**

Toys

❖ Take turns with a child in adding blocks to a structure. Since the child's concern is usually to make it taller, your participation can help make the stack longer or wider. A good rule-of-thumb for safety is to build towers only as high as a child's shoulder. Allow children to knock down towers they have built.

❖ Occasionally two children may cooperate in stacking blocks. When this happens, acknowledge that both children are working together. **Luis, you and your friend, Chantel, are stacking blocks.** However, do not expect the interaction to last long. In a few seconds one or the other will lose interest and return to solitary play. Children at this age usually do not play together for any extended period of time.

❖ When you give different shapes for the sorting box to two children say, **Deshay, can you put your shape in the box?** When both children's hands eagerly try to stuff their shapes into the box at the same time say, **Oh, Deshay wants to put her shape in the box and Miguel wants to put in his shape, too. Deshay, you sit on my lap until Miguel gets his piece in the box.** Patiently help the children take turns putting their shapes into the holes. As they work say, **Deshay and Miguel, you are learning to share. Friends share toys. God gives us friends. I'm glad we're friends. Friends love each other.**

God's Wonders

(Use only with teacher supervision. Store items out of children's reach.)

❖ Provide children with a fresh breeze by using a hand fan (make a fan by accordion-folding a sheet of paper). As children enjoy the breeze, comment about the fun they are sharing. **Can you feel the air blowing on your cheek? It feels good! Veronica is smiling. Veronica likes the feel of the cool air, and so does Seth. Seth and Veronica are friends.**

Music and Rhythm

❖ Provide simple rhythm instruments (such as two wood blocks or tambourines) for children to play as they listen to "Friends" and "My Friends" from the Active Time Songs on the *I Love to Sing!* cassette/CD. Join with them in making music. Comment about the instrument each child is playing, helping children become aware of each other.

Devotional

Take some time to read the story of David and Jonathan's friendship found in 1 Samuel 18—19:7. Notice how the circumstances of David and Jonathan's friendship changed drastically. At first, everything seemed rosy. Jonathan, King Saul, Saul's servants and all the people liked David. Friendship flourishes easily when things are going well.

But by the beginning of chapter 19, Saul's love for David has turned to raging jealousy. Now Saul seeks to turn Jonathan against David. Here comes the test of true friendship. Braving the wrath of his father the king, Jonathan stands up for his friend. It would have been so easy to bend, but Jonathan stood firm in the face of enormous pressure.

How strong are the friendships among the staff in your department? Are you merely acquaintances who happen to work together in the same room? Are you easily compatible only as long as everything runs smoothly? Or have you built relationships that help you sustain each other when pressure comes?

As you teach children about friendships, nurture your relationships with the others who work with you. Pray for them, asking God's Spirit to knit your hearts together as He did the hearts of David and Jonathan.

Getting to Know Parents

Send notes or postcards to the parents of children in your nursery to say thank-you for all the ways they make the nursery a good place to be. Comment on a specific way in which the parent has contributed to the nursery, such as a smile, toy donated to the nursery, suggestion offered or time spent helping in the nursery. If there are many children in your nursery, divide this task among the caregivers. Or plan to write one or two notes each week.

Parents need all the support and encouragement that they can get to do their job well. As nothing breeds success like success, your specific affirmation of something a parent is doing well will increase confidence in his or her current parenting abilities and ability to acquire more parenting skills.

Your service reminder: _____

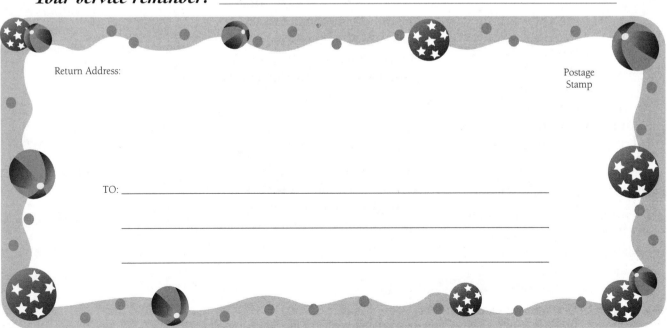

Return Address:

Postage Stamp

TO: _____

_____

_____

Clip Art

Clip art is an eye-catching way to enhance
and decorate nursery handbooks and brochures,
bulletin announcements, recruiting letters,
parent and teacher newsletters, forms and posters.

Cut and paste the following illustrations
to add interest to all your nursery communications.

Clip Art Page

Clip Art Page

Clip Art Page

Clip Art Page

Clip Art Page

Nursery Smart Pages • 249

Clip Art Page

 # *Index*

Index

Every nursery needs the Father's touch.

Let the little children come to Him…with **Little Blessings**. Gospel Light's all-new resource kit for babies and toddlers lets you provide the little ones in your church with great child care—and so much more! Every piece has been designed to help you nurture children physically, emotionally—and spiritually!

A great nursery begins with good training. This informative video prepares nursery workers for a vital ministry with the most complete baby and toddler information available.

How to Grow and Nurture a Quality Nursery

UPC 607135.001942

Decorate your nursery with these colorful posters featuring photos of happy babies, Bible stories, easy-to-sing songs and theme-related activities.

Little Blessings Nursery Posters

ISBN 08307.19059

It's the complete nursery program for loving God's little ones! From help for recruiting and training nursery workers to great music and fun instant activities, this kit provides everything you need to guide your little ones as they take their first steps in God's kingdom. Music comes on both CD *and* cassette!

Little Blessings Nursery Program

UPC 607135.001188

Little ones love to wiggle and giggle…and so will you! This portable, easy-to-use "easel" book includes 144 fun, creative activities you can do with babies or toddlers at a moment's notice.

**"I Love to Wiggle and Giggle!"
Instant Activities with Babies & Toddlers**

ISBN 08307.19032

You, too, will enjoy these delightful tunes on a reproducible CD or cassette. Includes upbeat songs for active play and gentle, soothing lullabies for calming little ones at quiet time.

**"I Love to Sing!"
Songs for Babies & Toddlers**

UPC 607135.001157 CD
UPC 607135.001140 Cassette

It's good news for God's little ones! Introduce babies and toddlers to great stories of the Bible with these 12 colorful, sturdy, non-toxic picture cards.

**"I Love to Look!"
Bible Story Picture Cards**

ISBN 08307.19040

A great gift for parents of babies and toddlers, this delightful package brings home the very best of *Little Blessings*. Includes the *"I Love to Look!"* Bible Story Picture Cards, the *"I Love to Wiggle and Giggle!"* Instant Activities easel book and the *"I Love to Sing!"* Songs for Babies and Toddlers cassette.

"I Love My Baby" Gift Pack

UPC 607135.002628

> " This is the most complete baby and toddler information I have seen in my 30 years in Christian education. **Little Blessings** is EXCELLENT! "
>
> **Willamae Myers
> Christian Educator**

Available at your local Christian Bookstore

Gospel Light

Gospel Light
Makes Sunday School
a Blast!

At every age level—from preschool to adults—
Gospel Light Curriculum

is designed to meet the particular

needs of that age group.

We make Bible learning fun,

And we take it seriously.

It's serious fun for your

Sunday School!

Ask your Gospel Light supplier for samples and more information.